Answers to Calvary Chapel's "Ten Reasons to Reject Preterism"

by Douglas Wilkinson

dougrwilkinson@yahoo.com

Other books by this author:
- *Making Sense of the Millennium*
- *Preterist Time Statements*
Available on Kindle and in print through Amazon.com

Table of Contents

Foreword

Calvary Chapel has had - and continues to have - a major influence on many believers. Unfortunately, that influence is not always positive or healthy. This is particularly true of their past emphasis and claims that the end of the age, the coming of the Lord was certain to occur in the modern generation. The misguided expectation created by the repeated false claims has caused disillusionment and discouragement among untold numbers of believers.

What is fascinating and discouraging about the Chapel is that there has been - and seemingly continues to be - an adamant refusal to acknowledge past false predictions. Instead of openly admitting that earlier predictions were undeniable failures, the leaders have simply "doubled down" on fostering a false sense of the imminent end. One has a right to ponder when- or if - the Chapel will ever wake up to the undeniable reality that they are guilty of fostering an unhealthy theological environment.

Now, in addition to not only refusing to admit their own failures, the leaders of Calvary Chapel have decided to attack the preterist movement (the view that all prophecy was fulfilled in the cataclysmic events of the end of the Old Covenant age in AD 70 - per Luke 21:22).

It is a positive and refreshing development to witness a longtime student of the Chapel - Douglas Wilkinson - to not only to begin pointing out the major failings of Chuck Smith and the Chapel, and the harm that has been done, but to respond to their charges of "heresy" against the preterist movement.

In this new book, Wilkinson, well familiar with Chapel beliefs and their charges, answers those claims head on. Particularly helpful in Wilkinson's book is his response to the "historical" issue that preterism was (supposedly) unknown in the early patristic writings. Wilkinson does a fine job of exposing this charge as misguided - indeed - self-contradictory. He actually turns this charge against the Chapel leaders! His analysis of those historical writings are insightful and "spot on" to say the least!

Wilkinson likewise does a fine job of pointing out the massive inconsistencies of the Chapel leaders when it comes to the language of imminence. On the one hand they dismiss the Biblical time statements that the end of the age was near in the first century, but then, they turn around and insist that that language must mean the end is near now! This is a glaring, major issue that Wilkinson explores and develops in an excellent manner. It is eye opening to say the least. It should give every Bible student a reason to re-think.

As with any book, one may find some things to differ with. But, anyone wanting to understand the charges being leveled against the rapidly growing preterist movement by the Calvary Chapel leaders and a solid response to those charges will find this book extremely helpful. I am happy to recommend it.

Don K. Preston (D. Div.)
President Preterist Research Institute
Ardmore, Ok.
www.eschatology.org
www.bibleprophecy.com

ON THE SIGNIFICANCE OF 70 A.D. AND DANIEL:

Chapter VIII — Of the Times of Christ's Birth and Passion, and of Jerusalem's Destruction.

Accordingly the times must be inquired into of the predicted and future nativity of the Christ, and of His passion, and of the extermination of the city of Jerusalem, that is, its devastation. For Daniel says, that "both the holy city and the holy place are exterminated together with the coming Leader, and that the pinnacle is destroyed unto ruin." And so the times of the coming Christ, the Leader, must be inquired into, which we shall trace in Daniel; and, after computing them, shall prove Him to be come, even on the ground of the times prescribed, and of competent signs and operations of His. Which matters we prove, again, on the ground of the consequences which were ever announced as to follow His advent; in order that we may believe all to have been as well fulfilled as foreseen.

- Tertullian[1]

Introduction

In the last few generations we've seen tumultuous changes in Christian eschatology. Entire systems of interpretation have been invented, discarded, or fragmented and then reformulated. For nearly 1900 years, a majority opinion existed on eschatology. But a little over a hundred years ago, that dominant approach of the church split into two distinct camps: postmillennialism and amillennialism. Postmillennialism's optimism about the increasing quality of life and civilization throughout the world was dealt a nearly fatal series of blows with the communist revolution, World War I, and World War II. Though the amillennial position remained historically orthodox and vaguely satisfying, its adherents didn't have much of a fire for spreading it. As a result, support for these positions started to fade in the 20th century.

Throughout church history, two minority positions called historicism and premillennialism had also found adherents.[2] However, about a hundred years ago the proponents of historicism, present through the Roman Catholic tradition and dominant in the Reformation, started to fade into history.[3] Historicism proposed that eschatological (or, end times) expectations could be seen unfolding throughout church history. In the final Reformed version, this meant that the seven bowls of wrath from Revelation (the last of the series of historical events to transpire before the second coming) represented recent events such as the French Revolution.[4] As historicists moved into the 19th Century, they expected the narrative of eschatology to wrap up, but that never happened. While historicism had provided some utility in creating fear and zealous rejection of Rome during the Reformation, its adherents started to dwindle because of the failure of the system.[5]

At the same time, a new variant of premillennialism called "dispensational premillennialism" started to gain ground. Premillennialism had been part of the church since its inception. It presumed that the New Testament era continued as the church age and that it would end in a climax at the second coming. After this, Christ would rule on earth from Jerusalem for 1,000 years. The dispensational variant was novel in Christian doctrine because it postulated a unique redemptive destiny between the physical descendants of Abraham, Isaac, and Jacob – Israel – and the Christian Church. By reanimating the literal land promises of the Old Covenant and assigning those to modern Jews, it paved the way for progressively more dramatic events in the history of European Jews and the residents of Palestine. The momentum towards a modern Jewish state began to build with the Niagara prophecy conferences of the late 1800s and with the publishing of the Scofield Reference Bible. The religious fervor surrounding World War I resulted in the Balfour Declaration, which was subsequently relied on as a legal basis for the establishment of the modern state of Israel.[6]

When the partnership between Jewish Zionists and Christian Zionists resulted in the founding of the nation of Israel in 1948, Christian focus on eschatology reached a fever pitch in America. The establishment of Israel in 1948 started a countdown in the minds of dispensationalists. The second coming and end of the world would happen within that generation (no more than 40 years).[7] But like the fate of the historicists before them, their hope in eschatology started to fade sixty or so years later when history proved their system of fulfillment wrong. Now, in 2016, we are left with a shrinking buy-in to those previous systems that are starting to be replaced by strange eschatological chimeras based on blood moon eclipses and Muslim invasions.[8] The general religious tone in America reflects an anxiety about the decline of Christianity in the west, which amillennialists and postmillennialists understand as a self-fulfilling prophecy as a result of looking for a rescue from this world instead of a rejuvenation of it.

The failure of dispensationalism has made room for a return to amillennialism and postmillennialism. However, the modern second look at these systems has resulted in a reevaluation of some of the original rationales for rejecting these systems in the first place. Like a great deal of Reformed theology, they had become too theoretical, ignoring the narrative of the Apostolic era. They were missing the tension and expectation of a second coming in the time of the Apostles.

In amillennialism and postmillennialism, there was no easy way to explain the connection between the tension seen in the New Testament narrative and their view of how this would play out in modern times. Premillennialism accepted this tension. Dispensationalism provided a superficially acceptable rationale for delaying this climax by saying that the church age starting at approximately Pentecost represents an interruption of this countdown. That meant that a pause button had been pushed just before the culmination of these events, and that the time statements of the New Testament can be taken literally as soon as the church is removed at the rapture and prophetic history is un-paused. When dispensationalism expired, the focus returned to these older systems, though there was no easy way to explain the failure of eschatological fulfillment described in the New

Testament time statements that predicted the second coming in the era of the Apostles.

Both amillennialism and postmillennialism are ways of explaining the expectation of the kingdom of God. But they also need a way to explain the fulfillment of the prophecies that allow for the beginning of that kingdom. Both systems had occasionally used rudimentary forms of preterism (realized or past fulfillment) for this. As modern scholarship has recognized the relationship between eschatological fulfillment and the implementation of the kingdom of God, stronger forms of preterism have started to spread aggressively.[9] In the strongest version of preterism, full preterism, the all eschatology in scripture is seen as fulfilled in early church history around the time of the Roman War. Most modern preterists don't look for a future Great Tribulation, Antichrist, or Mystery Babylon. It's not that they don't believe in them, as John MacArthur seems to think.[10] It's just that they see these elements of eschatology as being fulfilled in the history of the Roman War and the destruction of Jerusalem in 70AD. This book is a defense of full preterism against the premillennial dispensational position taken by Calvary Chapel.[11]

Teachers of premillennial futurist eschatology have a big problem with strong variants of preterism. In the case of Calvary Chapel, the persistent teaching of an imminent second coming is a core theme in their sermons. This should not come as any surprise. The church was founded by the late Chuck Smith in the heyday of the dispensationalist movement in the 1960s. Modern Israel had only been founded a few years before, and eschatological fervor surrounding events in the Middle East (the 1967 and 1973 wars elevated the tension) were sizzling in the minds of conservative American Christians. Dispensational premillennialism wasn't just a theological position. It was the primary lens through which most Evangelical Christians viewed everything in their lives including war, politics, economics, and planning for their personal futures in areas such as marriage, college, and having children. [12]

This book is a response to specific charges against preterism made by the Calvary Chapel church in Aurora, Colorado. On the Calvary Chapel Aurora apologetics webpage, they provide a ten-point refutation of preterism.[13] In reviewing this document and discussing it with friends who attend that church, it struck me that the ten points they cite represent common objections to preterism. I decided to use their handy list of talking points as the outline for a book addressing their claims. I found in talking to people personally, and debating the issue on the Internet, that the short format of a page-long post was simply not adequate to provide the depth that I think is needed to refute their claims. Instead, in each of the following chapters I provide argumentation and documentation against each of their assertions. In each case, I lead with a quote in italics from their publication. The rest of the chapter addresses their argument in detail. Because there is some redundancy in the Calvary Chapel talking points, and because it's possible that readers will simply skip to the chapters that address the points they're most interested in, there may be some redundancy in my arguments. I've tried to keep that to a minimum. For the most comprehensive experience, I ask you to work through the whole book from beginning to end, since some of my arguments build on each other. I hope that you, the reader, will find my arguments persuasive.

My arguments are based on a wide sample of preterist thought. In some cases, the various preterist camps engage in vigorous debates between each other on ways to explain past fulfillment. All of them are dedicated to historical scholarship and the Evangelical principle of the primacy of scripture. I've included references from these various camps to demonstrate the different ways that preterists try to answer objections to their systems. Examples of these camps include Don Preston's Covenant Eschatology,[14] Kurt Simmons' Bimillennial Preterism,[15] and Ed Stevens' traditional preterism based on an ancient literal rapture.[16] I also explain where my position, Perpetual Millennium Preterism, deviates from these systems. All of these camps agree that the second coming was an event associated with the Roman War in the first century, and that there are no additional events yet to be fulfilled in prophetic scripture.

My argument is based on three assumptions. The first will probably surprise you: I agree completely with premillennial dispensationalists such as John MacArthur that the Olivet Discourse (Matt. 24, Mark 13, Luke 21) describes the second coming of Christ. I agree that the imagery of Great Tribulation; Christ coming on clouds; the eclipse of sun, moon, and stars; and the gathering of the elect are all unmistakable indications of the second coming. But this creates a crisis. If that discourse was fulfilled in the Roman War in 66-73AD (as many early church writers claim), it violates the doctrine of a future second coming. This crisis is behind the argumentation of John MacArthur in his book *The Second Coming* (cited by Calvary Chapel as part of their background research for their paper). MacArthur makes the point that agreeing to any part of the Olivet Discourse being completely fulfilled in the Roman War of 66-73AD is tantamount to abandoning premillennialism. He and I agree on the gravity of the situation, though we come to opposite conclusions. As you'll see below, I cite numerous early church sources that agree with me that the Olivet Discourse was fulfilled in the Roman destruction of Jerusalem in 70AD. If those sources are correct, and we can agree that the Olivet Discourse describes the second coming, then dispensational premillennialism fall apart as a theological system.

Second, I agree with the usual Calvary Chapel approach that we want to be cautious in our use of early church writings when making theological arguments. Premillennial dispensationalists are famous for being suspicious historical creeds, especially of the Reformed ones. The Baptist variety of creeds carry some doctrine from the Reformation, but generally don't have strong Calvinist views. Calvary Chapel evolved from a mix of conservative Baptist and Charismatic influences (generally descended from Methodist teaching) so that they embrace traditional non-Reformed views of free will, and resist strong versions of predestination.[17] As a result of suspicion about the Roman Catholic Church and the creeds that come from the Reformation, they almost never teach about either historic systems of Christian doctrine or the writings of early church fathers. While I enjoy studying this era, I can appreciate why Evangelicals generally don't spend much time there: the early church fathers are at least a little bit wrong about almost everything, and are completely wrong about some pretty important stuff. This creates some problems for the Calvary Chapel approach. Some of their most important arguments are based on a perceived lack of preterist thought in early church writings. I'll address the question of why they would use those writings to make their case when they otherwise tend to avoid studying them. I'll point out that though we can occasionally find some interesting thoughts in early church writings, their material is of questionable value. If in any situation we fall back on scripture itself as a guide, I am confident I can show that preterism will be the result.

Third, I agree that scripture trumps historic doctrine and creeds. This might make some creedalists cringe, so I'll remind them that the Reformed creeds stipulate that they aren't as authoritative as scripture. The motto of the Reformation is Semper Reformanda (Always Reforming). This should mean that whatever can be solidly proven from scripture is authoritative, regardless of whether someone has noticed it or missed it in the past.

Keeping these three assumptions in mind, let's take a look at the Calvary Chapel critique of preterism.

Introduction Endnotes

[1] http://www.sacred-texts.com/chr/ecf/003/0030189.htm.

[2] Historicism started as a form of partial preterism. As history continued, it became distinct since it spread the majority of fulfillment over a larger and larger expanse of history. Preterism, on the other hand, identified most of prophetic fulfillment in a single cluster of events centered on the Roman War in the first century.

[3] There have been several phases of historicist thought since the first century. The earliest, because it defined eschatology as the unfolding drama of the rise of Christianity under Constantine, is now looked at as a sort of preterism. By modern historicism I mean the historicism proposed by the Reformers, where the Roman Catholic Church is seen as Mystery Babylon and the bowl judgments are associated with the Reformation itself.

[4] http://www.preteristcentral.com/The%20Road%20Back%20to%20Pre terism.html.
This excellent article by Kurt Simmons provides important background to the history of eschatology in the church. Simmons' point is that although preterism is clear in scripture, and was echoed throughout early church writings, church politics and the delay of fulfillment caused several incompatible views to arise. This at least proves that current eschatology is not founded primarily on scripture, but progressively fragmenting tradition.

[5] In a post-mortem of historicism, it can be seen that attempting to peg ongoing events of history to progressive events in prophecy (specifically the seals, trumpets, and bowls of Revelation) results in the exhausting of material. Once the bowls were assigned to the Reformation and the French Revolution there was no room left for future events. Traditional partial preterism has proposed an empty middle section between the initial fulfillments in the Roman War and the mysterious future Gog/Magog war, thus remaining much more resilient.

[6] Philip Jenkins, *The Great and Holy War*, p.135ff.

[7] The arguments in chapter 1 focusing on the Greek term *genea*, or "generation," become important here. In earlier dispensational Zionist thought, "this generation" meant those who were alive at the time of the founding of the Jewish nation in 1948. As that interpretation was invalidated by history, it became more common to see the argument by

the Calvary Chapel writer addressed in this book, which is that "this generation" was those alive at the time of the initiation of the Great Tribulation.

[8] The original Reformation-era version of historicism assigned the meaning of the seven trumpets of Revelation to the aggression of Islam against the Byzantine Empire. It is likely in my opinion that we will see a return to this motif, where the seven bowls will start to be seen as a fulfillment of the 20th century rise of Islam per Joel Richardson in *The Islamic Antichrist*. Since this will allow for a reformulation of dispensationalism I expect them to move in this direction over the next generation.

[9] http://www.gty.org/resources/sermons/61-23/the-certainty-of-the-second-coming-part-1.
John MacArthur refers to this dynamic in a 1991 broadcast of *Grace to You*. The reference is in a lesson on the relationship between 2 Peter 3 and the second coming:

"These names have caused a great impact on seminaries, universities, therefore professors, therefore students, therefore pastors and spiritual leaders; therefore, they have impacted the church. Some of those names you may recognize, some you will not, but I say again, if you were a seminary student you would recognize them all and you maybe need to know a little bit about their influence. First of all, a man by the name of Adolf Von Harnack, some years back, wrote a book, *What is Christianity?* In his writings, which have been extremely influential in contemporary theology, you read this, "The kingdom of God comes by coming to the individual, by entering into his soul and laying hold of it. True, the kingdom of God is the rule of God; but it is the rule of the holy God in the hearts of individuals; it is God himself in his power. From this point of view everything that was dramatic in the external and historical sense has vanished; and gone, too, are all the hopes for the future." End quote. Adolph Von Harnack is saying there is no Second Coming, there is no future kingdom. It is only a spiritual reality in the present. He rejected completely all eschatological aspects of the kingdom of God. Another very familiar writer, I remember reading quite a number of his works when I was a seminary student, is a man by the name of C.H. Dodd, who wrote one particular book called Parables of the kingdom. This book has influenced many contemporary theologians. And if you were to try to understand Dodd more fully, you would come to the conviction, without equivocation, that he denies any literal Second Coming of Jesus Christ. He states, "That since the Lord did not in literal truth return on the clouds of heaven during the '30s of the first century, to expect Him thus to return in the twentieth century is to go contrary to primitive Christianity which is true Christianity." As a matter of fact, C.H. Dodd taught that the doctrine of the Second Coming is a myth. And I'm quoting, "The least inadequate myth of the goal of history is that which molds itself upon the great divine event of the past known in its concrete actuality and depicts its final issue in a form which brings time to an end and places man in eternity. The least significant myth is the Second Coming of the Lord and the Last Judgment." End quote. He taught, in fact, did C.H. Dodd that the New Testament teaching of the Second Coming is sub-Christian. Karl Bart, a well-known purveyor of what came to be known as Neo-Orthodoxy, held to what he called a timeless eschatology in which the coming of Christ is no longer understood as a future literal return of Christ. But said Bart, quote, "It is a timeless symbol for the endless earnestness of eternity in every existential situation." End quote. Whatever in the world that means. Rudolf Bultmann, again well known to theological students, set out to make a life effort to quote/unquote "demythologize the New Testament." He concluded, "Among the mythological elements in the New Testament which must be reinterpreted and, therefore, no longer taken literally are the following: heaven, hell, the resurrection of Jesus Christ, the Second Coming of Christ, and the future day of judgment." Bultmann also claims to find support for his view in the writings of Paul. Paul, he admits, gave teachings about apocalyptic future events like the Second Coming and the final judgment. But, he says, "This is mythical eschatology. And so Paul must be demythologized." One more comes to mind, familiar to theological students, Jürgen Moltmann, another German. Moltmann, in vain...you look into his writings and try to find anything on the Second Coming of Christ that is not so totally ambiguous that it's absolutely nonsense. He is ambiguous on the Second Coming. He is ambiguous on the Day of Judgment. He is ambiguous on a future resurrection. He is ambiguous on a new heaven and a new earth. His comments are vague. His comments are abstract. His comments are imprecise. And they tell us that he is doing everything possible to evade having to even deal with such issues. I would say this small group of men have, as much as anybody, influenced modern contemporary theology in the church. And the bottom line is they deny the Second Coming of Jesus Christ. They deny the Day of the Lord's judgment. You say, "Why are you telling us this?" Because it is very important for you to understand that what Peter is dealing with in this chapter, we are dealing with today. The false teachers who were plaguing the believers to whom Peter writes are also plaguing the church today."

[10] John MacArthur, *The Second Coming*, p.28.

[11] Because in many places it is convenient and illuminating to include the interaction between premillennialism, amillennialism, and postmillennialism, I have included commentary on how these systems play off of each other. In most cases, references to amillennialism apply to postmillennialism as well, so I simply refer to amillennialism as a way of addressing the contrast with premillennialism.

[12] See Gary DeMar's *Last Days Madness* and *End Times Fiction*. This focus on modern fulfillments of prophecy is irrational since the next event in their eschatological calendar is an unannounced rapture. According to their own system, at least as taught by more theologically careful dispensationalists, there is no Biblical prophecy that needs to be fulfilled before this rapture happens, so theoretically nothing in the newspaper could have anything to do with fulfilled prophecy. Since this catching away to heaven could supposedly happen at any time in church history, the idea that being ready for the rapture should be informed by the events of the Middle East as told in a daily newspaper is nonsensical.

[13] Calvary Chapel, "Ten Reasons to Reject Preterism."

[14] Covenant Eschatology emphasizes the place of the transition from the Old Covenant to the New Covenant. It proposes that prophetic writings related to eschatology (not all prophecy is eschatology) are meant to describe that transition. Since that transition occurred in the first century, it is in fact fulfilled. Covenant Eschatology proposes that the millennium was the period of transition found in the New Testament writings. Typically, their view of resurrection, the corporate body view (CBV) is seen as the rebirth of the nation of God's people under the New Covenant.

[15] Bimillennial Preterism emphasizes the historicity of preterism and proposes a different millennium from Covenant Eschatology. Kurt Simmons, the leader of this group, has compiled extensive historical evidence of fulfillment that can be seen in regular history. His knowledge of Roman and Jewish history in the era is the basis of his system. He sees the thousand-year periods of the detention of Satan and the rule of the saints as independent of each other, though they are completed by 70AD. Kurt's view of the resurrection is based on an individual body view (IBV).

[16] Ed Stevens is the proponent of a system that represents a more traditional Reformed theology combined with an excellent understanding of the history of the early church and its writings. He is also a proponent of a literal rapture of the church in 66AD. This rapture position is by definition an IBV or IBD (Immortal Body at Death). This

position provides a potentially critical explanation for the historicity of preterism and Reformed doctrine. His rapture position is explained in *Expectations Demand a First Century Rapture.* Another important book arguing for a first-century rapture is *Taken to Heaven in 70* by Ian Harding. Harding focuses on the promise that at the same moment in the parousia all living and dead Christians will receive their promise of full knowledge and reward. This has been a notoriously difficult problem for Covenant Eschatology as proposed by Don Preston. The problem is that it is difficult to argue that Christians who lived on earth through the parousia in fact received full reward before arriving in heaven at the end of their lives.

[17] Roger Olson, *Arminian Theology: Myths and Realities*, p.44. Olson proves that the earliest understanding of Arminianism was solidly in the creedal Reformed tradition, though in modern times the term "Arminian" has come to mean something else. I regretfully am relying on the modern understanding of the term for sake of space to differentiate the matter.

Chapter 1: Matthew 24:34

Calvary Chapel Statement:

Matthew 24:34 says "Assuredly, I say to you, this generation will by no means pass away till all these things take place."

This is hands down the number one verse Preterists use as a proof text. They say "this generation" refers to the generation Jesus is speaking to and that "all these things" were fulfilled with the destruction of Jerusalem in AD 70.

But, when we read the verse in context with the previous verses of Matthew 24, we see that Jesus had just explained the signs leading up to His Second Coming. These events which Jesus talks about are devastating, cataclysmic and global and they are just too massive to be about the destruction of Jerusalem in AD 70.

So, in response to the disciples [sic] earlier questions as to "what will be the sign of Your coming" (verse 3), Jesus says that after these things take place, the generation alive at this time i.e., a future generation, will not pass away and will see these things come to pass.

Charges:

- Matthew 24:34 is the primary proof text used to prove preterism.
- Matthew 24 describes the signs related to the second coming.
- These events are too global to be part of a local judgment.
- A future generation will not pass away until they see the events of the Olivet Discourse take place.

The Calvary Chapel author starts with Matthew's version of the Olivet Discourse.[18] He is relying here on John MacArthur's assertion in *The Second Coming* that the whole theology of preterism is based on a single verse in this chapter, Matthew 24:34, "Truly, I say to you, this generation will not pass away until all these things take place."[19] In reality, there are more than 360 New Testament time statements that preterists can use to make their case.[20] The consensus of those statements make it impossible to sweep away the evidence that the New Testament authors were predicting the second coming in the first century. If a single one of those statements, and Matthew 24:34 is a very powerful one, turns out to be a bona fide prediction that the second coming was going to happen in the lifetime of the Apostles, then all futurist modes of eschatology are invalidated. To assert otherwise is to accept that scripture is terribly flawed.

This challenging realization was addressed by C. S. Lewis in *The World's Last Night*:[21]

> But there is worse to come. "Say what you like" we shall be told, "the apocalyptic beliefs of the first Christians have been proved to be false. It is clear from the New Testament that they all

expected the Second Coming in their own lifetime. And, worse still, they had a reason, and one which you will find very embarrassing. Their Master had told them so. He shared, and indeed created, their delusion. He said in so many words, 'this generation shall not pass till all these things be done.' And he was wrong. He clearly knew no more about the end of the world than anyone else.

It is certainly the most embarrassing verse in the Bible. Yet how teasing, also, that within fourteen words of it should come the statement 'But of that day and that hour knoweth no man, no, not the angels which are in heaven, neither the Son, but the Father.' The one exhibition of error and the one confession of ignorance grow side by side. That they stood thus in the mouth of Jesus himself, and were not merely placed thus by the reporter, we surely need not doubt. Unless the reporter were perfectly honest he would never have recorded the confession of ignorance at all; he could have had no motive for doing so except a desire to tell the whole truth. And unless later copyists were equally honest they would never have preserved the (apparently) mistaken prediction about "this generation" after the passage of time had shown the (apparent) mistake.

Lewis, in sparring with his imaginary foe, considered the claim by Jesus that "this generation shall not pass till all these things be done" to be the most embarrassing verse in the Bible. He is heartened to see that immediately afterwards there is an explicit claim of ignorance on Jesus' part about the timing of these events. In Lewis' mind, the fact that "no one knows the day or hour" means that Jesus could have been wrong when he delivered the Olivet Discourse.

The problem with Lewis' position is that it fails to take into consideration passages describing how much the Apostles would eventually learn. For instance, in John 14:26, "But the Helper, the Holy Spirit, whom the Father will send in my name, he will teach you all things and bring to your remembrance all that I have said to you (ESV)," we see that the Holy Spirit was not only going to remind the Apostles of Jesus' words (presumably so that they could quote him correctly while writing the four gospels over the next few years), but he was going to teach the Apostles new information. These Apostles then turned around and made more than 300 claims, separate from quotes of Jesus in the gospels, that the second coming would be in the first century.

Consider Jesus' advice in Luke 21:8: "many will come in my name, saying . . . 'The time is at hand!' Do not go after them."[22] If, after the era of the Olivet Discourse, there were no further authoritative revelations by God to the Apostles, so that the Apostles would have a correct understanding of God's intentions in eschatology, what do you think should be made of the Apostle Paul's advice to the Philippians: "Let your reasonableness be known to everyone. The Lord is at hand"?[23] In the first case, Jesus is telling his followers not to go after those who will say "the time is at hand." In the other, the most famous and prolific Apostle, Paul, tells his readers excitedly, "The Lord is at hand!" Whose advice are we supposed to follow?

We know from history that the early Christians took Christ's advice from the Olivet Discourse to heart during the Roman War. The purpose of the Olivet Discourse was to teach first-generation believers the signs before the coming of Christ in judgment, such as the surrounding of Jerusalem by armies. They were told exactly what to do to save themselves from death at the hands of the Romans. Since they took Jesus' instruction seriously, according to Josephus there is no record of Christians dying in Jerusalem in the Roman siege because they all fled the city as instructed.[24] There was meaningful information passed in the discourse that was utilized by that generation. They took Jesus' advice quite literally. It was not idealistic or spiritualized advice meant to be useful to every generation.[25]

In MacArthur's opinion, all of these time statements are simply designed to keep believers on their toes throughout all of church history.[26] Calvary Chapel teaches the same doctrine. Having been raised on it in the 1980s through Calvary Chapel radio sermons, I didn't see the inherent deceptiveness of it until I started to think critically about the hundreds of time statements made in plain language to the original audience.

Imagine you were the recipient of the following advice, **"You also, be patient. Establish your hearts, for the coming of the Lord is at hand."**[27] If you lived your whole life and the promise never materialized, would you be disappointed? Would you conclude that the person giving you the advice shouldn't be trusted? It seems odd to me that denominations that are bent on absolute literal interpretation would deliberately and unapologetically spiritualize advice like, **"Children, it is the last hour, and as you have heard that antichrist is coming, so now many antichrists have come. Therefore we know that it is the last hour."**[28]

Likewise, if you were told by an Apostle to expect rescue, like the Thessalonians were, I'm sure that you would wonder about his authority, knowledge, and his supposed representation of God if it didn't happen the way the Apostle told you it would:

> This is evidence of the righteous judgment of God, that you may be considered worthy of the kingdom of God, for which you are also suffering—since indeed God considers it just to repay with affliction those who afflict you, and to grant relief to you who are afflicted as well as to us, when the Lord Jesus is revealed from heaven with his mighty angels in flaming fire, inflicting vengeance on those who do not know God and on those who do not obey the gospel of our Lord Jesus. They will suffer the punishment of eternal destruction, away from the presence of the Lord and from the glory of his might, 10 when he comes on that day to be glorified in his saints, and to be marveled at among all who have believed, because our testimony to you was believed. (2 Thess. 1:5-10 ESV)

If you'd received this encouragement in the midst of persecution where your friends and family were being killed for following Christ, but you eventually found out that he wasn't actually supposed to come for at least another 2,000 years, you would probably find such a promise manipulative or dishonest. Similar promises or admonitions are found in the writings of James, Peter, Paul, and John. They are diverse in their construction and vocabulary, but unanimous in their perspective. They can't possibly result in confusion about the point that the Apostles were making: cheer up, be ready, don't quit, the coming of the Lord is at hand. Statements like this permeate the New Testament. Because of the hundreds of similar statements throughout the New Testament, if none of the Olivet Discourse material were available to preterists we would still have more than enough scripture to make our case.

The next argument by Calvary Chapel is based on an assumption about the scope and description of the second coming and the signs leading up to it. The Calvary Chapel author essentially says that Jesus couldn't have been referring to the generation alive at the time of his teaching because he was talking about the second coming (an event that follows seven years of worldwide disaster and supernatural events), and obviously the second coming hasn't happened.

That is circular reasoning. The author has done nothing to prove his definition of the second coming and the signs leading up to it. Therefore, we have no objective way to know why he thinks it hasn't happened. He is guessing at Jesus' definition of the second coming instead of proving it through scripture, where there is clear precedent on which to draw.

I'll start with a quick description of the signs leading up to the climax by looking at Luke's version of the Olivet Discourse:

> And they asked him, "Teacher, when will these things be, and what will be the sign when these things are about to take place?" And he said, "See that you are not led astray. For many will come in my name, saying, 'I am he!' and, 'The time is at hand!' Do not go after them. And when you hear of wars and tumults, do not be terrified, for these things must first take place, but the end will not be at once." Then he said to them, "Nation will rise against nation, and kingdom against kingdom. There will be great earthquakes, and in various places famines and pestilences. And there will be terrors and great signs from heaven. But before all this they will lay their hands on you and persecute you,

delivering you up to the synagogues and prisons, and you will be brought before kings and governors for my name's sake. This will be your opportunity to bear witness. Settle it therefore in your minds not to meditate beforehand how to answer, for I will give you a mouth and wisdom, which none of your adversaries will be able to withstand or contradict. You will be delivered up even by parents and brothers and relatives and friends, and some of you they will put to death. You will be hated by all for my name's sake. But not a hair of your head will perish. By your endurance you will gain your lives.

"But when you see Jerusalem surrounded by armies, then know that its desolation has come near. Then let those who are in Judea flee to the mountains, and let those who are inside the city depart, and let not those who are out in the country enter it, for these are days of vengeance, to fulfill all that is written. Alas for women who are pregnant and for those who are nursing infants in those days! For there will be great distress upon the earth and wrath against this people. They will fall by the edge of the sword and be led captive among all nations, and Jerusalem will be trampled underfoot by the Gentiles, until the times of the Gentiles are fulfilled. (Luke 21:7-24 ESV)

There is no indication in the passage above that the events preceding the second coming are anything other than regular historic events that include wars, persecutions, and famine. There is also no indication at all that it applies to anyone other than the original recipients of the passage. The description preceding the second coming is easily accommodated by the events leading up to the sacking of Jerusalem in 70AD as it is clearly described by Josephus.[29]

Moving forward to the description of the second coming itself, we can look backwards into the Old Testament to define the prophetic images of the New Testament that are used to define it. With this, we will have an objective standard to work from. The goal should be to find examples of the description of the second coming in scripture, define those terms according to a previous precedent in scripture, then examine these descriptions to see if they have already occurred in history. Below is the description of this event from Matthew 24. Our task is to find clear explanations for second coming related imagery in the Olivet Discourse. Instead of relying on our imagination for the definition of these images, we need to use scripture to guide us. Matthew 24 says:

> ... the sun will be darkened, and the moon will not give its light, and the stars will fall from heaven, and the powers of the heavens will be shaken. Then will appear in heaven the sign of the Son of Man, and then all the tribes of the earth will mourn, and they will see the Son of Man coming on the clouds of heaven with power and great glory. (Matt. 24:29-30 ESV)

That's very intense imagery. It has led people to expect to see these things happen literally, as if they were part of a CGI-based science fiction movie. The problem with CGI is that it causes us to make anachronistic assumptions about the imagery of scripture. For us, seeing bigger-than-life, impossible events come true on film is part of our normal life. We tend to subconsciously think that these things can literally come true in our own lives. The fact that there are no fires or sound in the vacuum of space doesn't seem to faze us as we blend CGI with literal scientific reality. While it's hard for westerners raised on a scientifically literal worldview to understand, hyperbolic prophetic imagery found in ancient literature is simply their attempt at CGI, or animation, in storytelling. They never expected it to be truly literal.

We'll use David's song celebrating the defeat of his enemies from 2 Samuel 22 as an example. In real history, David's enemy Saul fell on his sword at the end of a hilltop battle. Tragically, David's good friend Jonathan was killed as well. This was done with arrows, swords, knives, sweat, and dirt. Here's how David describes what happened when a few thousand men run around sweating and stabbing each other:

> And David spoke to the Lord the words of this song on the day when the Lord delivered him from the hand of all his enemies, and from the hand of Saul. He said, "The Lord is my rock and my fortress and my deliverer, my God, my rock, in whom I take refuge, my shield, and the horn of my salvation, my stronghold and my refuge, my savior; you save me from violence. I call upon the Lord, who is worthy to be praised, and I am saved from my enemies. For the waves of death encompassed me, the torrents of destruction assailed me; the cords of Sheol entangled me; the snares of death confronted me. In my distress I called upon the Lord; to my God I called. From his temple he heard my voice, and my cry came to his ears. Then the earth reeled and rocked; the foundations of the heavens trembled and quaked, because he was angry. Smoke went up from his nostrils, and devouring fire from his mouth; glowing coals flamed forth from him. He bowed the heavens and came down; thick darkness was under his feet. He rode on a cherub and flew; he was seen on the wings of the wind. He made darkness around him his canopy, thick clouds, a gathering of water. Out of the brightness before him coals of fire flamed forth. The Lord

thundered from heaven, and the Most High uttered his voice. And he sent out arrows and scattered them; lightning, and routed them. Then the channels of the sea were seen; the foundations of the world were laid bare, at the rebuke of the Lord, at the blast of the breath of his nostrils." (2 Sam. 22:1-16 ESV)

Now, let's examine the imagery. I'll point out below where elements of this imagery were never meant to be taken literally:

- God is not a rock.
- God does not have horns.
- Death doesn't have waves, and David wasn't literally surrounded by them.
- No torrent of destructive water literally assailed David.
- Sheol doesn't have cords.
- Death doesn't literally have snares.
- God does not have ears.
- There is no record of an earthquake during the battle.
- No matter how you define the "heavens," they cannot tremble and quake.
- God does not have nostrils.
- God does not have a mouth.
- God is not a dragon, that fire would shoot out of his mouth.
- God does not shoot flaming coals from his body.
- There is no record of the atmosphere of the earth changing shape during the battle.
- God does not have feet, and it's not clear how darkness can exist under them because he is light.
- God does not need to ride a Cherub to ride in order to fly.

- The wind does not have wings.
- In spite of darkness shrouding him, somehow flame and fire come from him.
- There is no record of arrows shooting out of God.
- There is no record of lightning in the battle.
- There is no record in the battle of the ocean receding so that you can see the bottom of the ocean.
- There is no record in the battle that the foundations of the world were seen.

The point of the list is to demonstrate that not a single constituent element of David's song literally happened in history. Not one. All of these examples are hyperbole, anthropopathisms, or anthropomorphisms. Bigger-than-life language is used to describe how God works in human history. God almost always uses human actors in un-miraculous circumstances to execute his judgment in history.[30]

If we can accept that hyperbolic images can be used to explain the importance of an event, though not the literal description of it, and we can go back to previous scripture to find similar examples for something like the description of the second coming, then we have compared scripture with scripture in order to form an objective, durable interpretation. Below is a list of the imagery found in Matthew 24:27-31 that we are going to attempt to define through previous Biblical precedent:

- The sun and moon won't give light.
- The stars will fall from heaven.
- The powers of the heavens will be shaken.
- The sign of the Son of Man in heaven.
- All the tribes of the earth will mourn.

- They will see the Son of Man coming on the clouds of heaven with power and great glory.
- He will send out his angels to the four winds to gather the elect.

The first time we see an explicit interpretation of imagery including the phrase "sun, moon, and stars" is Genesis 37:9, where they did not represent literal astronomical bodies. Instead they were symbolic of Joseph's father, mother, and eleven brothers. It was not uncommon in Hebrew thought for these terms to represent family or power relationships. Moving on to prophetic uses:

> Behold, the day of the Lord comes, cruel, with wrath and fierce anger, to make the land a desolation and to destroy its sinners from it. For the stars of the heavens and their constellations will not give their light; the sun will be dark at its rising, and the moon will not shed its light. I will punish the world for its evil, and the wicked for their iniquity; I will put an end to the pomp of the arrogant, and lay low the pompous pride of the ruthless. (Isaiah 13:9-11 ESV)

In actual history, this prophecy was fulfilled by an invasion of the Assyrians in 689BC. So in prophetic "day of the Lord" imagery, the first prophetic use of the eclipse of the sun and moon simply has to do with the invasion of a foreign military. Since such a military invasion often includes an overthrow of the government, or at least a diminishing of that government's power, there is probably some extension of the meaning of this imagery to the power systems supporting the kingdom. However, the point is that it doesn't mean that the astronomical bodies were literally changed in some way. Likewise, below we see a similar, interesting description of the judgment of the "whole earth" in Isaiah, where the astronomical bodies are actually judged:

> On that day the Lord will punish the host of heaven, in heaven, and the kings of the earth, on the earth. They will be gathered together as prisoners in a pit; they will be shut up in a prison, and after many days they will be punished. Then the moon will be confounded and the sun ashamed, for the Lord of hosts reigns on Mount Zion and in Jerusalem, and his glory will be before his elders. (Isaiah 24:21-23 ESV)[31]

My final reference of the more than 20 uses of "sun and moon" in prophetic texts (if I took the time I am confident I could make the case that they all follow the same pattern) is found in Isaiah:

> Whereas you have been forsaken and hated, with no one passing through, I will make you majestic forever, a joy from age to age. You shall suck the milk of nations; you shall nurse at the breast of kings; and you shall know that I, the Lord, am your Savior and your Redeemer, the Mighty One of Jacob. Instead of bronze I will bring gold, and instead of iron I will bring silver; instead of wood, bronze, instead of stones, iron. I will make your overseers peace and your taskmasters righteousness. Violence shall no more be heard in your land, devastation or destruction within your borders; you shall call your walls Salvation, and your gates Praise. The sun shall be no more your light by day, nor for brightness shall the moon give you light; but the Lord will be your everlasting light, and your God will be your glory. Your sun shall no more go down, nor your moon withdraw itself; for the Lord will be your everlasting light, and your days of mourning shall be ended. Your people

shall all be righteous; they shall possess the land forever, the branch of my planting, the work of my hands, that I might be glorified. (Isaiah 60:15-21 ESV)

There's an interesting plot twist in this passage. In Isaiah 13 we saw that the day of the Lord was a military invasion in ancient history where the sun and moon stopped shining, though there is no indication that this literally happened. In Isaiah 24 we saw a hint of the sun and moon as characters to be judged (echoing the concept of the powers of the heavens being shaken) at the time they stop shining. Here, in Isaiah 60, we see that they were replaced by God himself (echoing the description of the New Jerusalem in Revelation 21-22). The sun and moon in prophetic literature figuratively represents non-God power or religious functions that are subjugated or replaced when God finally fixes the world spiritually (cf. Psalm 110). This would make sense with the preterist interpretation of the eclipse of the old sun, moon, and stars in the Olivet Discourse. In preterism, these represent elements of the Temple and the Jewish religion, as well as the other idolatrous religions dedicated to demonic worship, which would be nullified by the Roman War and replaced by the fully functioning Kingdom of God.

The sun, moon, and stars are not meant to be understood as the literal astronomical objects in these passages. Likewise, the global language used in all of the passages quoted in this chapter only applied to small Middle Eastern cities or nations. An excellent example of this is in Isaiah 34, where in the oracle against Edom the sky was described as rolling up like a scroll. In actual history, this passage was fulfilled by a military invasion that resulted in the end of their world. There is no reason that use of the same language used in the New Testament has to apply to any grander scale.

Next, we'll look at the phrase ". . . and they will see the Son of Man coming on the clouds of heaven with power and great glory" from Matthew 24:30 (ESV). Most people would start with the ascension of Christ in Acts 1:11 to define Jesus' return to the earth on the clouds. There, he is said to "come" or "arrive" on clouds just like he left.[32] I argue that all of the evidence up to this point indicates that Jesus is going to return in judgment in some way associated with clouds according to Old Testament precedent, so we will start in the Old Testament to see how these ideas have been combined. Below is one of the most important eschatological references to "coming on clouds":

> I saw in the night visions, and behold, with the clouds of heaven there came one like a son of man, and he came to the Ancient of Days and was presented before him. And to him was given dominion and glory and a kingdom, that all peoples, nations, and languages should serve him; his dominion is an everlasting dominion, which shall not pass away, and his kingdom one that shall not be destroyed. (Dan. 7:13-14 ESV)

It's hard to overstate the importance of this passage. Premillennialists and other futurists have no problem seeing this as a description of the second coming. We agree with them on that. They run into a problem, however, when we pay close attention to the constituent elements and the imagery. Four beasts are described. Premillennial theologians stipulate that they represent the kingdoms of Babylon, Medo-Persia, Greece, and Rome. We agree with them. The fourth beast, Rome, makes war with the saints, overcoming them. Preterists take this as the Roman Empire's persecution under Nero in the time of the Apostles. Because of the obvious, inescapable reference to Rome, premillennialists are required to propose a future rebuilt

Roman Empire in the era of the Great Tribulation in order to fulfill this passage.[33] However, you'll notice no reference to a rebuilt Roman Empire. Premillennialists are forced to propose that this empire will be rebuilt because it is obviously involved in the passage, but the rebuilding itself is fabricated out of a necessity. It is an entirely made up concept required to keep the premillennial system from falling apart.

Once the beast has overcome the saints, he is captured and presented before a court in heaven and judged. He is then thrown into fire to be destroyed (a clear reference to this is found in Great White Throne Judgment and the Lake of Fire of Revelation 20-22). Immediately after this vision, Daniel sees a vision in which "one like a son of man" came with the clouds of heaven. It's at this moment that the full expression of the Son of Man's kingdom becomes a reality. There appears to be a direct connection between this passage in Daniel and the description of the climax of events in Matthew 24.

Premillennialists are in a bit a bind with this as the "Second Coming" because it is at this point that the function of the Lake of Fire begins. In their system, the Lake of Fire judgment shouldn't happen until 1,000 years after the second coming. Amillennialists have a much easier time with this sequence because of their timing of the final judgment. But, either way, this is a definitive passage. It is probably the direct reference cited by Jesus in the Olivet Discourse for the eschatological coming of the son of man on clouds. According to John F. Walvoord in *Every Prophecy of the Bible*:

> The coming of the Son of man (v.13) could be
> understood to refer to the coming of Jesus

> Christ as the Messiah in His second coming, as Christ Himself used this expression "a Son of man" in many reference to himself in the New Testament (Matt. 8:20; 9:6 10:23; 11:19; 12:8, 32, 40, etc.).
>
> This passage referred to Jesus Christ in his incarnation approaching the "Ancient of Days" (Dan 7:13), an obvious reference to God the Father. The reference to giving Him complete authority over all people would be fulfilled in His millennial kingdom which, as far as dominion is concerned, will continue forever (v.14).[34]

The original hearers of Christ, or readers of their works, were Jews steeped in Daniel and other Old Testament prophets. They knew the imagery involved like the back of their hands. Just as they associated his label "Son of David" as a fulfillment of the promise in the Davidic covenant, they would have recognized Christ's label of the Son of Man as a reference to this prophetic climax. When he said that they would see him coming in the clouds in power and great glory, he was telling them that at the point of fulfillment in the Olivet Discourse, the parallel prediction in Daniel 7 would be fulfilled.

We've seen that the time that Jesus comes in clouds will be the time when he receives his kingdom. It should not be controversial to say that this happens in conjunction with the battle of Armageddon. Since it's possible that the "cloud" terminology is associated with the battle itself, next, we'll look at other uses of "coming in the clouds" in reference to the arrival of God in judgment. Ezekiel 38 is our first example:

> Be ready and keep ready, you and all your hosts that are assembled about you, and be a guard for

> them. After many days you will be mustered. In the latter years you will go against the land that is restored from war, the land whose people were gathered from many peoples upon the mountains of Israel, which had been a continual waste. Its people were brought out from the peoples and now dwell securely, all of them. You will advance, coming on like a storm. You will be like a cloud covering the land, you and all your hordes, and many peoples with you. (Ezek. 38:7-9 ESV)

This passage starts with a description of a military invasion on the land of the people of God. It describes the army that is coming against them as being like a storm, and their armies like a cloud covering the land. These invaders do so because God directs them to do so. They are the method by which God comes in judgment. This imagery is not unusual in the Old Testament. Invading armies are seen in numerous places such as Isaiah 28 as God coming like a cloud or a storm:

> Behold, the Lord has one who is mighty and strong; like a storm of hail, a destroying tempest, like a storm of mighty, overflowing waters, he casts down to the earth with his hand. (Isaiah 28:2 ESV)

In this case, he did so on earth in the form of an invading army that conquered another nation. Similar imagery is used in Jeremiah to describe the invasion of the Babylonians to punish the Southern Kingdom:

> Behold, he comes up like clouds; his chariots like the whirlwind; his horses are swifter than eagles— woe to us, for we are ruined! O Jerusalem, wash your heart from evil, that you may be saved. How long shall your wicked thoughts lodge within you? (Jer. 4:13-14 ESV)

In fact, as Don Preston points out in *Like Father Like Son, On Clouds of Glory*, God is consistently seen using cloud imagery to indicate divine wrath carried out by human militaries in regular history.[35] In other words, when God comes on a cloud he's doing so in human history as a military invasion by a foreign army. Since a key hermeneutical principle is that the Old Testament should help us define prophetic imagery, the burden of proof in this case is on the futurist to prove that coming in or on clouds means something other than its historic, Biblical use. The Biblical precedent is for cloud imagery to describe a military invasion. Nowhere do any of the New Testament authors redefine the imagery. The preterist argument is that the imagery was fulfilled by the Roman War beginning in 66AD. There is no Biblical precedent for futurists to assume that "coming on clouds" means Jesus riding a cumulous surf board.

It should come as no surprise, then, that every Old Testament use of the phrase "day of the Lord" is a military disaster due to punishment inflicted by God.[36] There was no attempt by the Apostles anywhere in the New Testament to redefine "the day of the Lord" or its method of fulfillment. If the original audience expected that the phrase "day of the Lord" or "coming on the clouds" meant a military disaster, it would have been up to the Apostles to clearly, explicitly redefine the terms. They never did. The only reasonable conclusion, then, is that the second coming was in fact a coming in judgment against Christ's enemies (Matt. 23) that was fulfilled by the Roman army just as the prophetic imagery would suggest.

The imagery of the Son of Man in heaven and the Son of Man coming on the clouds were tied closely together, so they were addressed as a unit. But we don't want to forget the mourning of the tribes of the earth. This language starts in prophetic imagery back in Isaiah 2. That prophecy is against "Judah and Jerusalem," and describes the "latter days" when final judgment will come against Israel. As the prophecy continues through to chapter 3, we find the following:

> In that day the Lord will take away the finery of the anklets, the headbands, and the crescents; the pendants, the bracelets, and the scarves; the headdresses, the armlets, the sashes, the perfume boxes, and the amulets; the signet rings and nose rings; the festal robes, the mantles, the cloaks, and the handbags; the mirrors, the linen garments, the turbans, and the veils. Instead of perfume there will be rottenness; and instead of a belt, a rope; and instead of well-set hair, baldness; and instead of a rich robe, a skirt of sackcloth; and branding instead of beauty. Your men shall fall by the sword and your mighty men in battle. And her gates shall lament and mourn; empty, she shall sit on the ground. (Isaiah 3:18-26 ESV)

Starting with this precedent, mourning is connected in prophetic literature with the "latter days" and judgment against Israel. We see this continued in passages that refer to mourning in association with judgment against Israel in Isaiah 22:12-14, 60:19-21, and 61:1-4. At the conclusion of Isaiah's prophecies associated with the second coming we see the anticipation of mourning, and the promise of comfort from mourning. In a parallel passage in Joel 2:5-13 we see a connection between the eclipse of the sun, moon and stars, a military disaster, and mourning by the people involved. With these passages as background, we'll now look at the passage in Zechariah 12 that is likely the source of the reference in the Olivet Discourse:

> And I will pour out on the house of David and the inhabitants of Jerusalem a spirit of grace and pleas for mercy, so that, when they look on me, on him whom they have pierced, they shall mourn for him, as one mourns for an only child, and weep bitterly over him, as one weeps over a firstborn. On that day the mourning in Jerusalem will be as great as the mourning for Hadad-rimmon in the plain of Megiddo. The land shall mourn, each family by itself: the family of the house of David by itself, and their wives by themselves; the family of the house of Nathan by itself, and their wives by themselves; the family of the house of Levi by itself, and their wives by themselves; the family of the Shimeites by itself, and their wives by themselves; and all the families that are left, each by itself, and their wives by themselves. (Zech. 12:10-14 ESV)

The most important point to see here is that the mourning is associated with eschatological judgment, and the geography in question is the land associated with Judah. Those who were mourning were Israelites. This is important because when it says "all the tribes of the earth will mourn" in most major translations, people unfamiliar with Biblical languages expand this geography to include the whole globe.[37] However, the Greek term behind this word is "ge." While it's possible that the term "earth" is the correct English word here, there is no reason to assume that it has to imply the whole globe. And, there is no particular reason to choose "earth" as opposed to "land," "territory," or "region." Given the precedent found in Zechariah, and the lack of knowledge of modern geography by Old Testament prophets, I argue that the proper term for this interconnected concept should have been "land," and that this should have been understood to be the land of Judah at the time of the day of the Lord. In other words, if we track the use of the term "mourn" in the prophecy, we are naturally limited to a fulfillment in the land of Judah with the target audience as the Israelites living there.

Next, we'll look at the final piece of second coming imagery connected to the Olivet Discourse. It should be obvious and unassailable that Mark 13:27 ("And then he will send out the angels and gather his elect from the four winds, from the ends of the earth to the ends of heaven") is a reference to the resurrection expected in Isaiah 11:12, Dan. 12:2-4, Matt. 3:12, Matt. 13:30, 24:31ff, 1 Cor. 15:50ff, 1 Thess. 4:13ff, Rev. 14:14ff, and others. The resurrection was clearly part of the day of the Lord (day of Christ, day of God, etc.), and was to occur at the culmination of eschatology. Premillennialism and amillennialism differ here again by proposing multiple resurrections as far as 1007 years apart.[38] But I think we can all agree that the resurrection is seen in the verse in question. If this is so, the second coming is definitely in view in the Olivet Discourse. I won't go into the nature of the resurrection here. All that is necessary at this point is for us to nail down the timing in the text.

Finally, we'll look at the term "generation" in Matthew 24. The Calvary Chapel writer confidently asserts that in Matthew 24, Jesus is only saying that the people alive at the time of the final fulfillment will survive until the completion of the fulfillment. It is unclear what sort of rhetorical power such a statement is supposed to have to the original audience since there isn't much question that the people who are alive to see something will be alive to see it. Relying on MacArthur's statement that all preterist theology is based on a misunderstanding of this term, he doesn't make a detailed defense of why the term should be understood as a future generation. He assumes that since the imagery associated *must* be future, then the generation *must* be as well. I've already shown that the imagery is best explained by comparing scripture with scripture, and that it was fulfilled by the Roman War. I could stop here in refuting this point. But, I'll push on to focus on how the New Testament uses "generation" to prove that there are no grounds for rejecting preterism because of this passage.

Though there other, and some earlier, definitions of "generation" sympathetic to the Calvary Chapel and John MacArthur position, one of the most important comes from the Scofield Reference Notes for Matthew 24:34:

> (Greek, "genea", the primary definition of which is, "race, kind, family, stock, breed"). (So all lexicons.) That the word is used in this sense because none of "these things," that is, the world-wide preaching of the kingdom, the great tribulation, the return of the Lord in visible glory, and the regathering of the elect, occurred at the destruction of Jerusalem by Titus, A.D. 70. The promise is, therefore, that the generation -- nation, or family of Israel -- will be preserved unto "these things"; a promise wonderfully fulfilled to this day.[39]

This quote is important because the Scofield Reference Bible is credited with making dispensationalism in the early 1900s. His position was very influential and set the tone for dispensationalists throughout that century. In this note Scofield is unambiguous that the primary definition of the term genea is "race, kind, family, stock, breed," and that "all lexicons" agree with him (though he doesn't tell us which ones).

The problem is that he is wrong. The following are both the Strong's and Thayer's definition for the term genea:

Strong's definition

G1074

γενεά

genea

ghen-eh-ah'

From (a presumed derivative of) G1085; a generation; by implication an age (the period or the persons): - age, generation, nation, time.

Total KJV occurrences: 42

Thayer's definition:

1) fathered, birth, nativity

2) that which has been begotten, men of the same stock, a family

2a) the several ranks of natural descent, the successive members of a genealogy

2b) metaphorically a group of men very like each other in endowments, pursuits, character

2b1) especially in a bad sense, a perverse nation

3) the whole multitude of men living at the same time

4) an age (i.e. the time ordinarily occupied be each successive generation), a space of 30 - 33 years

If you were to only read Scofield, you would not know that the most highly respected English lexicon, Strong's, lists the primary definition of genea as, "a generation; by implication an age (the period or the persons): - age, generation, nation, time." While it is an option for genea to mean race, no mainstream, or even ancient, English language Bible has used the term this way in text (ESV, NLT, RSV, NKJV, NIV, NASB, WEY, Darby, ASV, KJV, YLT, GW, HCSB, NASB77, NASB95, ISV, JUB, KJV-1611, LEB, LITV, EMTV, Geneva, ABP, BBE, Bishops Bible 1568, CEV). And, while it is true that in some cases there are footnotes explaining that optional terms such as age, or race exist for genea, none of the translation committees have chosen those terms. Why?

The reason is that the context clearly shows that the original hearers of Jesus' teaching were the group who should have expected to see the fulfillment. In Matthew 24, the term "they" is used eight times for either the targets of judgment or the angels who'd bring it. Not one time is it used to describe a believer in the future. Instead, the term "you" is used 21 times for the original target audience to indicate that the people hearing the discourse would be the ones who needed to be warned about its fulfillment. A few of the examples are:

> And Jesus answered them, "See that no one leads **you** astray. (Matt. 24:4 ESV)

> And you will hear of wars and rumors of wars. See that **you** are not alarmed, for this must take place, but the end is not yet. (Matt. 24:6 ESV)

> Then they will deliver **you** up to tribulation and put **you** to death, and **you** will be hated by all nations for my name's sake. (Matt. 24:9 ESV)

> See, I have told **you** beforehand. So, if they say to **you**, 'Look, he is in the wilderness,' do not go out. If they say, 'Look, he is in the inner rooms,' do not believe it. (Matt. 24:25-26 ESV)

In addition to these obvious indications that Jesus was telling the Disciples about things that they would experience, we have clues from the surrounding context about the scope of "generation." The discourse that includes the Olivet Discourse actually begins in chapter 23, where Jesus scolds the Jewish leadership. As part of a chiasm, chapter 23 contains the first use of the term "generation," while chapter 24 has the second. Chapter 23 acts as the left book end for the topic of Christ's coming, and chapter 24 acts as the right book end. This helps us define what generation is in view.[40] Portions of the chiasm below are quoted from David Currie's *What Jesus Really Said About the End of the World.*[41]

A. This generation (23:36)

B. Gathering the rejected (23:37)

C. See the Son of Man (23:38-39)

D. Going away (24:1a)

Z. Preach the gospel to all of the world (24:14)

D'. Appearing (24:30a)

C'. See the Son of Man (24:30b)

B'. Gathering successful (24:31)

A'. This generation (24:32-34)

No one I'm aware of alleges that the use of "generation" in Matthew 23 refers to anyone other than the Pharisees that Jesus was scolding. Since this is so, the second reference to it should have a direct reference to the first one. If "this generation" in Matthew 24 refers to the Jews in the New Testament era, then there is no reason that it is about anything other than the Roman War. If it's about the Roman War, and as we've seen above, preterists and premillennialists agree that the Olivet Discourse is certainly about the second coming, then the coming of the Romans as a tool used by God for judgment was the earthly manifestation of the second coming of Christ in glory.[42]

One final connection I'll make to define "generation" in Matthew 24 is with a matching passage in Matthew 16:

> From that time Jesus began to show his disciples that he must go to Jerusalem and suffer many things from the elders and chief priests and scribes, and be killed, and on the third day be raised. And Peter took him aside and began to rebuke him, saying, "Far be it from you, Lord! This shall never happen to you." But he turned and said to Peter, "Get behind me, Satan! You are a hindrance to me. For you are not setting your mind on the things of God, but on the things of man." Then Jesus told his disciples, "If anyone would come after me, let him deny himself and take up his cross and follow me. For whoever would save his life will lose it, but whoever loses his life for my sake will find it. For what will it profit a man if he gains the whole world and forfeits his soul? Or what shall a man give in return for his soul? For the Son of Man is going to come with his angels in the glory of his Father, and then he will repay each person according to what he has done. Truly, I say to you, there are some standing here who will not taste death until they see the Son of Man coming in his kingdom." (Matt. 16:21-28 ESV)

Here, we see that Jesus taught the Disciples about prophetic events in his own future, and then their own. In teaching about the final individual's destiny he describes that judgment as happening to the Disciples when he comes with his angels in the glory of his Father. It is at the time that the Son of Man's kingdom arrives that the audience will be judged. That will happen before everyone present tastes death.[43] This cannot be a reference to the transfiguration mentioned in the next chapter because each man wasn't repaid for his works at that time. Instead, the connecting language of "coming with his angels" is found in Matthew 24:31, "And he will send out his angels with a loud trumpet call, and they will gather his elect from the four winds, from one end of heaven to the other." This event must have happened before all of the Disciples died. Since the judgment in Matthew 16 had to have happened before the Disciples died, to the generation that was alive at the time, premillennial dispensationalism is impossible.

Summary:

The second coming happened right on time, in exactly the way it was predicted. The fact that our modern imaginations don't match the way scripture predicts and describes the real fulfillment of prophecy doesn't mean that God was unfaithful. It means that we were programmed, sometimes unconsciously, to see it that way. The generation living to hear the Olivet Discourse is the one that saw the fulfillment of these events. The scope of the prediction matches a local judgment just as similar language had predicted throughout the Old Testament. Jesus and the Apostles were not wrong. God did not change his mind. The Olivet Discourse was not a dual prophecy with part of it waiting mysteriously at least 2,000 years to be fulfilled.

Chapter 1 Endnotes

[18] Other versions of this speech are given in Mark 13 and Luke 21. A full analysis of the lesson can't be done without comparing all three of these lessons. But, as a hermeneutical point of audience relevance, each of these lessons as recorded in different books should be adequate to convey the basic point of the discourse.

[19] In *The Second Coming*, p.10, John MacArthur begins his assault on preterism by saying, "Hyper-preterists build their whole theology on a misunderstanding of Christ's words in Matthew 24:34 . . ." This is clearly untrue. See the Recommended Reading page for books that approach preterist theology from several different angles.

[20] Douglas Wikinson, *Preterist Time Statements*.

[21] C.S. Lewis, *The World's Last Night and Other Essays*.

[22] This is Luke's version of the Olivet Discourse. This version is significantly different than the ones found in Matthew and Mark. It clearly described the crisis at hand as Jerusalem being surrounded by armies, and by comparing the texts we can clearly see that this invasion was the abomination that would desolate Jerusalem.

[23] Philippians 4:5 (ESV); Credit goes to Don Preston for his observation of this dynamic.

[24] Josephus, *Wars of the Jews, Book 6*:
http://sacred-texts.com/jud/josephus/war-6.htm.

[25] It's not at all clear how the instruction for believers to flee to the mountains is supposed to be helpful when the universe is melted as part of the coming judgment. Likewise, if we are going to take the advice literally, I expect that most Zionist Christians would be surprised to find out that they will be arrested and beaten by Jews in synagogues as part of the Great Tribulation (Mark 13:9).

[26] John MacArthur, *The Second Coming*, p.59.

[27] James 5:8 (ESV).

[28] 1 John 2:18 (ESV).

[29] Josephus, *Wars of the Jews, Book 6*:
http://sacred-texts.com/jud/josephus/war-6.htm.

[30] I'm not denying that miracles happen. Clearly, at some points in the Biblical narrative miraculous events happen where God personally breaks into history. However, as I show in this chapter this is not typically the case with "the day of the Lord." The Biblical precedent is that these events are always military invasions by human civilizations carrying out judgment by God.

[31] Once again, this passage shows the sun, moon, and stars being affected by a military invasion. In this case, they are actually judged and punished, which indicates that in prophetic imagery these bodies do not represent real astronomical objects. Instead, I think it's more likely that they represent the "host of heaven" as the supernatural Divine Council that managed human affairs in pagan nations in the Old Testament, or under the Old Covenant. The sun, moon, and stars do not literally refer to the objects in space, and the objects in space are not literally affected by military battles on earth. See David Curtis' YouTube series on spiritual warfare, https://www.youtube.com/watch?v=1IWhVVxavA4; http://digitalcommons.liberty.edu/cgi/viewcontent.cgi?article=1092&context=fac_dis.

[32] The Greek term here is *erchomai.* It does not necessarily mean return. It simply says that Jesus will "come" or "arrive" in the same way as you saw him go into heaven, presumably somehow related to clouds. A comparison of the ascension to the events of Revelation 5:1ff, and the subsequent acknowledgement of the session of Christ in Acts 2, should give us pause in presumptively assigning Acts 1:11 to the second coming. However, plausible preterist arguments have been made to accommodate such a second coming application, so I will focus my efforts on those in this book.

[33] Amillennialists tend to apply the prophetic events of Daniel to the Hellenistic era in Palestine, having fulfillment in the campaign of Antiochus Epiphanies. Their position is not directly engaged by my argument.

[34] John F. Walvoord, *Every Prophecy of the Bible,* p.231-32.

[35] Don K. Preston, *Like Father Like Son, On Clouds of Glory,* p.71.

[36] Douglas Wilkinson, *Making Sense of the Millennium.*

[37] The ESV, NLT, RSV, NKJV, NIV, NASB, ASV, KJV, and YLT all use the term "earth."

[38] Premillennialism has two literal out-of-the-grave resurrections, one at the beginning of the millennium and one at the end, whereas amillennialism has the first resurrection as spiritual regeneration and the second as literal at the end of time.

[39] Scofield Reference Notes, Matthew 24:34, e-Sword.

[40] David Currie, *What Jesus Really Said about the End of the World*, p.32. In a chiasm, an argument is made self-referential to help define the scope or imagery in it. The order of argument is A, B, C, C', B', A'. In each case, the first example of the letter introduces a character or term and the second one refers back to the original one in some way. With this structure identified in Matthew 23-24 in reference to the term "generation," it is rhetorically impossible for the second use of "generation" be a different class of people than the first use.

[41] Currie makes a very powerful case that the Olivet Discourse is about the destruction of the Temple in Jerusalem. Unfortunately, he doesn't follow his own observations to their logical conclusion. Instead, he falls back on the Magisterium and concedes that the whole discourse has a double meaning. There is no evidence of this in the text, but historical doctrine requires that he takes this position.

[42] L.S. Chafer, *Major Bible Themes*, p.308; and Gary DeMar, https://americanvision.org/1689/norman-l-geisler-generation/. DeMar documents that Norman Geisler supports genea translated as "race."

[43] Stanley Toussaint, *Behold the King,* p.209.

Chapter 2: Revelation 1:1

Calvary Chapel Statement:

Revelation 1:1 says, "The Revelation of Jesus Christ, which God gave Him to show His servants--things which must shortly [Greek: tachos] take place. And He sent and signified it by His angel to His servant John.

See also Revelation 2:16; 11:14; 22:12 where the word quickly is used.

Preterists will say that Jesus was coming quickly and soon after John wrote these words, but is this the meaning that John was trying to convey?

The words quickly [Greek: tachus] and soon [Greek: tachos] mean "shortly, quickly, speedily or swiftly". They don't convey the idea of a "soon" event but "an event that when it comes will be swift and quick".

- ○ *Vines Expository of the Old and New Testament Words says that tachus means, "swift, quick" and signifies "quickly".*
- ○ *Thayer's Greek-English Lexicon says that tachus means "quickly, speedily"*

John was not referring to when the event would happen but in what manner the event would take place. These events would come upon us "swiftly and suddenly" because "the day of the Lord so comes as a thief in the night."

(1 Thessalonians 5:2). In other words, they would come swiftly.

Charge:

- Tachus and tachos describe the rapidity of the event, not the immediacy.

This complaint against preterism is based on a failure to understand the depth and richness of the eschatological time statements in the New Testament. In reviewing the ten points provided by Calvary Chapel, only two of them directly address time statements. At best, they are addressing three references in the synoptic Gospels and two similar references in Revelation. As mentioned earlier, there are more than 360 direct or indirect eschatological time statements in the New Testament. None of these statements indicate that the second coming might be thousands of years in the future. Some of them might indicate that the timing is vague. But all of them can be argued to mean that the timing is very close. Futurists need to make every one of these statements fit in the second category (they admit that none of them fit in the first category). If a single one of them ends legitimately in the third category, then preterism is the result. They might dodge a few of these statements, but the full barrage is overwhelming.

I will not be hitting you with the full barrage. If you want that, take a look at my book *Preterist Time Statements*.[44] Below, I will be demonstrating that the Calvary Chapel argument in Revelation is at best naïve. I think you'll find that there is no way the Calvary Chapel analysis holds water. We'll start with the full definitions of tachos in Strong's and Thayer's as found in e-Sword.[45] I've found that this format is helpful because it allows the reader to confirm what I'm saying free of charge:

Strong's definition

tachos

takh'-os

From the same as G5036; a brief space (of time), that is, (with G1722 prefixed) in haste: - + quickly, + shortly, + speedily.

Thayer's definition

tachos

1) quickness, speed

Next, I'll provide the non-eschatological uses of the term. The quotes are all in the ESV (I haven't seen much of a difference in this case in other popular translations). I use non-eschatological uses as a baseline before moving into the eschatological uses because the examples are less likely to be manipulated out of theological bias in the author's eschatology. I'll comment in a few cases on what I think are important points brought out by the text:

> Now when Herod was about to bring him out, on that very night, Peter was sleeping between two soldiers, bound with two chains, and sentries before the door were guarding the prison. And behold, an angel of the Lord stood next to him, and a light shone in the cell. He struck Peter on the side and woke him, saying, "Get up quickly." And the chains fell off his hands. And the angel said to him, "Dress yourself and put on your sandals." And he did so. And he said to him, "Wrap your cloak around you and follow me." And he went out and followed him. He did not know that what was being done by the angel was real, but

thought he was seeing a vision. (Acts 12:6-9 ESV)

In this passage, Peter found himself in jail destined to be killed at Herod's next opportunity. An angel came to rescue him. The angel told Peter to "get up tachos." Now, does it make sense for Peter to have coiled his legs underneath him in anticipation of springing into action at some unknown future date? Of course not. Does it make sense for Peter to have immediately started moving, though at a lazy pace? Of course not. Having been through three months of Marine drill instructors yelling "quickly!" or "hurry up!" at me, I think I understand the position Peter was in. He was being ordered to move now, and with maximum speed! It makes no sense to dichotomize the two concepts, as you'll find throughout the rest of the examples.

> When I had returned to Jerusalem and was praying in the temple, I fell into a trance and saw him saying to me, 'Make haste and get out of Jerusalem quickly, because they will not accept your testimony about me.' (Acts 22:17-18 ESV)

Here, again, we see the idea of both immediate and fast movement.

> Festus replied that Paul was being kept at Caesarea and that he himself intended to go there shortly. (Acts 25:4 ESV)

Here, the idea of immediacy is associated with the passage, though the speed of the movement is ambiguous. If you were going to use this passage as a controlling precedent, you'd come to the opposite conclusion of the Calvary Chapel writer. In this case you wouldn't know how quickly Festus was going to move (by foot, horse, or boat), but you'd know it was going to happen very soon.

> He said, "In a certain city there was a judge who neither feared God nor respected man. And there was a widow in that city who kept coming to him and saying, 'Give me justice against my adversary.' For a while he refused, but afterward he said to himself, 'Though I neither fear God nor respect man, yet because this widow keeps bothering me, I will give her justice, so that she will not beat me down by her continual coming.'" And the Lord said, "Hear what the unrighteous judge says. And will not God give justice to his elect, who cry to him day and night? Will he delay long over them? I tell you, he will give justice to them speedily. Nevertheless, when the Son of Man comes, will he find faith on earth?" (Luke 18:2-8 ESV)

Again, in this case giving justice speedily is connected to the idea of no delay. It doesn't necessarily mean that the justice needs to happen in a fast manner once it starts (though I'm sure it would). But it does demand that it at least happens without delay. Again, this is exactly the opposite of what the Calvary Chapel writer asserts.

This exhausts the uses of tachos outside of eschatology. If you had only the previous examples as a baseline, you would have to conclude that the term is primarily addressing immediacy, and only secondarily (if at all) the actual speed of the action. So, you'd have to say that the word at least means that something had to happen immediately. You might even conclude that it means the opposite of what the Calvary Chapel writer proposes.

Next, we'll look at eschatological uses outside of Revelation 1:

The God of peace will soon crush Satan under your feet. The grace of our Lord Jesus Christ be with you. (Rom. 16:20 ESV)

And he said to me, "These words are trustworthy and true. And the Lord, the God of the spirits of the prophets, has sent his angel to show his servants what must soon take place." (Rev. 22:6 ESV)

In both of these cases, the ESV translators have chosen to translate the term as "soon." Again, the rapidity of the event in question is not stated. The following are the terms that various translations use for tachos in Revelation 1:1:

"soon": ESV, NLT, RSV, NIV, NASB95, HCSB, NASB77

"before long": WEY

"shortly": NKJV, DARBY, ASV, KJV,

"quickly": YLT, GW

"before you know it": MSG

As you can see for yourself, there is no indication that the term tachos excludes the idea of "soon" or "shortly." This assertion has no foundation whatsoever in the rest of scripture's use of that term, which can only lead us to the conclusion that their interpretation is based on theological necessity. If it means that Christ will return soon (with or without rapid movement), preterism is the result. They have to avoid this possibility at all costs.

The following is the primary passage in the Calvary Chapel argument:

The revelation of Jesus Christ, which God gave him to show to his servants the things that must soon take place. He made it known by sending his angel to his servant John, who bore witness

> to the word of God and to the testimony of Jesus Christ, even to all that he saw. Blessed is the one who reads aloud the words of this prophecy, and blessed are those who hear, and who keep what is written in it, for the time is near. (Rev. 1:1-3 ESV)

I think you can clearly see that the meaning of tachos in verse 1 naturally carries the meaning of a near-term fulfillment. But even if this use of the term broke free of all precedent found in the New Testament, so that it only defined the rapidity of the event and the timing of it remained ambiguous, the Calvary Chapel position still cannot stand. Their disaster comes in verse 3, "Blessed is the one who reads aloud the words of this prophecy, and blessed are those who hear, and who keep what is written in it, for the time is near." The Calvary Chapel writer conveniently left that verse out of his argument. I think he did so because it destroys his case. The time of the second coming was both "soon" and "near."

In case you think that there is a chance that "near" in verse 3 doesn't mean "near" in proximity of time, take a look again at the definitions of the words from Strong's and Thayer's:

Strong's definition

ἐγγύς

eggus

eng-goos'

From a primary verb ἄγχω agchō (to squeeze or throttle; akin to the base of G43); near (literally or figuratively, of place or time): - from, at hand, near, nigh (at hand, unto), ready.

Thayer's definition

ἐγγύς

eggus

1) near, of place and position

1a) near

1b) those who are near access to God

1b1) Jews, as opposed to those who are alien from God and his blessings

1b2) The Rabbis used the term "to make nigh" as equivalent to "to make a proselyte"

2) of time

2a) of times imminent and soon to come pass

Below, I've provided both non-eschatological and eschatological uses of eggus, the term translated as "near":

> So because of the Jewish day of Preparation, since the tomb was close at hand, they laid Jesus there. (John 19:42 ESV)

> He said, "Go into the city to a certain man and say to him, 'The Teacher says, My time is at hand. I will keep the Passover at your house with my disciples.'" (Matt. 26:18 ESV)

> In speaking of a new covenant, he makes the first one obsolete. And what is becoming obsolete and growing old is ready to vanish away. (Heb. 8:13 ESV)

> From the fig tree learn its lesson: as soon as its branch becomes tender and puts out its leaves, you know that summer is near. So also, when you see all these things, you know that he is near, at the very gates. (Matt. 24:32-33 ESV)

I think you can see that when you look at all of the evidence there is no doubt that Revelation 1:1-3 indicates that the events would happen in short order. I encourage you to follow up on similar types of arguments by using online or computer-based searches. You don't have to know Greek to do so. All you have to know is how to use a dictionary and a concordance. Two of my favorite free tools to do such research (there are others) are e-Sword (a free computer Bible program with an easy to use lexicon and concordance system) and Interlinear Scripture Analyzer or ISA (a free computer bible program with a powerful concordant view presentation). You can find these programs at:

www.e-sword.net

www.scripture4all.org

Please use these tools to test the things I'm saying. Test the things apologists such as the Calvary Chapel writer says. Be a good Berean.

Summary:

In Revelation 1, the use of tachos means "near" and the use of eggus two verses later means "at hand." Used together, they demand that the action happen in short order. At the risk of running up the score against the Calvary Chapel writer, I have avoided listing the more than 360 similar eschatological time statements in the New Testament.[46] The evidence that fulfillment was promised to happen in that generation is overwhelming.

As I addressed in chapter 1, the only option left to Evangelical futurists is to follow the line of thought advanced by John MacArthur in *The Second Coming*. He can clearly see the danger to futurist eschatology presented by the New Testament time statements. If Jesus and the

Apostles were being honest and had any credibility at all, then the second coming had to have happened in that generation. If they were wrong, then scripture, and our conception of their reliability, is profoundly flawed. This is why MacArthur says that these times statements weren't meant to be taken literally. Instead, they were meant to be spiritualized by their readers. They weren't meant to be truthful warnings or encouragements to those who first received them. They were only meant to prompt Christians to sanctification in all generations.

Chapter 3: Early Church Fathers

Calvary Chapel Statement:

The Early Church Fathers in their writings never mentioned that Jesus' Second Coming already occurred.

Charlie Campbell, Director of Always Be Ready Apologetics Ministry says that "The idea that Jesus came back in A.D. 70 was a foreign idea during the first five centuries of the church and then only mentioned sporadically after that until about 400 years ago. It wasn't until the early 17th century—when preterist thinking was applied by the Jesuit Catholic scholar named Alcazar to the book of Revelation—that it was given very serious consideration."

If Jesus Christ's Second Coming had already occurred, don't you think the early church fathers would have found it significant to at least mention it once?

Charges:

- The idea that Jesus came back in the destruction of Jerusalem was foreign to the church prior to 500AD.
- It is only sporadically found afterwards.
- It wasn't until Alcazar's book that preterism was taken seriously.
- The church fathers should have mentioned such an important event.

There is quite a bit of overlap in the arguments between this chapter and the next. I'll try to keep them somewhat segregated, but you'll notice that the charges are similar enough that there is bound to be some redundancy in my remarks. This chapter will rely heavily on the research done by Ed Stevens, John Bray, Riley O'Brien Powell, Francis Gumerlock, and Gary DeMar.[47]

The difficulty of this chapter is that, while it presents some real challenges to preterism, it reveals even more about the illegitimate assumptions of premillennialism. My question to them is, are you sure you want to go there?

The issue at hand is whether or not the patristic writers (those early church writers who commented on Christianity in the first few hundred years) are reliable sources of doctrine. In order for them to be reliable, they would have to meet a number of criteria. First, they would have to be creating documents that are reliably dated. Second, they would have to be writing within objective orthodoxy, meaning that they would have to be correct about what they are saying. Third, they would have to rely on inside knowledge passed down to them from the Apostles so that their understanding of scripture is superior to the study of the text by itself. Fourth, when early writers disagree there must be some way to tell which one is correct. Fifth, the formulations of doctrines that are handed down to modern theology must be substantially similar to the modern version so that the modern theology can claim orthodoxy.

The problem with each of these criteria is that they are not true. First, there is no objective way to know when any of the patristic documents (generally grouped under the Ante-Nicene Fathers, or ANF, collection) were actually created. This includes several important early documents such as the Epistle of Barnabas, the Didache, 1 Clement, The Shepherd of Hermas, and the epistles of Ignatius.[48] These examples are critical because they represent the writings most likely to bridge the New Testament/ANF writings, or 70AD – 110AD.

Because they are notoriously hard to date, we have to be careful of the conclusions we draw from them. Ed Stevens has proposed, and is doing deep historical research to prove, that the Epistle of Barnabas was actually written before 70AD. If his thesis is correct, then one of the most important traditional examples of a post-70AD document looking forward to the second coming, instead becomes one potentially looking forward to the destruction of Jerusalem. Likewise, there is good scholarly evidence that the Didache was written before that critical date (see below). It is an open question whether or not Paul's associate Clement is the Clement of Rome who wrote 1 Clement. If so, then it is quite possible that it was written early as well. The Shepherd of Hermas was a popular early church fiction that served a similar role as Pilgrim's Progress in the Reformation era. But it presents all sorts of doctrinal problems to modern theology, so it might be better to group it with curious apocryphal writings than to embrace its stance on eschatology.[49] If that particular book is doctrinally off base, then we have to wonder what group of Christians contributed to its content. Were they Christians who were passing down oral tradition from the Apostles (in which case we'd assume they were correct), or were they from a later generation who was groping to make sense of New Testament texts that had been compiled, though they had no guidance in their interpretation? And, finally, there is a real question about the dating of Ignatius' epistles. While they don't contain much about eschatology other than a vague sense of still anticipating a future resurrection, there is a real question in scholarship about whether or not they are authentic. They might, on the other hand, be a later forgery meant to reinforce Roman Catholic Church views on authority in church leadership. If this later suspicion is correct, then they should have no bearing at all on our consideration of early writings. If all of these works were either written before 70AD or are illegitimate, then we have very little to go on in the first generation of the church after the destruction of Jerusalem.

The second point is that ANF writings would have to represent objectively correct, orthodox teachings since it is only meaningful to use them in arguing eschatology if they represent correct Apostolic doctrine. There are several problems with this. To start with, it is widely accepted that all sorts of strange doctrine exists within ANF writings (i.e., soteriology, Christology, eschatology, and theology proper). This brings up the question of how this could possibly be. Why would people who were supposedly the direct religious descendants of the Apostles write divergent opinions about Christian doctrine? What kind of authority would these people have if they didn't agree with each other? Clearly one of them must be wrong. So which one?

We see this issue quite clearly in the early church's opinion on the millennium. Very early, some writers adopted an essentially Jewish view, seeing the millennium as a literalistic 1,000-year reign of Jesus in a rebuilt, giant, ideal Jerusalem. Some writers mocked this, with a powerful legend including the Apostle John publically rejecting the proponent of this approach.[50] In the end, scholars are clear that a number of different schools existed very early in church history. However, if they have some authority that preterists are to be measured against, how is it possible that there were different schools so early in Christianity? If this is true, how can patristic writers as a group be generically used to refute preterism? In order to say that a single one of those factions had the truth, so that this is the basis on which we should be measured, we'd have to take sides that would create major theological problems in modern Christianity.

An excellent example of this is that the chiliast (or literal earthly millennium premillennialist) debate still rages. Modern American Christians have no idea that the church consciously declared their eschatology heretical in 381AD, and that some form of either amillennialism or postmillennialism was the dominant orthodox approach of the church. Since premillennialists are the dominant force in American Christianity, you almost can't blame them for not realizing that their view isn't supposed to be an option. Obviously, it's been very persuasive. But the fact remains that premillennial eschatology, according to the early church, is an impossible heresy. So, are we sure we want to use early church writings as a standard?

Third, for any of the early church writings to be persuasive in our time we would have to be persuaded that they represented Apostolic doctrine handed down from the pre-70AD era. Unfortunately, none of those writers claim this.

All ANF writers cite scripture of both the Old and New Testaments to justify their beliefs. The good news is that this indicates that the scripture was compiled quite early, and that everyone seemed to agree on the content. The problem is that since they seem to rely on only their analysis of the text, they don't propose to bring any more to the table than any other generation who studied scripture closely. If those writers made a point of repeatedly relying on what they'd been told that the Apostles believed, then this would not be an issue. But they did not. That means that any generation with superior access to texts and tools to analyze them is more likely to come up with the right interpretation than the first generation.[51] With our modern research methods, which have clearly shown that the Olivet Discourse and the 70-Weeks prophecy of Daniel are unambiguous constituent elements of the second coming, we are in an excellent position to point out the historical strength of preterism.

Fourth, if we find ourselves in a situation where ancient writers disagree, we need to have a way to declare a winner. It is clear that there is disagreement in that generation, but how do we know who should win? In the early church, correct doctrine was usually established simply as a result of winning a war or assassinating a rival group.[52] In one example, in the Second Council of Ephesus in 449AD, the bishop Flavian had his brains beaten out on the floor of the meeting room to make the point to the rest of the delegates that a certain view of Christology would be the only one accepted.[53] Teamwork was the order of the day. Since whichever institutional church won the kinetic battle tended to win the doctrinal one, it is extremely dangerous to assume that their doctrine should have some sort of control over our modern analysis.

Fifth, while the allegation is that preterism isn't embraced by any of the early church writers, the assumption is that the early church writers did embrace modern systems such as premillennialism. But what if the modern opponents of preterism can't trace the roots of their eschatology back to the early church? This is exactly the bind that Calvary Chapel finds itself in. Though premillennialism can be found generically in the early church (having evolved from simply reading Revelation 19-22 sequentially as if it should be fulfilled chronologically), the early version of premillennialism, presumably based on inside knowledge passed on from the Apostles, would be unrecognizable to modern premillennial advocates. According to leaders like Irenaeus, the early church's premillennialism was fundamentally based on the assumption that there was going to be 6,000 years of human history before the final 1,000 years, the perfect era, kicked in.[54] They took this quite literally. If we are to assume that they got this interpretation through some Apostolic legend (which is the only thing that gives the early church any interpretive authority over the modern church), then we would have to conclude that this version of premillennialism is correct. The problem is that it has been invalidated by history. They expected the final 1,000 years to happen at any moment in the first few hundred years of the church. We are now nearly 2,000 years into their future and still waiting. Just like dispensationalism expired because the second coming didn't take place within a generation of the founding of Israel, premillennialism as a paradigm died when the 6,000 years of history expired sometime in the first few hundred years of the church.

For the early church premillennialists to have any authority at all they would have to have based that 6,000-year paradigm on inside knowledge passed down outside of scripture from the Apostles. But they were wrong. We have to assume the Apostles were never wrong. Therefore, the early church premillennialists did not have inside knowledge. If the early church premillennialists were wrong because they had no inside knowledge, then modern premillennialists have no foundation for criticizing the orthodoxy of preterism. Also, since the earlier version of premillennialism represented the orthodox version of it (meaning simply the original version of it), and since the modern premillennialists follow a completely different foundation for their eschatology, modern premillennialists would be just as unorthodox as they claim the preterists are. Do the modern premillennialists want to admit that their system is based on a paradigm that was proven invalid more than 1,500 years ago, and was actually declared heretical at the Constantinople council in 381AD (something never done to ancient preterists)?

The source of terminology favored by futurists is also an issue. It is the definition of irony that the person who invented the terms "second coming" and "second advent" did so in a book that deliberately, powerfully refutes and completely invalidates dispensationalism. Justin Martyr wrote *Dialog with Trypho, the Jew*[55] in approximately 160AD with the specific intent of proving that God had rejected the Jews for good. As part of that conversation he is the first person in church history to use the popular terms "second coming" and "second advent." That was about 130 years after the Olivet Discourse was given by Jesus. Justin invented the terms "second coming" and "second advent" in order to prepare the field to discuss an earthly millennium as part of an argument that the Jews had been rejected by God. It's a wonder that Calvary Chapel and similar dispensationalists embrace these terms or concepts since their entire view of ecclesiology, Christian Zionism, and the modern eschatological expectation is based on the position that Justin was arguing against.

In another stroke of irony, although Martyr dedicated *Dialog with Trypho, the Jew* to combatting the idea of the Jews remaining the people of God, he still seemed to be heavily affected by their worldview and hermeneutic.[56] Because of this, he was one of the first chiliasts, or millennialists, in the church. This position, which expected a 1,000-year literal kingdom of God on earth ruled by Christ from Jerusalem, was eventually made heretical by the church in the 381 Constantinople edition of the Nicene Creed.[57] Justin's literalistic version of the second coming was necessary to set up his literalistic version of the thousand-year reign of the saints. So, the one overly literalistic position that was eventually declared a heresy (the thousand-year earthly kingdom) could only have been created through the invention of a second one that fatefully became very popular in eschatological studies. In other words, Justin's eschatology was a mess.

Before we go further, Justin's writings (as well as Tertullian's and Irenaeus') bring up an interesting series of questions that I'd encourage you to keep in mind while reviewing all early church writings. First, does it matter what the early church fathers thought about the second coming when all modern systems of theology strenuously reject at least one of the positions of all of these writers?[58] For instance, early church premillennialism was based on the paradigm of six thousand years of earth history having already elapsed. They were looking forward in the very near future to the seventh literal thousand years, which would be the Millennium.[59] That system was invalidated by history. Therefore, early premillennialism was invalidated. If early premillennialism, which is rejected by modern theologians, is the baseline used for the criticism of preterism, how much power is there in this? Is it fair for modern premillennialists to borrow some of the vocabulary of the early church, while rejecting the fundamentals of their system, and then claim to be representing those early positions?

Second, does it matter that we can prove through powerful research tools available to us, but not available to them, that their own positions are incoherent and self-contradictory? In my book *Making Sense of the Millennium*, I point out that the early church eventually developed a loose doctrine of amillennialism based on the fulfillment of at least part of Daniel 7 (see below) and Revelation 20.[60] It was from Revelation 20 that they got the idea that the saints were reigning in heaven in the amillennial paradigm. And Daniel 7 is the source for the comment in the 381AD Constantinople version of the Nicene Creed (written specifically to make chiliasm, or premillennialism, heretical) that insists on a present kingdom that would last "forever, forever and ever." Through modern analytical tools, Duncan McKenzie was able to prove in *The Antichrist and the Second Coming* (Vols. 1-2) that the events of Daniel 7 related to the judgment of the saints, and were reflected in both Revelation 20:4-6 and 11-15.[61] In Daniel they appear to be one complex event in one vision. In Revelation they appear to be two visions separated by 1,000 years. The saints' portion of Revelation 20 (vs. 4-6, 11-15) was actually meant to be seen as a single event in history per Daniel 7.[62] This means that amillennialism was correct to see the saints reigning in heaven during the church age. It was also right to see the kingdom of God lasting forever and ever. But amillennial supporters haven't done the comparative analysis to see that the "forever and ever" reign had already started when the saints began to reign.[63] These observations have only been a standard part of analyzing scripture since a systematic approach to explaining theology has been combined with easy access to both concordance and computer search technology. Since some of this analysis proves ancient interpretations were myopic and incoherent, how much weight should we give their authors? How wrong do early church authors or paradigms have to be before we set them aside?

Third, why do we care what their opinion was on the matter if they don't claim to be basing their opinion primarily on a tradition handed down by the Apostles, but instead only claim to rely on scripture? You might be surprised to learn this, but none of the authors for whom we have extant writings claim to have written their work based primarily on tradition passed down from the Apostles.[64] And, since they are all logically incoherent at least on some level, this shouldn't be surprising. For the sake of argument, let's say Justin had inside knowledge passed on by the Apostles. We would assume that he used that knowledge to write *Dialog with Trypho, the Jew*. Unfortunately for Calvary Chapel, in that book he argues that premillennial dispensationalism, their primary interpretive framework, was completely wrong. Justin's point to Trypho, his imaginary interlocutor, is that the Jews were permanently rejected by God. Justin would scoff at the idea that the modern state of Israel was either a regathering of the Jews or any indication at all that God considered the Jews his people. Calvary Chapel leadership would certainly want to push back on that. So how much power exists in their argument when the book from which it comes destroys their very own system?

But they might be tempted to embrace popular writers like Clement. He was a proponent of a flesh-based resurrection just like Calvary Chapel. However, at one point in *The First Epistle of Clement* he attempted to prove that there would be a flesh-based resurrection of humans based on the story of the Phoenix bird raising up from the dirt in Arabia every 500 years.[65] He also proposed that Jesus had to be at least 50 years old because the term "master" had been used for him. Does anyone really thing these early church writers were basing their views on some sort of inside knowledge passed directly from the Apostles? Do we really want to base our opinions on observations such as these? On the other hand, if these writers were just making sense of scripture as best they could, why should their opinions be any more qualified than ours?

While Justin's imagination of the second coming or second advent might have been different than his successors,[66] the terms he invented stuck. But strangely, they came to mean different things to different systems of eschatology.[67] This happened incrementally over the years, resulting in radical differences in postmillennialism, amillennialism and premillennialism. In addition, since it was at least 130 years from the Olivet Discourse until the term was invented, it is anachronistic to focus simply on this term (no one writing before 170AD could have used the term because it hadn't been invented yet). Instead of simply looking for early writers who proposed that the "second coming" had already happened, I propose instead that we look at two elements of the second coming that modern premillennial theologians demand could only be fulfilled by the second coming: The Olivet Discourse and the fulfillment of Daniel's 70-Weeks prophecy. In modern premillennial terms, if these events were fulfilled then the second coming has happened. Anyone claiming that these events were fulfilled in the past might as well be saying that the second coming had already happened.

I stipulated in the opening of this book that the Olivet Discourse is a description of the second coming. Some premillennial writers such as Wayne House and John MacArthur agree, seeing the danger of allowing any of the Olivet Discourse to describe anything other than the second coming.[68] Therefore, if I can prove that a patristic author thought that the Olivet Discourse was fulfilled in the Roman War, then he is de facto asserting that the second coming happened at that time whether he came to that conclusion consciously or not, and whether he used the vocabulary "second coming" or "second advent" or not. For that writer to also be a futurist only means that his eschatology is incoherent, not that I'm wrong. But the futurists have to make a decision: Either we both use old sources that are incoherent or we both throw them out. They can't keep them for their purposes and deny them for mine.

As an example, Clement of Alexandria (cited below) is crystal clear that he thinks major elements of the 70th Week of Daniel and the Olivet Discourse were fulfilled in the events of the first century Roman War. But he also expects a future second coming. Futurists would say that this means that he is against preterism. I'd say that he has stipulated to a major preterist argument (though he didn't use the term preterism because it didn't exist at the time, just as he never used the term "second coming," and so might not have been aware of its invention only few years before). So, do we keep him or throw him out? If we have an early church author (as I'll point out, it'll turn out to be a large number of them) who has an eschatology that is incoherent and inconsistent, how much should we care if he didn't notice something that seems clear to us as a result of detailed textual analysis? Likewise, again, should Calvary Chapel use authors whose positions were antagonistic to their own in order to fight against modern enemies?

Let's start with Justin Martyr. As I mentioned earlier, Justin was the inventor of the terms "second coming" and "second advent" in about 160AD.[69] He did so in order to describe the process used to implement the thousand-year reign of Christ on earth in similar worldwide, fleshly imagery. One of his major goals in his formulation of his vocabulary and rhetoric is to prove that the Jews had been permanently rejected by God. This rejection was based on the Roman War and other calamities that they'd faced. They'd been killed and enslaved, and the Christians had been blessed. Justin's only conclusion was that the Jews had been rejected and the Christians had been chosen to replace them. Below is a short excerpt from his dialog, which is dedicated to this point:

> CHAPTER XXV -- THE JEWS BOAST IN VAIN THAT THEY ARE SONS OF ABRAHAM.
>
> Those who justify themselves, and say they are sons of Abraham, shall be desirous even in a small degree to receive the inheritance along with you; as the Holy Spirit, by the mouth of Isaiah, cries, speaking thus while he personates them: 'Return from heaven, and behold from the habitation of Thy holiness and glory. Where is Thy zeal and strength? . . .

Justin moves on in chapter XXXI to connect this thought to the "second advent":

> But if so great a power is shown to have followed and to be still following the dispensation of His suffering, how great shall that be which shall follow His glorious advent! For He shall come on the clouds as the Son of

man, so Daniel foretold, and His angels shall come with Him. These are the words: 'I beheld till the thrones were set; and the Ancient of days did sit, whose garment was white as snow, and the hair of His head like the pure wool. His throne was like a fiery flame, His wheels as burning fire. A fiery stream issued and came forth from before Him. Thousand thousands ministered unto Him, and ten thousand times ten thousand stood before Him.

This passage is critical. Justin clearly shows that the fulfillment of Daniel 7 is the second coming. There is no doubt about this. I, and all preterists that I'm aware of, agree with him on this point. Justin then goes on to argue that John the Baptist was in fact the Elijah that was to come per Zechariah and Malachi. Again, we agree. After asserting that John the Baptist was a fulfillment of the first phase of this prophecy we see this important section:

CHAPTER LI -- IT IS PROVED THAT THIS PROPHECY HAS BEEN FULFILLED.

And when I ceased, Trypho said, "All the words of the prophecy you repeat, sir, are ambiguous, and have no force in proving what you wish to prove." Then I answered, "If the prophets had not ceased, so that there were no more in your nation, Trypho, after this John, it is evident that what I say in reference to Jesus Christ might be regarded perhaps as ambiguous. But if John came first calling on men to repent, and Christ, while[John] still sat by the river Jordan, having come, put an end to his prophesying and baptizing, and preached also Himself, saying that the kingdom of heaven is at hand, . . .

Justin is arguing that John the Baptist played a major role in the prophecies related to Jesus' first advent. He also argues that John was associated with anticipating the second advent. Unfortunately, he sees that second one as being very far into the future in contrast with passages like Malachi 4 and the references to them in the New Testament.[70]

Also interesting is Justin's application of the description of the New Heaven and New Earth in Isaiah 65 to the thousand-year reign of Christ. He is probably the first author to make the drastic mistake, which Calvary Chapel follows, of using Isaiah 65 to describe something other than the New Heaven and New Earth. Instead of leaving the descriptions in the passage under that category, he assigns them to the Millennium (I argue that it's actually both).[71]

> CHAPTER LXXXI -- HE ENDEAVOURS TO PROVE THIS OPINION FROM ISAIAH AND THE APOCALYPSE.
>
> For Isaiah spake thus concerning this space of a thousand years: 'For there shall be the new heaven and the new earth, and the former shall not be remembered, or come into their heart; but they shall find joy and gladness in it, which things I create. For, Behold, I make Jerusalem a rejoicing, and My people a joy; and I shall rejoice over Jerusalem, and be glad over My I people. And the voice of weeping shall be no more heard in her, or the voice of crying.

The passage from Justin above is somewhat confusing. Although he is a futurist, he seems to be using the definitive passage in scripture for the New Heaven and New Earth and applying it to the Millennium. The term New Heaven and New Earth is only elsewhere found in Revelation 21-22 and 2 Peter 3. Both of these uses are based on the precedent of Isaiah 65-66, so these three chapters should be our primary or foundational source for what the New Heaven and New

Earth would be like. But there's a problem. According to Isaiah and Revelation there is still death and evangelism in this period. While members of the New Jerusalem are uniquely blessed, you still have normal life going on in the rest of the world.

The problem is that in both premillennial and amillennial doctrine, the New Heaven and New Earth only come about after the universe is melted and rebuilt in order to cleanse it of all evidence of the sin of Adam. This cleansing function runs very deep in their theology and is an unavoidable step in redemption given the early church fathers' (from Justin through Augustine) view of cosmology (essentially, physics). Forgetting for a moment that premillennialism and amillennialism disagree about whether there is 1,000 years between the second coming and the New Heaven and New Earth, there is no room in either theological system for death and evangelism after they have started.

However, Justin, either through incoherence or sloppiness (according to futurist eschatology), asserts exactly that. In his view the Millennium happens at the same time as the New Heaven and New Earth (at least in the way that he handles this passage), so there is both death and evangelism during this period. The implications of this are staggering. And I agree with him. I make my case in *Making Sense of the Millennium* that theologians have missed the parameters of the New Heaven and New Earth in Isaiah (even if they are a type and shadow, the dynamics still exist) and so mis-formulated eschatology from very early on.

This brings up an interesting situation for Calvary Chapel. They assume that Justin is right about the definition and description of the second coming. By claiming that Justin coined the terms "second coming" and "second advent" with some sort of authority (whether by mysterious Apostolic tradition or by excellent exegesis) they are supposedly able to refute preterism by saying that Justin didn't believe it had already happened. However, Justin also claimed that their definitions of the role of John the Baptist and at least the New Heaven and New Earth are completely wrong, not to mention the permanent rejection of the Jews as the people of God. In these cases, Justin agrees with preterists more than futurists. I agree with Justin that there needed to be a second coming. I simply disagree with him on the timing and purpose of it. I happen to agree with Justin's formulation of applying Isaiah 65 to the Millennium,[72] though I disagree with the fleshly nature that is usually imposed on the thousand-year reign of the saints. In other words, I agree with Justin about parts of almost everything he said; Calvary Chapel (and most futurist theologians) disagree with almost everything he has said, but use the terminology he invented in his argument to anchor their eschatology.

I'll wrap up our look at Justin with two quotes from him in his first apology regarding the judgment that had just happened against the Jews.

CHAPTER XLV -- CHRIST'S SESSION IN HEAVEN FORETOLD.

These are his words: "The Lord said unto My Lord, Sit Thou at My right hand, until I make Thine enemies Thy footstool. The Lord shall send to Thee the rod of power out of Jerusalem; and rule Thou in the midst of Thine enemies. With Thee is the government in the day of Thy power, in the beauties of Thy saints: from the womb of morning hare I begotten Thee." That which he says, "He shall send to Thee the rod of power out of Jerusalem," is predictive of the mighty, word, which His apostles, going forth from Jerusalem, preached everywhere; and though death is decreed against those who teach or at all confess the name of Christ, we everywhere both embrace and teach it.[73]

CHAPTER XLVII -- DESOLATION OF JUDAEA FORETOLD.

That the land of the Jews, then, was to be laid waste, hear what was said by the Spirit of prophecy. And the words were spoken as if from the person of the people wondering at what had happened. They are these: "Sion is a wilderness, Jerusalem a desolation. The house of our sanctuary has become a curse, and the glory which our fathers blessed is burned up with fire, and all its glorious things are laid waste: and Thou refrainest Thyself at these things, and hast held Thy peace, and hast humbled us very sore." And ye are convinced that Jerusalem has been laid waste, as was predicted. And concerning its desolation, and that no one should be permitted to inhabit it, there was the following prophecy by Isaiah: "Their land is desolate, their enemies consume it before them, and none of them shall dwell therein." And that it is guarded by you lest any one dwell in it, and that death is decreed against a Jew apprehended entering it, you know very well.

The first of these two quotes shows Justin applying terminology usually reserved for the millennial reign to his own era, extending it back to the Apostles. He doesn't see the reign of Christ in his kingdom as a physically dominating one, in spite of the mention of his "rod of power," etc. In this, he's practically an amillennialist. He's not being particularly consistent with this, since if he were pressed on the matter, he would say that the Millennium is still future to him. This passage just goes to show the arbitrary nature of his exegesis.

In the second section, we see critical prophecies from Isaiah 64 normally applied to the second coming being applied to the destruction of Jerusalem before Justin was writing. In other words, it seemed to be common knowledge to him that the judgment against Jerusalem predicted in Isaiah 64 had already happened. I would point to Don Preston's extensive audio teaching on Zion in Isaiah to make a detailed argument that this must be applied to the second coming.[74] If Justin has argued for a past second coming in one section (whether he realizes it or not) and a future second coming in a second section, does he have any credibility left on the matter? If his argument is more often consistent with preterism than with premillennial dispensationalism (he didn't know these terms, of course, so we are only going by the elements of his arguments), should futurists be using him as a source for their argument against preterists?

To summarize, Justin asserts that there will be a second coming of Christ. Both premillennialists and preterists agree with this, though we disagree with the timing. Justin establishes that Daniel 7 is a description of the second coming. Again, premillennialists and preterists agree on the dynamic, though we disagree on the timing. Justin powerfully argues that the Jews are no longer the chosen people of God. Preterists would have no problem with this by loosely following what's known as supersessionism.[75] Calvary Chapel would choke on it. But, his argument is powerful and crystal clear. Do they still want to claim that he has inside knowledge or authority on eschatology?

Continuing, Justin says that John the Baptist was supposed to arrive before the day of the Lord. Preterists agree with the

New Testament that Elijah already came in the person of John the Baptist. Calvary Chapel leaders will say that this prophecy failed in the first century so that Elijah has to come back again in the future. Justin argues that Isaiah 65-66 applies to the New Heaven and New Earth. Preterists agree. In my variant of preterism I'd also agree with him that it applies to the Millennium.[76] However, Calvary Chapel teaches, as does all futurist teachers I'm aware of, that Isaiah 65-66 defines the Millennium but not the New Heaven and New Earth. I've heard them refer to Isaiah's version of the New Heaven and New Earth as an initial phase of it, but they'd argue that they are still looking for the real, final New Heaven and New Earth. Clearly, absolute reliance on early church writers is a bad idea.

Next, we'll move on to Clement of Alexandria, another very important writer from the generation after Justin. Clement's *Stromata* provides us with a clear description of his interpretation of Daniel's 70-Weeks prophecy:

> That the temple accordingly was built in seven weeks, is evident; for it is written in Esdras. And thus Christ became King of the Jews, reigning in Jerusalem in the fulfilment of the seven weeks. And in the sixty and two weeks the whole of Judaea was quiet, and without wars. And Christ our Lord, "the Holy of Holies," having come and fulfilled the vision and the prophecy, was anointed in His flesh by the Holy Spirit of His Father.
>
> In those "sixty and two weeks," as the prophet said, and "in the one week," was He Lord. The half of the week Nero held sway, and in the holy city Jerusalem placed the abomination; and in the half of the week he was taken away, and Otho, and Galba, and Vitellius. And Vespasian rose to the supreme power, and destroyed

> Jerusalem, and desolated the holy place. And
> that such are the facts of the case, is clear to him
> that is able to understand, as the prophet said.[77]

Without any question, Clement of Alexandria (who never used the terms "second coming" or "second advent" in *Stromata*), writing in about 190AD, is saying that the entire 70-Weeks prophecy of Daniel was fulfilled in the Roman War against Jerusalem in 70AD. This is exactly what preterists argue. Calvary Chapel teachers would say that Clement is absolutely wrong. Preterists would not say that Clement actually understood the implications of what he said. But if Clement said that the 70-Weeks prophecy was fulfilled, and there is no evidence that he was aware of the newly coined term "second coming," and the 70-Weeks prophecy is acknowledged by all premillennialists as being synonymous with the "second coming," then how can premillennialists claim that no one from the ancient world thought that the second coming had already happened? If, on the other hand, Clement thought that the 70-Weeks prophecy was fulfilled, and that there was still a future second coming, how can premillennialists use him as a source of reliable opinion since they would argue that he is absolutely, fundamentally wrong about his eschatology?

Finally, we'll jump forward a few hundred years to about 325AD and look at Eusebius, one of the most important writers of early Christianity. His book *The Church History* (or, *Ecclesiastical History*) is recognized as the most important early history of the church. But he wrote other things as well. One of the most important of these was *Theophania*.[78] This book has a strange history because it was recovered from obscurity having been translated into Aramaic. There doesn't seem to be any doubt that it was originally written in Greek, but no Greek copies exist. So how might this have happened?

The editor of the recovered copy, Samuel Lee, points out that someone as important as Eusebius would have had all of his works compiled by the Roman Catholic Church for their library. For him to have written a book that wasn't noticed by them, or at least declared to be lost, would have been nearly impossible. So, if there is no Greek copy of his book in their library, and the only copy was written in a language that reflects geography that they did not control, his conclusion is that there is a strong possibility that there was a deliberate attempt by the Roman Catholic Church to suppress the book.[79] This is an important factor when considering fragmentary evidence of preterism in church history.

In Eusebius' case, *Theophania* was found and eventually translated into English by Lee. Lee concludes the book with an interesting compilation of Eusebius' position on eschatology found inside. In a nutshell, he is a full preterist with an end date based on the work of Constantine and the founding of the Roman Catholic Church. He saw the success of the church as the breaking in of the New Heaven and New Earth. Importantly, his position, which can be seen in fragments in places like *Ecclesiastical History* was never condemned by the church. If Eusebius was the most important historian of the early church and thought that all prophecy had been fulfilled by ancient events, but he was never condemned for it, then why are modern preterists condemned for similar beliefs?

To flesh out Eusebius' position a bit further, we need to review an unambiguous, though long, quote of his position on the 70 Weeks of Daniel:[80]

This, then, was the very time that Daniel, inspired by the divine spirit, marked when he said, "I Daniel understood in the books the number of the years, what was the word of the Lord to Jeremiah the prophet, for the fulfilment of the desolation of Jerusalem seventy years, and I turned my face to the Lord my God, to present my prayer and petition." Then after his prayer the Angel prophesied to him of the seventy weeks, and told him at what point to begin to reckon the time, saying, ". . .

And if you reckon the succeeding period from that date up to King Herod and the Roman Emperor Augustus, in whose times our Saviour was born on earth, you will find it amounts to 483 years, which are the seven and sixty-two weeks of the prophecy of Daniel. From the sixty-sixth Olympiad to the 186th Olympiad there are 121 Olympiads, or 484 years, an Olympiad consisting of four years, during which time Augustus the Roman Emperor, in the fifteenth year of his reign, gained the kingdom of Egypt and of the whole world, under whom Herod was the first foreigner to ascend the Jewish throne, and our Lord and Saviour Jesus Christ was born, the time of His birth synchronizing with the fulfilment of the seven and sixty-two weeks of Daniel's prophecy.

And afterwards comes the one remaining week, separated from them and divided by a long interval, during which occurred all the other events that are predicted in between, all of which being foretold in the middle of the oracle were fulfilled; they run in the following way: "After the seven and sixty-two weeks the Unction shall be cast out, and there is no judgment in it. And he will destroy the city and the Holy Place with the leader that cometh, and they shall be cut off as by a flood, and until the end of the completion of the war by destructions" . . .

"And the city, and the holy place, he will destroy, with the governor that cometh." Here again I understand the rulers of foreign stock who succeeded him to be meant. For as above he named the High-Priests, Christs and Governors, saying, "Until Christ the Governor," in the same way after their time and after their abolition there was no other ruler to come but the same Herod of foreign stock, and the others ruled the nation in order after them, in whose company and by whose aid, using them as his agents, that hateful bane of good men is said to have destroyed the city and the Holy Place. And indeed he destroyed of a truth the whole nation, now upsetting the established order of the priesthood, now perverting the whole people, and encouraging the city (which stands metaphorically for its people) in impiety. And Aquila agrees with my interpretation of the passage, translating thus, "And the people of the governor that cometh will destroy the city and the holy place." Meaning that the city and the Holy Place arc not only to be ruined by the leader to come, whom I have identified in my interpretation, but also by his people. And you would not be far wrong in saying, too, that the Roman general and his army arc meant by the words before us, where I think the camps of the Roman rulers are meant, who governed the nation from that time, and who destroyed the city of Jerusalem itself, and its ancient venerable Temple. For they were cut off by them as by a flood, and were at once involved in destruction until the war was concluded, so that the prophecy was fulfilled and they suffered

> utter desolation after their plot against our
> Saviour, which was followed by their extreme
> sufferings during the siege. You will find an
> accurate account of it in the history of Josephus.

There is not much doubt here that Eusebius is saying that the 70th Week of Daniel was completely fulfilled in the first century.[81] If this is true, and like MacArthur we confidently say that the last week of that prophecy can only happen at the second coming, then we are saying that Eusebius was proposing the second coming had already happened (whether he realized the implication of his position or not).

Don Preston conclusively proves that the six elements of the 70th Week prophecy could only be fulfilled at the climax of the eschaton, at the second coming and resurrection. There is no way to have those six points fulfilled and then have any further prophecy from Israel's calendar unfulfilled (MacArthur would agree). And remember, we agreed with MacArthur that Daniel's 70 Weeks and the Olivet Discourse (all of it, since we are stipulating that it is fulfilled as a unified event) were synonymous with the second coming of Christ.[82]

Do we have anything from Eusebius about the Olivet Discourse?

> Chapter VII.--The Predictions of Christ.

> 1. It is fitting to add to these accounts the true prediction of our Saviour in which he foretold these very events. 2. His words are as follows: "Woe unto them that are with child, and to them that give suck in those days! But pray ye that your flight be not in the winter, neither on the Sabbath day. For there shall be great tribulation, such as was not since the beginning of the world to this time, no, nor ever shall be." 3. The

historian, reckoning the whole number of the slain, says that eleven hundred thousand persons perished by famine and sword, and that the rest of the rioters and robbers, being betrayed by each other after the taking of the city, were slain. But the tallest of the youths and those that were distinguished for beauty were preserved for the triumph. Of the rest of the multitude, those that were over seventeen years of age were sent as prisoners to labor in the works of Egypt, while still more were scattered through the provinces to meet their death in the theaters by the sword and by beasts. Those under seventeen years of age were carried away to be sold as slaves, and of these alone the number reached ninety thousand. 4. These things took place in this manner in the second year of the reign of Vespasian, in accordance with the prophecies of our Lord and Saviour Jesus Christ, who by divine power saw them beforehand as if they were already present, and wept and mourned according to the statement of the holy evangelists, who give the very words which he uttered, when, as if addressing Jerusalem herself, he said: 5. "If thou hadst known, even thou, in this day, the things which belong unto thy peace! But now they are hid from thine eyes. For the days shall come upon thee, that thine enemies shall cast a rampart about thee, and compass thee round, and keep thee in on every side, and shall lay thee and thy children even with the ground." 6. And then, as if speaking concerning the people, he says, "For there shall be great distress in the land, and wrath upon this people. And they shall fall by the edge of the sword, and shall be led away captive into all nations. And Jerusalem shall be trodden down of the Gentiles, until the times of the Gentiles be fulfilled." And again: "When ye shall see Jerusalem compassed with armies,

then know that the desolation thereof is nigh."
7. If any one compares the words of our Saviour with the other accounts of the historian concerning the whole war, how can one fail to wonder, and to admit that the foreknowledge and the prophecy of our Saviour were truly divine and marvellously strange. 8. Concerning those calamities, then, that befell the whole Jewish nation after the Saviour's passion and after the words which the multitude of the Jews uttered, when they begged the release of the robber and murderer, but besought that the Prince of Life should be taken from their midst, it is not necessary to add anything to the account of the historian.[83]

Clearly, Eusebius is claiming that these elements of the Olivet Discourse have already been fulfilled. Preterists agree. Premillennialists absolutely don't agree, and if Eusebius had come to the conclusion that this was synonymous with the second coming they would condemn him. Since he was convinced that the work of Constantine did in fact fulfill this prophecy they should condemn him. But I've never seen them do it in print. The church has not done so for the last 1,500 years. Why not?

In this section, we've seen major church figures (there are many others) who will stipulate that parts of both of these passages have been fulfilled. Clement of Alexandria, Tertullian, Julianus Africanus, Eusebius of Caesarea, Ambrosiaster, Isidore of Seville, Isho'dad of Merv, Andrew of Saint Victor, and Peter of Blois are all cited as writing that the 70th Week was completely fulfilled.[84] Just because they didn't know of the term "second coming," or didn't have a coherent eschatology that made the correct connections between seemingly disconnected passages, doesn't mean that in our modern systematic approach to theology we can't use them as sources to make our point. Since we have proven that early writers clearly stipulated to elements of an ancient fulfillment of the second coming, whether they realized or not, are we still going to say that according to modern analysis no one in church history has identified the second coming has having happened?

With the exception of Eusebius, I'm not necessarily saying that these authors consciously realized that this is what they were admitting to when they wrote. But just as other elements of theology such as Christology or justification are derived by bits and pieces of what earlier writers formulated (sometimes without realizing the implications of what they were saying) I think the development of eschatology follows the same dynamic.

The complex theory of justification by faith and penal substitutionary atonement are two excellent examples. No one taught either doctrine in its fully formed system for at least 1,500 years. But if you're a Reformed Christian you believe that the early writers were seeing glimpses of it, and groping in the same direction that the Reformation was able to successfully flesh out. I'd argue that the same doctrinal evolution should be allowed for eschatology.

But if that isn't granted to modern preterists by the reader, then Eusebius' position sets an interesting precedent for an alternative outlook: If the church has always been able to accept a complete fulfillment of second coming imagery and eschatology as of 325AD, according to one of the most important writers in church history, how can preterism be considered heretical? Eusebius was never condemned for his position. Luis Alcasar based his 1600AD preterist formulation on Eusebius' assumptions. In reality, that position (a very strong version of preterism based on the fulfillment of all prophecy in the events of the conversion of the Roman Empire in the era of Constantine) had been around since the 300s AD.[85]

In addition to these ancient writers, numerous middle-age and modern writers claim that the 70 Weeks of Daniel and then Olivet Discourse were at least partially fulfilled in the Roman War.[86] They do not generally realize that in doing so they have conceded that the second coming happened at the same time too. Again, John MacArthur and those in his camp can see this crisis clearly. I propose that given the options available at this point, modern Christians are forced into one of two positions: 1) Since the Olivet Discourse describes the second coming, the Olivet Discourse could not have been fulfilled in any way in the Roman War, or 2) since the Olivet Discourse describes the second coming, we are logically driven to acknowledge that this was already fulfilled, no matter how emotionally disturbing that is to us. If it wasn't fulfilled then we have to walk away from ancient writers who said it was, and stop comparing our enemies to the writings of ancient writers who stipulate so.

Summary:

The theme of this chapter is that premillennial dispensationalists should probably avoid going down the road of comparing modern eschatology to ancient Christian doctrine. It hurts them far more than it helps them. It's hard to overemphasize how important it is that early Christian writers considered the Olivet Discourse and 70-Weeks prophecy of Daniel to be fulfilled in the events of the Roman War. If dispensationalists want to use these writings to point out the lack of systematic preterism, they do so at the expense of impaling their own system. According to early Christian writings, premillennial dispensationalism (the eschatology of Calvary Chapel) is completely wrong. Though fragments of preterism can be seen in ancient writings, the fundamentals of dispensationalism are completely foreign to them.

It's correct to say that there were no early church writers who claimed that the "second coming" had already taken place. One possible reason we don't see it in early writings is that the term hadn't been invented or wasn't widespread when they wrote. Another reason is that they only saw the doctrine in bits and pieces, and it took many years of analysis to see how it fit together, just like the doctrines of Christology and justification. Once this was done for eschatology, the unity and importance of both Daniel's 70-Weeks prophecy and the Olivet Discourse became obvious. It has been shown that a large number of writers have argued that these two events were fulfilled in the events of the Roman War. Therefore, the position that these events fulfill the meaning of the second coming can't be considered heretical.

Chapter 3 Endnotes

[44] Douglas Wilkinson, *Preterist Time Statements*.

[45] e-Sword, http://www.e-sword.net/ (Last accessed 4/1/16).

[46] Regarding *tachus* mentioned in the Calvary Chapel argument, it does nothing to improve their argument. The Strong's definition is: Neuter singular of G5036 (as adverb); *shortly*, that is, *without delay*, *soon*, or (by surprise) *suddenly*, or (by implication of ease) *readily:* - lightly, quickly. The Thayer's definition is simpler: 1) quickly, speedily (without delay).

[47] Ed Stevens, *Final Decade Before the End*; John Bray, *Matthew 24 Fulfilled*; Riley O'Brien Powell, http://www.thelivingquestion.org; Francis Gumerlock, *Revelation and the First Century*; Gary DeMar and Francis Gumerlock, *The Early Church and the End of the World*.

[48] http://www.earlychristianwritings.com/text/1clement-lightfoot.html (Last accessed 4/18/16). The passage below makes it clear that Clement was writing before the destruction of the Temple by the Romans in 70AD.

"1 Clem 41:2 Not in every place, brethren, are the continual daily sacrifices offered, or the freewill offerings, or the sin offerings and the trespass offerings, but in Jerusalem alone. And even there the offering is not made in every place, but before the sanctuary in the court of the altar; and this too through the high priest and the aforesaid ministers, after that the victim to be offered hath been inspected for blemishes."

[49] In the Shepherd of Hermas the author describes all sorts of strange interpretations of Biblical language associated with the New Jerusalem. No Evangelical church in America would allow such strange teachings, but for some reason the eschatological conclusions of the book are supposed to be binding on us. Consider, for example, the following:

http://www.earlychristianwritings.com/text/shepherd.html (Last accessed 4/18/16).

CHAPTER XVII

"I understand, sir," I replied. "Now, sir," I continued, "explain to me, with respect to the mountains, why their forms are various and diverse."

"Listen," he said: "these mountains are the twelve tribes, which inhabit the whole world. The Son of God, accordingly, was preached unto them by the apostles." "But why are the mountains of various kinds, some having one form, and others another? Explain that to me, sir." "Listen," he answered: "these twelve tribes that inhabit the whole world are twelve nations. And they vary in prudence and understanding. As numerous, then, as are the varieties of the mountains which you saw, are also the diversities of mind and understanding among these nations. And I will explain to you the actions of each one." "First, sir," I said, "explain this: why, when the mountains are so diverse, their stones, when placed in the building, became one colour, shining like those also that had ascended out of the pit." "Because," he said, "all the nations that dwell under heaven were called by hearing and believing upon the name of the Son of God. Having, therefore, received the seal, they had one understanding and one mind; and their faith became one, and their love one, and with the name they bore also the spirits of the virgins. On this account the building of the tower became of one colour, bright as the sun. But after they had entered into the same place, and became one body, certain of these defiled themselves, and were expelled from the race of the righteous, and became again what they were before, or rather worse."

[50] In this legend, the Apostle John enters a public bath and runs into Cerinthus, at which point John tells everyone to run for it because Cerinthus is a terrible heretic. The historical problem with this legend is that John would have been in his 90s at that point, so there is a question whether the story was meant to describe the collision between another John, John the Presbyter, and Cerinthus. But the point stands: The anti-chiliast school of Christianity powerfully rejected the idea of a literal 1,000-year reign on earth. They acted on this by making such a proposal heretical in 381AD.

[51] The issue of doctrinal evolution in the first few centuries of the church is poorly understood by most Evangelicals. The following is a paragraph describing the five-way fight between church regional power centers in the early church. The implications for basing doctrine off early church writing should be obvious:

"The Alexandrian church claimed a distinguished ancestry with a list of rulers that traced back to St. Mark the Evangelist, but we know very little about the succession of orthodox bishops before the famous theologian and philosopher Clement of Alexandria, around 190. This obscurity may reflect some embarrassed rewriting by later church historians. In fact, Alexandria had a very distinguished Christian history from apostolic times, but much of it was, by later standards, wildly heretical and overly willing to draw on the insights of pagan philosophy or Judaism. Egypt was the home of the greatest early Gnostics, Basilides, and Valentinus, and probably several others, and before Clement, no non-Gnostic Christian enjoyed anything like the same degree of prestige in Alexandria. Only later, as Orthodox non-Gnostics secured their position, did they feel the need to invent a respectable spiritual ancestry for themselves, in the form of an artificial list of suitably orthodox bishops." Philip Jenkins. *Jesus Wars,* p.91.

[52] Ibid, 3.

[53] Ibid, 36.

[54] http://www.earlychristianwritings.com/text/irenaeus-book5.html.

[55] Justin Martyr, "Dialogue with Trypho." http://www.earlychristianwritings.com/text/justinmartyr-dialoguetrypho.html (Last accessed 4/3/16).

[56] Lapide, "Cerinthus with his followers are meant here. He was the first heresiarch after Simon Magus to deny, in S. Paul's time, the resurrection. See Eusebuis (Hist. Lib. Vii. c. 23, and lib. Iii. c. 28) and Epiphanius (Hares. 28). Cerinthus was a champion of Judaism, and, founding his opinions on Jewish traditions, he referred all the prophecies about the Church and the Gospel law to an earthly kingdom, and to riches, and to bodily pleasures. In the same way he afterwards perverted the meaning of Revelation xx. 4, and became the parent of the Chiliasts, or the Millennarian heretics."

[57] http://web.mit.edu/ocf/www/nicene_creed.html (Last accessed 5/4/16). Stuart G. Hall, *Doctrine and Practice of the Early Church.*

[58] If we think it does matter, then we have to take into account the various statements they made and their implications. Below is an interesting list of quotes by early authors compiled by Riley O'Brien Powell. They come from an excellent (and much longer) list found on her blog site, http://livingthequestion.org/historic-quotes/ (Last accessed 5/4/16).

100: The Odes of Solomon "Because He is my Sun and His rays have lifted me up and His light hath dispelled all darkness from my face. In Him I HAVE acquired eyes and HAVE SEEN His HOLY DAY: The way of error I have left, and have walked towards Him and have received salvation from Him, without grudging. I HAVE put on INCORRUPTION through His name: and have put off corruption by His grace. DEATH HAS BEEN DESTROYED before my face: and Sheol bath been abolished by my word".

150: Melito – *Homily of the Pascha* "Who will contend against me? Let him stand before me. It is I who delivered the condemned. It is I who gave life to the dead. It is I who RAISED UP THE BURIED. Who will argue with me? It is I, says Christ, who DESTROYED DEATH. It is I who triumphed over the enemy, and having trod down Hades, and bound the Strong Man, and HAVE SNATCHED UP MANKIND TO THE HEIGHTS OF HEAVEN."

175: Irenaeus – *Against Heresies* "the temple constructed of stones was indeed then rebuilt (for as yet that law was observed which had been made upon tables of stone), yet no new covenant was given, but they used the Mosaic law until the coming of the Lord; but from the Lord's advent, the new covenant which brings back peace, and the law which gives life, has gone forth over the whole earth, as the prophets said: "For out of Zion shall go forth the law, and the word of the Lord from Jerusalem ; and He shall rebuke many people; and they shall break down their swords into ploughshares, and their spears into pruninghooks, and they shall no longer learn to fight."

500: Andreas "And I saw, when he had opened the sixth seal, and behold there was a great earthquake, and the sun became as black as sackcloth of hair, and the whole moon became as blood. And the stars from heaven fell upon the earth, as a fig-tree casteth its green figs when it is shaken by the wind." [Apocalypse 6:12-13] "There are not wanting those who apply this passage to the siege and destruction of Jerusalem by Titus."

Tertullian ~200 AD "The Founder of Western Theology"

CHAP. VIII.– OF JERUSALEM'S DESTRUCTION: "Accordingly the times must be inquired into of the predicted and future nativity of the Christ, and of His passion, and of the extermination of the city of Jerusalem, that is, its devastation. For Daniel says, that "both the Holy City and the Holy Place are exterminated together with the coming Leader, and that the pinnacle is destroyed unto ruin" And so the times of the coming Christ, the Leader, must be inquired into, which we shall trace in Daniel; and, after computing them, SHALL PROVE HIM TO HAVE COME, even on the ground of the TIMES PRESCRIBED, and of competent signs and operations of His. Which matters we prove, again, on the ground of the consequences which were ever announced as to follow HIS ADVENT; in order that we may BELIEVE ALL TO HAVE BEEN as well FULFILLED AS FORESEEN.

Athanasius 345 AD "It is, in fact, a sign and notable PROOF of the COMING OF THE WORD that Jerusalem no longer stands."

Chrysostom 380 AD "For I will ask them, Did He send the prophets and wise men? Did they slay them in their synagogue? Was their house left desolate? Did ALL the VENGEANCE COME UPON THAT

GENERATION? It is QUITE PLAIN THAT IT WAS SO, and NO MAN NO MAN GAINSAYS IT."

[100 AD] "Do you see that His discourse is addressed to the Jews, and that He is speaking of the ills that should overtake them? And let not any man suppose this to have been spoken hyperbolically; but let him study the writings of Josephus, and LEARN THE TRUTH of the sayings." Commentary on Matthew 24:21

"Remembering this saving commandment and all those things which CAME TO PASS for us: the cross, the grave, the resurrection on the third day, the ascension into heaven, the sitting down at the right hand, THE SECOND AND GLORIOUS COMING AGAIN." – St Chrysostom's Divine Liturgy

Attend, O Lord Jesus Christ our God, from thy holy dwelling place and from the glorious throne of thy kingdom, and come to sanctify us, O thou that sits with the Father above, and that are invisibly PRESENT HERE WITH US. – St Chrysostom's Divine Liturgy

You brought us forth from non-existence into being, and RAISED US UP AGAIN when we had fallen, and left nothing undone until you had brought us to heaven and bestowed upon us your future kingdom." Prayer of the Anaphora – Eucharistic Prayer

Eusebius 314 AD "The Father of Church History" "And ALL THIS PROPHECY of what would result from their insolence against the Christ has been CLEARLY PROVED TO HAVE TAKEN PLACE ... afterwards from that day to this that God turned their feasts into mourning, despoiled them of their famous Mother-City, and destroyed the holy Temple therein when Titus and Vespasian were Emperors of Rome, so that they could no longer go up to keep their feasts and sacred meetings... in return for their rejection of the Word of God; since with one voice they refused Him, so He refuses them." – Demonstratio Evangelica, BOOK X

"When we see WHAT WAS of old FORETOLD for the nations FULFILLED in our own day, and when the lamentation and wailing that was predicted for the Jews, and the burning of the Temple and its utter desolation, can also be seen even now to HAVE OCCURRED ACCORDING TO PREDICTION, surely we must also agree that the King who was prophesied, the Christ of God, HAS COME, since THE SIGNS OF HIS COMING have been shown in each instance I have treated to HAVE BEEN CLEARLY FULFILLED." Demonstratio Evangelica (Proof of the Gospel); BOOK VIII

"If any one compares the words of our Saviour with the other accounts of the historian (Josephus) concerning the whole war, how can one fail to wonder, and to admit that the foreknowledge and the prophecy of our Saviour were truly divine and marvelously strange." Book III, Ch. VII

"And the people of the governor that cometh will destroy the city and the holy place." Meaning that the city and the Holy Place arc not only to be ruined by the leader to come, whom I have identified in my interpretation, but also by his people. And you would not be far wrong in saying, too, that the Roman general and his army arc meant by the words before us, where I think the camps of the Roman rulers are meant, who governed the nation from that time, and who destroyed the city of Jerusalem itself, and its ancient venerable Temple. For they were cut off by them as by a flood, and were at once involved in destruction until the war was concluded, SO THAT THE PROPHECY WAS FULFILLED ... You will find an accurate account of it in the history of Josephus." – Demonstratio Evangelica "Proof of the Gospel", BOOK VIII

Hippolytus of Rome ~200 AD

Come, then, O blessed Isaiah; arise, tell us clearly what did you prophesy with respect to the mighty Babylon? For thou didst speak also of Jerusalem, and YOUR WORD IS ACCOMPLISHED. For you spoke boldly and openly: "Your country is desolate, your cities are burned with fire; your land, strangers devour it in your presence, and it is desolate as overthrown by many strangers. The daughter of Zion shall be left as a cottage in a vineyard, and as a lodge in a garden of cucumbers, as a besieged city."

What then? HAVE NOT THESE THINGS COME TO PASS? ARE NOT THE THINGS ANNOUNCED BY YOU FULFILLED? Is not their country, Judea, desolate? Is not the holy place burned with fire? Are not their walls cast down? Are not their cities destroyed? Their land, do not strangers devour it? Do not the Romans rule the country? And …Thou art dead in the world, but YOU LIVE IN CHRIST." (resurrection!) – Fragments of Dogmatic and Historical Works

Irenaeus ~174 AD Early Church Father

CHAP. IV.– THE DESTRUCTION OF JERUSALEM WAS PUT IN EXECUTION BY THE MOST WISE COUNSEL OF GOD. 1. Further, also, concerning Jerusalem and the Lord, they venture to assert that, if it had been "the City of the Great King," it would not have been descrtcd. This is just as if any one should say, that if straw were a creation of God, it would never part company with the wheat;…so also [was it with] Jerusalem, which had in herself borne the yoke of bondage under which man was reduced, who in former times was not subject to God when death was reigning ... 2. Since, then, THE LAW originated with Moses, it TERMINATED WITH JOHN as a necessary consequence. Christ had come to FULFILL it: wherefore "the law and the prophets were" with them "until John. "And therefore Jerusalem, taking its commencement from David, and fulfilling its own times, must have an End of legislation when the New Covenant was revealed."

(Riley's note: The New Jerusalem, the New Heavens and Earth ARE the New Covenant that was revealed from Heaven by God, given to US and is where he dwells with US NOW! The "End" that was spoken of in Scripture was Covenantal and fulfilled in the past. What great news for us!)

Origen ~ 100s "I challenge anyone to prove my statement untrue if I say that the entire Jewish nation was destroyed less than one whole generation later on account of these sufferings which they inflicted on Jesus. For it was, I believe, forty-two years from the time when they crucified Jesus to the destruction of Jerusalem." Contra Celsum, 198-199

(Riley's note: This quote below supports the idea of Revelation's main theme as a story about God giving his Old Covenant wife, Israel, a bill of divorcement, i.e. the scrolls that are read of her misgivings in court, before the Judge. And of his taking his New Covenant Bride, New Jerusalem, New Heavens and Earth, or all who are in the body of Christ, spiritually 'married' to God. For more on this, see *The Book of Revelation Made Easy* by Dr. Kenneth Gentry, who did his dissertation on this).

"Therefore he, also, having separated from her [Old Covenant Israel], married, so to speak, another [New Covenant Israel], having given into the hands of the former the bill of divorcement; wherefore they can no longer do the things enjoined on them by the law, because of the bill of divorcement. And a sign that she has received the bill of divorcement is this, that Jerusalem was destroyed along with what they called the sanctuary of the things in it which were believed to be holy, and with the altar of burnt offerings, and all the worship associated with it...Jerusalem was compassed with armies, and its desolation was near, and their house was taken away from it... And, about the same time, I think, the husband wrote out a bill of divorcement to his former wife, and gave it into her hands, and sent her away from his own house...COMMENTARY ON THE GOSPEL ACCORDING TO MATTHEW, Book 2. sec. 19.

Dom Toutee (1790) "St. Chrysostom shows that the destruction of Jerusalem is to be ascribed, not to the power of the Romans, for God had often delivered it from no less dangers; but to a special providence which was pleased to put it out of the power of human perversity to delay or respite the extinction of those ceremonial observances." St. Cyril.

[59] Gary DeMar and Francis Gumerlock, *The Early Church and the End of the World.*p.46-47; *The Epistle of Barnabas:*
http://www.ccel.org/ccel/schaff/anf01.vi.ii.xv.html
http://www.ccel.org/ccel/lightfoot/fathers.ii.xiii.html.

[60] Douglas Wilkinson, *Making Sense of the Millennium.*

[61] Duncan McKenzie, *The Antichrist and the Second Coming* (Vol. 2), p.7.

[62] Rev. 20:1-3, 7-10 refer to a one thousand-year detention of Satan, and the events to transpire after that thousand years. In v.3 we see he is detained, "until the thousand years were ended. After that he must be released for a little while." The primary mistake of interpreters has been to apply this expiration to both Satan's and the saints' thousand years. In reality, it only applies to Satan's detention. In other words, they are both given a symbolic, or figurative detention. In Satan's case, it ends just before his demise. In the case of the saints, in Daniel 7:18, 22, 27 and Revelation 22:5, their reign is explicitly said to last "forever, forever and ever."

[63] Standard amillennialism argues that this is in 30AD, but I argue in my book that it starts in 70AD; also see James Jordan, *Through New Eyes.*

[64] The possible exception here is Ignatius, whose opinion on eschatology can be summed up as his looking forward to the return of Christ. We have no detailed explanation of his interpretive system. It is unlikely that he had one, since such things were only fleshed out as the church evolved. Other characters such as Polycarp and Papias were said to have studied under the Apostles, but this is not verified and we don't have their extant writings. In addition, highly respected early church writers such as Eusebius had low views of Papias.

[65] Philip Schaff, http://www.ccel.org/ccel/schaff/anf01.ii.ii.xxv.html.

[66] There is some question about whether the early writers expected the next crisis to be the melting of the universe, as modern amillennialism sometimes proposes, or a literal thousand-year gluttonous banquet.

[67] Given the importance of the traditional definition of the second coming, it's surprising to me that the different eschatological traditions don't argue more between each other about it. It is simple for them to push back against a preterist understanding of the event, but they don't

seem to realize that their own uses are mutually exclusive. They are no less mutually exclusive than a comparison to preterism. For instance, amillennialism proposes that the second coming can only happen after the end of the Millennium, after the Gog and Magog war, and includes the melting of the universe to set up resurrection, final judgment, and the eternal state. The premillennial version is much less dramatic (the scope is trillions of times smaller). For premillennialists, the second coming is essentially the return of Christ at the end of the battle of Armageddon in order to defeat the enemies of the Jews and set up a 1,000-year kingdom on earth. Their favorite passages for describing this kingdom are Isaiah 65-66 and Zechariah 13-14. In those passages, the kingdom starts off small (Jesus has little initial effect), but eventually grows to take over the whole world. At the end, Jesus is mysteriously deposed or neutered to make room for the final Gog and Magog battle. With the dramatic difference in definition of the second coming between these systems, it's amazing to me that they are fixated on the only slightly smaller scope found within preterism.

[68] John MacArthur, *The Second Coming;* www.pre-trib.org. All partial preterists that I'm aware of and some premillennialsts would disagree, saying that the Olivet Discourse was fulfilled in 70AD up to some vague and disagreed upon point (in Matthew's version generally around vs. 30-34). I don't think that they are being as consistent on this point as the premillennialists, such as John MacArthur, who see the issue more clearly.

[69] http://www.earlychristianwritings.com/text/justinmartyr-dialoguetrypho.html.

[70] Don K. Preston, *Elijah Has Come.*

[71] Douglas Wilkinson, *Making Sense of the Millennium.*

[72] Douglas Wilkinson, *Making Sense of the Millennium;* Douglas Wilkinson and Jerel Kratt, *Three Views on the Millennium in Preterism* (Not yet released as of 7/3/16).

[73] http://www.earlychristianwritings.com/text/justinmartyr-firstapology.html.

[74] Don K. Preston and William Bell, *Two Guys and a Bible: Zion.* Podcast.

[75] This basic position is also known as replacement theology. Regretfully, as in most theology, this basic position is poorly understood and almost never fairly described by dispensationalists. I know this from

growing up in dispensationalism and hearing thousands of hours of their teaching. I have never heard supersessionism or replacement theology defined by dispensationalist teaching without at least an implicit assertion that it means antisemitism. This is simply not true. Antisemitism in the church comes from futurist eschatology. It is caused by a failure to see that the enemy of the church, the Jews in the New Testament narrative, were already punished for their misdeeds. Once that punishment was inflicted there was no more natural animosity between Christians and Jews. But eschatology based on a futurist paradigm keeps that animosity alive. It is behind the partially correct approach of Justin Martyr in *Dialog with Trypho* and, more importantly, Martin Luther in *The Jews and Their Lies*. In both cases, if a proper understanding of eschatology was adopted this tension would have evaporated. The Father's people are those who follow the Son. The Jews, and other Israelites, of the New Testament age who were true believers made the transition to the New Covenant. They recruited billions of Gentiles in their wakes. In this age, everyone is invited to join because the gates of the New Jerusalem are never shut.

[76] Most preterists would say that the millennium applied to the period from 30AD to 70AD.

[77] http://www.earlychristianwritings.com/text/clement-stromata-book1.html.

[78] http://www.tertullian.org/fathers/eusebius_theophania_01 preface.htm.

[79] A similar campaign was conducted to suppress "Origenism."

[80] Eusebius of Ceasarea, Ecologues on Daniel via Gumerlock, *Revelation and the First Century,* 194; http://www.tertullian.org/fathers/eusebius_de_10_book8.htm.

[81] Likewise, Eusebius is clear in *The Proof of the Gospel* 2:214 that Zechariah 14, a favorite passage of dispensationalists for describing the second coming and the implementation of the Millennium, was also fulfilled by the Roman War; Gary DeMar and Francis Gumerlock, *The Early Church and the End of the World.* p.21-24.

[82] Don K. Preston, *70 Weeks Are Determined For ... The Resurrection.*

[83] Phillip Schaff, *Proof of the Gospel Book III Chapter VII.*

[84] Gary DeMar and Francis Gumerlock, *The Early Church and the End of the World*, p.86-90; *Francis* Gumerlock. *Revelation and the First Century*, p.191-198.

[85] Luis de Alcasar, Vestigio Arcani Sensus in Apocalypsi [An Investigation of the Secret Meaning of the Apocalypse] (Antwerp: Martinus Nutius, 1614, 1619).

[86] John Chrysostom, John Lightfoot, John Calvin, Philip Doddridge, Thomas Newton, John Gill Martin Luther, Ralph Laon, R.C. Sproul, Jay Adams, and many more, Francis Gumerlock, *Revelation and the First Century*, p.191-198.

Chapter 4: Christians Lived Through the Event

Calvary Chapel Statement:

The Christians that lived through the destruction of Jerusalem in AD 70 believed that the Second Coming of Jesus was still a future event.

For example, the didache, an early church order document which is dated between AD 80 and AD 100 provides evidence that the early Christians believed Jesus' second coming was still in the future.

Dr. John MacArthur says in his book The Second Coming that the didache was "certainly used and cited in the early centuries by many Church Fathers (as well as by the historian Eusebius). So its early existence is well documented... This document proves that those who actually lived through the events of A.D. 70 regarded Matthew 24:29-31 – and the entire Olivet Discourse – as yet-fulfilled prophecy."

Charges:

- Christians lived through the events of 70AD and still considered the second coming to be in their future.
- The Didache, dated after 70AD, asserts the same.

While the Calvary Chapel assertion would seem to be common sense, it's actually based on a combination of anachronism and false assumptions. As we've just seen in the previous chapter, it's anachronistic (assuming that something about a later time period applies to a previous one) to expect the earliest members of the church to use the terms "second coming" or "second advent." Those terms wouldn't be invented until about 100 years after Jerusalem was destroyed by the Romans. The survivors of the Roman War couldn't be thinking of it in modern terms. As pointed out in the previous chapter, fundamental elements of the second coming such as the Olivet Discourse and Daniel's 70-Weeks prophecy were in fact assumed to be fulfilled by the early church, though they didn't always use the term "second coming" when explaining their view. So, it's not clear on what John MacArthur is basing his opinion.

Their false assumption is based on the fact that Christian history is very poorly documented in the 40-year period immediately following the 70AD destruction of Jerusalem. Both the Calvary Chapel writer and John MacArthur assert that Christians (we have to assume they mean average Christians since the leadership known to us in the New Testament had been essentially wiped out by 70AD) still considered the second coming to be in the future. Based on what? The fact that average people did so generations later? Between widespread illiteracy among common people and the unfortunate fact that very few ancient writings of any king have survived, they have nothing on which to base their assertion in this chapter.

If one takes the position (as I do) that all of the New Testament was written before 70AD, that several important books such as the Epistle of Barnabas and the Didache were written before 70AD (see below), and that the first extant writings after this date belong to Ignatius (who wrote after 105AD), we would have no way of knowing what the average person thought in that era since none of what they might have written survived.[87] Instead, we have an approximately 40-year gap before the beginning of the handful of letters or apologies written by church leaders, known to us as the Ante-Nicene writings.[88] These were produced starting at least 70 years after Christ's ministry, with only a small number completed before 200AD. And again, as I document throughout this book, a large number of these leaders stipulate that the Olivet Discourse and/or the prophecies of Daniel were in fact fulfilled by the Roman destruction of Jerusalem. In modern terms, this would mean that they are arguing that the second coming had already happened, though this is itself an anachronism since they didn't seem to realize how interconnected Biblical eschatology is.

Starting with what we know of the beliefs of average Christians in the New Testament era is one way to figure out what the average person in 70AD thought. In the Apostolic era there was a great deal of confusion about eschatology. This is clearly behind the controversies of 1 and 2 Thessalonians, as well as the actions of Hymenaeus in 1 and 2 Timothy. When most commentators expound on these passages, one of the most important things that they tend to skip is an explanation for the confusion of the target audience. Paul had personally taught these audiences about a proper understanding of eschatology in face-to-face Bible classes. But they seemed to have had a great deal of difficulty remembering or understanding what they'd been taught.

This is a stunning fact. You'd think that if an Apostle had taught a Bible class describing what was going to lead up to the second coming, and then exactly what would happen during the second coming, that you wouldn't confuse that climactic historical event for another one. This audience should have had its act together. But, the Thessalonians almost immediately got confused when comparing current events with Paul's teaching. This has important implications for eschatology in early church writings. None of the early church writers whose works are available to us (Papias would be an exception if his works had survived) claimed to be interpreting scripture based on anything other than the text itself. They did not claim to have inside knowledge passed down by oral tradition from the Apostles. If there was no oral tradition, so that the background rationale wasn't provided by the Apostles, then it's unsurprising that there has been so much confusion in Christian theology. And, if the original hearers of the Apostles were constantly getting it wrong, we should probably give each other a break in modern debates on the topic.

As Don Preston asks in his excellent book and audio series *The Hymenaean Heresy: Reverse the Charges*,[89] how is it possible that the Thessalonians, and later Hymenaeaus, could have thought that the events in question had already happened? If the ancient Christians were premillennial dispensationalists, the next thing they would have expected was the rapture. Even if they believed they were left behind at the rapture, we would assume that they would not have seen a point in writing a letter to Paul to find out why, since surely he wouldn't have been left behind! And, in any case, if the day of the Lord and resurrection had already happened, according to premillennial doctrine they would have somehow missed the second coming. What are the odds of that?! If the ancient Christians were amillennial, they would have assumed that at the day of the Lord the universe had melted into plasma. Surely they wouldn't have missed that! Regardless of which eschatological school you follow, do you think it's possible that someone taught by an Apostle could be this confused about whether or not it had already happened?

Or does it seem more likely that they confused contemporary events with what they'd been taught by Paul because Paul described the second coming as something that would happen in regular history, in their lifetimes. As Don Preston and Ed Stevens point out in their books, there were several events in the era of the writing of 2 Thessalonians that could have been candidates for the day of the Lord from the point of view of the Christians in Thessalonica. Remember, according to the precedent of scripture "the day of the Lord" was simply a military catastrophe of some kind. Since they were expecting this catastrophe to be a military disaster against the Jews, we should start there.

A good candidate for the Thessalonians' confusion about the day of the Lord against the Jews can be seen in the events of Passover, 50AD.[90] On that date, in Jerusalem, 20,000 - 30,000 Jews were slaughtered by the Romans because of a riot related to the festival.[91] Keeping in mind that the Thessalonian epistles were written in the early 50s AD, if all you knew about the day of the Lord was that a foreign military was going to destroy the Jews in Jerusalem at the day of the Lord, and you got word that such a disaster had happened, would you have then questioned Paul about whether or not this fulfilled the prophecy? Would it make sense to send him a letter or messenger requesting clarification? If so, this might have been his response:

> Now we request you, brethren, with regard to the coming of our Lord Jesus Christ and our gathering together to Him, that you not be quickly shaken from your composure or be disturbed either by a spirit or a message or a letter as if from us, to the effect that the day of the Lord has come. Let no one in any way deceive you, for it will not come unless the apostasy comes first, and the man of lawlessness is revealed, the son of destruction, who opposes and exalts himself above every so-called god or object of worship, so that he takes his seat in the temple of God, displaying himself as being God. Do you not remember that while I was still with you, I was telling you these things? (2 Thess. 2:1-5 ESV)

Paul is simply saying, "No. This couldn't have been the fulfillment. I already told you. Other things have to happen first." Paul's response would mean that the events were due to happen in that generation, involving people who were already alive and identified in person to his audience. If Paul is responding to their question about their historical circumstances by telling them that other historical circumstances have to happen first, he is implying that they were nearly correct. There was nothing wrong with their interpretation of the day of the Lord as some sort of temporal, historical disaster. If this is true, the entire modern conception of the second coming is completely wrong

Obviously, even though an Apostle had taught them face to face about how these events would unfold, there was still some confusion. This only increased as the apostasy of 2

Thessalonians 2:3 set in. In the parallel comment in the Olivet Discourse, we find that most Christians were going to fall away from the faith in that climactic time (Matt. 24:12). Paul's only criticism of his audience was to remind them of the signs that he said they would see leading up to this event. He didn't criticize them for thinking that a regular historical disaster could have been mistaken for the day of the Lord. Since a significant number of Christians were confused about eschatology in the time of the Apostles, and since part of the crisis running up to the second coming included a falling away or martyrdom of the majority of Christians, it's no wonder that 50 years after the deaths of the Apostles the leadership weren't writing accurately about it. And, in any case, there is no record at all of what the average Christian thought on the topic.

Turning to what little evidence we do have of the opinions of average people in the early church, while there are no long-format writings by average Christians in the post-70AD period, we do find a few interesting artifacts from short-format writings such as grave markers or catacomb inscriptions. This would be a good way to retrieve information about what the average person believed about the normal circumstances of their lives, and would also betray some important theological background. For instance, for the Calvary Chapel member who is still expecting either a rapture or the resurrection according to 1 Thessalonians 4, there has been no change in the location or condition of dead believers since the time of the New Testament when Paul was writing. The dead are still in the Hadean realm, with the good guys waiting in Abraham's Bosom. At the rapture or resurrection, then, we are still expecting the dead in Christ to rise from the Hadean Realm and to be "snatched" into the air (rapturo in Latin, or harpazo in Greek) to be with the Lord forever.[92]

So, what would it mean to us theologically to see the following inscription on a grave marker from the very early church: "Zoticus laid here to sleep; 'Raptus eterne domus,' Snatched home eternally." "In Christ; Alexander is not dead but lives beyond the stars, and his body rests in this tomb."?[93] In any modern seminary, those early Christians would get an "F" on their paper about the rapture, the resurrection and the eternal state. This is because in fact the second coming hasn't happened, and the "rapture" (AKA the "snatch"), hasn't occurred. Zoticus was not in fact "snatched home eternally." And, since according to most conservative theology the dead in Christ are raised from paradise (a compartment of Hades) at the resurrection, Alexander is not in fact living beyond the stars.[94] It's possible that the average Christian of the time simply didn't know what he was talking about. This might reinforce that they were living in a soup of confusion on eschatology, so their opinions about a future second coming are not authoritative. On the other hand, if the average Christian in that age thought the resurrection has already happened, then futurists have a problem because this means that they thought the second coming was in the past (whether they knew it from that vocabulary or not). So, if they are wrong then their opinions are suspect, and the Calvary Chapel assertion is unfounded. If they were right, then the Calvary Chapel assertion is simply wrong. Which is it?

Another interesting comment comes from the Eastern Orthodox Church liturgy. The Eastern Orthodox Church is very ancient, and has had a comparatively stable theology throughout its existence. Though it is loosely amillennial, eschatology is not emphasized. Doctrinal teaching tends to be done through their liturgy and to a large extent art. The following is an intriguing passage found in their prayer for the Eucharist. It is a prayer of thankfulness for things that God has already brought to pass:

> Remembering this saving commandment and all those things which have come to pass for us: the cross, the tomb, the resurrection on the third day, the ascension into heaven, the sitting at the right hand of God the Father, the second and glorious coming.[95]

It is strange that in its liturgy the Eastern Orthodox Church would describe the second coming as having happened already. If you were to ask an Eastern Orthodox theologian if the church still expects a future second coming, he would say "yes." It's possible that this phrase was meant proleptically (meaning that it is so sure to happen that it is described in the past tense). But, it is also possible that some echo of ancient preterist thought is represented in this comment, and the church simply hasn't gotten rid of it.

Another strange dynamic comes from the way that the Eastern Orthodox Church describes its path to sanctification. In the New Testament, the Apostles consistently anchor their admonitions for holy living on the judgment that is "about to come." The New Testament crisis is the motivation behind everything that the Apostles teach. But, instead of an obsession about preparation for an impending eschatological crisis as is seen in the New Testament, the Eastern Orthodox Church emphasizes theosis, or becoming like God in a lifelong, contemplative process. The process as they describe it is more contemplative and solemn, but is not energized by a judgment that is about to take place. Why the change of tone? What theology justifies moving away from the Biblical way of motivating Christians?

We can also take a look at the Syriac Church of the East. Most western Christians are almost completely ignorant of this very ancient church.[96] It is well accepted in the west that most of the Apostles moved east in the first generation of the church. What isn't well known is that they had a tremendous impact. It turns out that by about 350AD the Syriac Church of the East spread to the tip of India, the Russian Steppes, and the eastern coast of China. For the first 1,000 years of the church they were by far the largest church by geography and population. They were eventually almost exterminated by the forces of history, primarily Islam.

But fortunately, the remnant of that church has moved to western countries for refuge in the last century. In conversations with members of those churches it was made clear to me that they don't have any tradition of teaching eschatology. In other words, they don't have a tradition of teaching about, or focusing on, the expectation of a second coming. One of the members told me that he grew up in that church and in 40 years of attendance couldn't remember having heard a single lesson on the topic. Instead, they focus almost exclusively on personal holiness and contemplation of God. Their approach to teaching about the second coming is very similar to the Eastern Orthodox Church. Why?

It seems to me that a tradition such as that might have come from a group of Christians where, from the very beginning of their growing church, the eschatological crisis wasn't on the horizon anymore. Remember, it was the impending crisis of a judgment "about to come" that provided the incubator for holiness in the New Testament. Why else would that church drop one of the major themes of scripture?

We might also question the likelihood that information about the Roman destruction of Jerusalem and its implications would be passed down successfully. Consider the ages and life expectancy of people at the time. Let's assume for the sake of argument that to be a well-informed Christian in 70AD you'd need to have been a Christian for several years, or have grown up in the church to about 25 years old (though theology in that age wasn't formulated systematically as we know it today, and you would not have had access to a full compilation of what we know as the New Testament). Also, it's estimated that the average life expectancy in the era was around 55 years. Finally, again, remember that Jesus predicted that the majority of the church would either be martyred or fall away in the Great Tribulation. Then, keeping in mind the confusion experienced by Paul in the churches he personally taught, the number of Christians who were alive in 70AD and who had a clear understanding of eschatological doctrine would be rather small. If that generation had told their kids that there was nothing further to worry about because the day of the Lord had already happened, it is likely that the core message of Christianity would have changed somewhat from the New Testament circumstances. That new message would simply have focused on Christian living and growth, and not on the impending disaster. It is also likely that almost everyone who was born or converted in the first generation after 70AD would have died and been replaced by another generation before the first writings began after 100AD. Finally, the first generations of writers (Ignatius, Tertullian, Origen, etc.) were Greek Gentiles who sometimes show little appreciation for the subtleties of Hebrew hermeneutics. As a result, the Greek-based church (with its literalistic mindset) two or three generations after 70AD literally expected to see the sky roll up like a scroll, or the sun to stop shining, or a city to descend from the sky in order for these prophecies to be properly fulfilled. All it would have taken is for a few people who wrote (already a very small sample of people) to quote elements of the New Testament expectation without understanding that they'd already been fulfilled in order to begin the interpretive momentum that we see today.

Another option is to propose a literal rapture in the late 60s AD. Ed Stevens is the premier proponent of this position within preterism.[97] He argues that all of the rapture expectation that is familiar in modern premillennial dispensationalism is well founded on scripture. But, he argues that the fulfillment happened in association with the Neronic persecution and the Roman War. For those worried about why there was no record of an ancient rapture, remember that the population of the world was comparatively small, the population of surviving faithful Christians at that point was very small, and those who were still around tended to be migrating as a means of survival (i.e., the flight to Pella). If the rapture were to happen overnight, it is not at all clear that the local non-Christians would have even noticed. And again, since there is almost nothing in writing surviving from that era, there is no reliable way to know if people noticed it or not.

The literal rapture position easily answers questions about widespread doctrinal confusion in early Christianity. It is common knowledge that early Christians had all sorts of strange ideas about doctrine, and that modern doctrinal formulations found in Evangelical Christianity would be very foreign to them. If Stevens is correct, everyone who accurately knew what was going on was instantaneously taken directly to heaven at the rapture. Those who became Christians in the first generation after the rapture (these conversions would have started only a few seconds after the rapture due to people finally responding to prior evangelization), were not well informed about doctrinal issues. Just as the Ante-Nicene writers claim, they would have gotten all of their ideas from reading scripture, not hearing oral tradition. So, the new post-second-coming Christians would have made predictable mistakes based on their Greek philosophical worldview and poor hermeneutics. Though he is in the minority in preterist circles, Stevens provides a simple, elegant way to answer this question and many others.

We'll close the chapter by looking at the single piece of specific evidence that MacArthur uses to make his argument. According to MacArthur, the Didache, an early primer on Christian doctrine, proves that the early church still expected the second coming because it was written after 70AD and includes passages such as the following:[98]

> 1 "Watch" over your life: "let your lamps" be not quenched "and your loins" be not ungirded, but be "ready," for ye know not "the hour in which our Lord cometh." 2 But be frequently gathered together seeking the things which are profitable for your souls, for the whole time of your faith shall not profit you except ye be found perfect at the last time; 3 for in the last days the false prophets and the corrupters shall be multiplied, and the sheep shall be turned into wolves, and love shall change to hate; 4 for as lawlessness increaseth they shall hate one another and persecute and betray, and then shall appear the deceiver of the world as a Son of God, and shall do signs and wonders and the earth shall be given over into his hands and he shall commit iniquities which have never been since the world began.
>
> Then shall the creation of mankind come to the fiery trial and "many shall be offended" and be lost, but "they who endure" in their faith "shall

be saved" by the curse itself. And "then shall appear the signs" of the truth. First the sign spread out in Heaven, then the sign of the sound of the trumpet, and thirdly the resurrection of the dead: but not of all the dead, but as it was said, "The Lord shall come and all his saints with him." Then shall the world "see the Lord coming on the clouds of Heaven."

It turns out that the date range for the writing of the Didache includes very early dates extending to the 50s AD. As Gary DeMar and Francis Gumerlock relate in *The Early Church and the End of the World*, "The definitive work on the Didache was written by the French Canadian Jean-Paul Audet who concluded that it was composed, almost certainly in Antioch, between 50-70."[99] DeMar quotes dates of writing as late as the mid-third century in his section on the dating of at least parts of the Didache, so it's possible that elements of it were added later. However, it is likely that the core of it was written very early. So, the existence of the Didache and its use by the early church proves nothing about the average believer's opinion of the second coming after 70AD. You wouldn't know it from MacArthur's claim. MacArthur gives no consideration to a possible pre-70AD date of writing. I'll give him the benefit of the doubt and say that he was simply ignorant of the scholarship on the topic. But, with that single example removed (or at least called a draw), and no other evidence presented to support his case, his allegation in this chapter falls flat.

While there were no long-format writings that we are aware of that have been proven to come from the period between 70AD and about 105AD, there is some hope in this regard. Francis Gumerlock has spoken in several venues (including his books cited here) about the fact that the compilation of church fathers in the Ante-Nicene Father collection represents only about 10% of the writings from the period, or an estimated 7,000 pages of material. That means that there is still more than 1,000,000 pages of material that has never been translated from Greek or Latin into English.[100] That means that only a limited, or fairly ancient, analysis of this information has ever been done by the western church. Hopefully, over the next hundred years, additional analysis of this material will lend some clarity to the expectation of the average person of the early church.

Summary:

We've seen in this chapter that it's disingenuous to expect testimony from average Christians in the early church as if they were Americans with Facebook or email that would provide a detailed record of their thoughts. Average people simply didn't have their thoughts recorded. And the later writers never claimed to have relied on the thoughts of average believers. There are preterist explanations for why the tradition of the 70AD second coming wasn't passed on. Finally, the Didache was likely written before 70AD, so using it as an argument against preterism proves nothing.

Chapter 4 Endnotes

[87] The same applies to the Epistle of Barnabas per Ed Stevens in *First Century Events in Chronological Order,* pre-publication, 2009; and *Final Decade Before the End.* International Preterist Association, 2014; private correspondence with Ed related to the dating of the Epistle of Barnabas and Didache.; John A.T. Robinson. *Redating the New Testament,* p. 323; Gary DeMar and Francis Gumerlock, *The Early Church and the End of the World,* p.28.

[88] Ed Stevens, private correspondence:

Dr. Wayne McCown (Sept 16, 2004 lecture at Northwestern Seminary) "If we actually map out the history of the first century following 70 AD and the collapse of Jerusalem, with the death of Paul and Peter preceding that, and Paul's writings and all the epistles he wrote having been finished before that, then there arises an **obscure dark period**, often labeled that, when chronological and historical charts were **not sure what was going on** between 70 AD and 90 AD. . . . what happened in the 70s and 80s? . . . it's a **dark period**, and we are not sure exactly what was going on . . ."

W.H.C. Frend (*The Early Church: From the Beginnings to 461*) "The years that followed the fall of Jerusalem are among **the most obscure** in the life of the primitive Church."

John A. T. Robinson (*Redating the New Testament*) Refers to the first three decades after AD 70 as "A **'tunnel period'** in which there was no evidence of literary remains . . ."

Williston Walker (*A History of the Christian Church* – third edition) "the forty years from 70 to 110 remain one of the **obscurest portions of church history.**

James Moffatt (*Introduction to the Literature of the New Testament*) "We should expect . . . that an event like the fall of Jerusalem would have dinted some of the literature of the primitive church, . . . [but] the catastrophe is **practically ignored** in the extant Christian literature of the [late] first century."

C.F.D. Moule (*The Birth of the New Testament*) "It is hard to believe that a Judaistic type of Christianity which had itself been closely involved in the cataclysm of the years leading up to AD 70 would not have **shown the scars** – or, alternatively, would not have **made capital** out of this signal evidence that they, and not non-Christian Judaism, were the true Israel. But in fact **our traditions are silent.**"

Jaroslav Pelikan (*The Emergence of the Catholic Tradition*)
"...one **looks in vain** for proof of a **bitter disappointment** over the postponement of the Parousia or of a **shattering** of the early Christian communities by the delay in the Lord's return..."

L.H. Gaston (*No Stone on Another: Studies in the Fall of Jerusalem in the Synoptic Gospels*) "There is **no unambiguous reference to the fall of Jerusalem** any place outside the gospels."

Philip Schaff (*History of the Christian Church* (Vol. 2)):

> There is no other transition in history **so radical and sudden**, and yet **so silent and secret**. The stream of divine life in its passage from the mountain of inspiration to the valley of tradition is for a short time lost to our view, and **seems to run under ground**. . . It is a remarkable fact that after the days of the Apostles no names of great missionaries are mentioned . . .

So for some strange reason we find no more apostolic missionary trips, church planting, or epistle-writing activity still going on after AD 70. Church Historians are still scratching their heads trying to figure out what happened to all those saints who are mentioned in the pages of our NT. Where did they go? Why don't we hear from at least one of them after AD 70 (Timothy, Titus, or even Apostle John)? We don't know when they died, where they died, where they were buried -- nothing! Every one of them vanish without a trace. Were they embarrassed into silence by the non-fulfillment of the Parousia? Were they embarrassed that their expectations of seeing, hearing, and experiencing the Parousia were not fulfilled? Are we to assume that the Parousia did not happen, therefore they all left the faith out of embarrassment? That would make Jesus and all the Apostles false prophets.

No, I suspect there is a better explanation for their silence and absence. They were taken to heaven just like Jesus and the apostles had promised (**Matt 24:31, John 14:3, 1 Thess. 4:17**). That is what left the huge hole in church history which church historians are still puzzled over. That is the reason why there are so few writings after AD 70, none of which are from the apostles or their co-workers. That is why the later writers in the early second century were so confused and doctrinally off-base on so many issues, especially eschatology. They did not have the apostles or any of the first generation of Christians left around to guide them. All they had were the NT scriptures.

There is a real historical conundrum here which has baffled historians for two thousand years. Silence and absence. Confusion and doctrinal deviancy. Eschatological chaos. How could that happen if any of the apostles (especially John) or their immediate disciples (like Timothy, Titus, Gaius, Aristarchus, or Tychicus) were still around? Why didn't at least one of them speak up to set the record straight?

Yet all we have in those first three decades after AD 70 is a profound silence at the very time we would expect dancing in the streets and shouting from the rooftops. That silence and absence is screaming "rapture." Otherwise we have to believe that every one of those pre-70 saints who remained alive until AD 70 **failed to see, hear, and experience what they were expecting to experience** at the Parousia. But if the Parousia did not occur **as they had expected**, they should have been complaining about it, and venting their frustration, confusion, and disillusionment. But we do not even have that! All we have is silence. Those Christians were not celebrating the fulfillment, nor complaining about the non-fulfillment, because they were no longer on earth. They were gone. They were taken to heaven just like Jesus and the apostles promised (**Matt 24:31, John 14:3, 1 Thess. 4:17**). So their life in heaven after AD 70 was indeed "*radically, profoundly different*" than their life on earth before AD 70.

Be sure to look up all the scriptures I mentioned above, and read them in their context. You will also want to read all the articles I have attached to this message.

[89] Don K. Preston, *The Hymenaean Heresy: Reverse the Charges.*

[90] http://sacred-texts.com/jud/josephus/war-2.htm.

[91] Another possible influence might have been the 50,000 Jews killed in Seleucua in 38AD, J. Marcellus Kik. *An Eschatology of Victory*, p.93.

[92] Most Christians don't appreciate that if the location of the dead has not changed since the New Testament, their loved ones are not necessarily in the presence of God after death.

[93] J.W. Hanson, *Universalism, the Prevailing Doctrine of the Christian Church During its First Five Hundred Years.*

[94] Andrew Perriman, *Hell and Heaven in Narrative Perspective.*

[95] http://oca.org/orthodoxy/the-orthodox-faith/worship/the-divine-liturgy/eucharistic-canon-anaphora.

[96] E.H. Broadbent, *The Pilgrim Church;* Leonard Verduin, *The Reformers and their Stepchildren;* Soro, *The Church of the East*; Phillip Jenkins, *The Lost History of Christianity.*

[97] Ed Stevens, *Expectations Demand a First Century Rapture.*

[98] http://www.earlychristianwritings.com/text/didache-lake.html.

[99] John A.T. Robinson, *Redating the New Testament*, p. 323; Jean-Paul Audet, *La Didache: Instructions des Apotres*; Michael W. Holms, ed., *The Apostolic Fathers: Greek Texts and English Translations*, p.247-248.

[100] Gary DeMar and Francis Gumerlock, *The Early Church and the End of the World,* p.40.

Chapter 5: The Dating of Revelation

Calvary Chapel Statement:

The late dating of the Book of Revelation can be demonstrated to be after AD 70.

In order for Preterists to claim that Revelation had largely or completely been fulfilled, they say it had to be written before the destruction of Jerusalem in AD 70 or around AD 65.

It's believed, and with good reason that the Book of Revelation was written by John around AD 95, during the time of the Roman Emperor Domitian's reign as Mark Hitchcock documents:

Domitianic Date of AD 95*: Hegesippus (AD 150), Irenaeus (AD 180), Clement of Alexandria (150-215), Tertullian (160-220), Origen (185-253), Dio Cassius (150-235), Victorinus (ca. 300), Eusebius (260-340), Jerome (340-419), Sulpicius Severus (ca. 400), Orosius (ca. 400), Primasius (ca. 540), Paulus Orosius (ca. 600), Andreas (ca. 600), The Acts of John (ca. 650), Venerable Bede (ca. 700).*

Neronic Date of 65AD*: Syriac Version of NT (508 & 616), Arethas (ca. 900), Theophylact (d. 1107).*

Nero was the Roman emperor who reigned from (AD 54-68) and Domitian was the Roman emperor who reigned from (AD 81-96).

Charges:

- Preterism doesn't make sense if Revelation was written in 95AD.
- Revelation can be demonstrated to have been written after 70AD.

While it's true that most modern conservative preterist arguments only make sense if Revelation was written before 70AD, a late date such as 95AD doesn't invalidate the preterist position. In fact, alternate early fulfillments have been proposed throughout church history. A fulfillment based on the Bar Kokhba revolt, Eusebius' full preterism based on the events surrounding Constantine and the Christian conquering of the Roman Empire, and Luis Alcazar's similar preterist position work just fine with a late date. In each of these cases, historical events other than the fall of Jerusalem in 70AD are used to fulfill the second coming prediction. To say that preterism categorically falls apart with a late dating of Revelation is a strawman.

More importantly, the most powerful argument for preterism, the time statements, severely challenge the futurist position no matter when Revelation was written. We looked at one section of time statements from Revelation 1 earlier. Now, we'll look at one that has an important connection to a key Old Testament prophet, Daniel. In Daniel 12 we see him receiving a vision that he doesn't seem to understand. He asks the angels to help him with it:

> I heard, but I did not understand. Then I said, "O my lord, what shall be the outcome of these things?" He said, "Go your way, Daniel, for the words are shut up and sealed until the time of the end. (Dan. 12:8-9 ESV)

Whatever the vision was about, it wasn't about events that would unfold in Daniel's lifetime. In fact, Daniel is told that it's about "the time of the end" at the "shattering of the holy people" mentioned earlier in Daniel 12. Moving to Revelation, most futurists aren't aware that there is a very similar passage there. In fact, you might say that is a deliberate reversal of the advice given to Daniel:

> And he said to me, "Do not seal up the words of the prophecy of this book, for the time is near. Let the evildoer still do evil, and the filthy still be filthy, and the righteous still do right, and the holy still be holy. Behold, I am coming soon, bringing my recompense with me, to repay everyone for what he has done. I am the Alpha and the Omega, the first and the last, the beginning and the end." (Rev. 22:10-13 ESV)

Here, we find that the author isn't allowed to seal up the words. The contrast with Daniel 12 is striking. It indicates that Revelation will be fulfilled in very near future. So, though the date of writing may control which historical events the fulfillment is assigned to, the time statement issue doesn't rely on the date of writing. It simply says, in the clearest possible language, that the "time is near."

It so happens that since a credible claim can be made that Revelation was written in the early 60s AD, "the end" in question makes sense to most preterists as the Roman War. This fits every other time indicator in the New Testament such as the assertion by Jesus that the current generation would not pass away until all of these things had taken place (Matt. 23-24). Any way you cut it, the time statements require an ancient fulfillment. "The time is near" can't mean 2,000 years and counting.

The fact that there have been ancient interpretations based on post-95AD fulfillment means that this chapter could easily end right here. But, I'll move on to try to prove that an early date of writing is in fact plausible, preserving the modern pre-70AD paradigm. By the end, I think you'll see that the early date is at least plausible.

The Calvary Chapel writer cites Mark Hitchcock's list to show that early writers were almost all advocates of the 95AD date, and that only a few writers supported a pre-70AD date. Francis Gumerlock's book, *Revelation and the First Century* refutes Hitchcock handily.[101] It turns out that the earliest proposed date for John's vision (though the actual recording of it in writing isn't strictly part of this theory) is 33AD. Gumerlock quotes a 12th-century writing called *Voyage of St. Brendan* in which the author claims that John received this vision, "when he was in anguish at the Last Supper, grief-stricken on hearing that Judas would betray the Lord."[102] Gumerlock then moves on to quote from several traditions with the proposed year or writing here in parentheses: Mingana Syriac (36-37AD), Epiphanius of Salamis (41-54AD), Apringius of Beja (41-54AD), Beatus of Liebana (50-53AD), History of John (54-68AD), Thomas of Harkel (54-68), Theophylact of Ochrida (59-62AD). Tertullian, Jerome, Origen, and others all argue that Revelation was written during the reign of Nero (54-68AD). In fact, Gumerlock demonstrates that there are several traditions for the dating of Revelation, and that there is no ancient consensus on this point.

In addition to the early authors cited by Gumerlock, Riley O'Brien Powell has compiled an extensive list of authors who make the argument that Revelation was written in the 60s AD.[103] Her excellent article has far more information than I'll provide here. But, with permission, I'll simply list for you the 62 modern authors she cites who support an early date:

Jay E. Adams, D.E. Aune, Greg L. Bahnsen, Joseph R. Balyeat, Arthur Stapylton Barnes, R. Bauckham, W. Bauer, W.F. Arndt and F.W. Gingrich, Ulrich R. Beeson, Albert A. Bell Jr., Charles Bigg, F.F. Bruce, Rudolf Bultmann, R. Carré, David Chilton, William Newton Clarke, Adela Yarbro Collins, W. Gary Crampton, Berry Stewart Crebs, Gary DeMar, George Edmundson, George P. Fisher, J. Massyngberde Ford, S.J. Friesen, A.J.P. Garrow, Kenneth L. Gentry, Robert McQueen Grant, Samuel G. Green, I. Head, Bernard W. Henderson, M. Hengel, David Hill, B. Kowalski, P. Lampe, Francis Nigel Lee, Peter J. Leithart, J.W. Marshall, A.D. Momigliano, Charles Herbert Morgan, C.F.D. Moule, Robert L. Pierce, T. Randell, James J.L. Ratton, J. W. Roberts, John A.T. Robinson, G. Rojas-Flores, C. Rowland, W. Sanday, J.J. Scott, Edward Gordon Selwyn, T.B. Slater, D. Moody Smith, A.G. Soeting, Charles Cutler Torrey, Cornelis Vanderwaal, J.W. Van Henten, G.H. Van Kooten, Arthur Weigall, Bernhard Weiss, A.N. Wilson, J. Christian Wilson, M. Wilson, Herbert B. Workman

In a book dedicated to the dating of Revelation, Kenneth Gentry does an exhaustive job of documenting the early date position.[104] His book, *Before Jerusalem Fell*, is considered by some to be the definitive guide on the topic. Gentry is a strong opponent of full preterism, so he did not write this book in an attempt to prove our point. In it, he makes several important observations that severely weaken the late-date advocates. I'll focus on what I think is the most important one below. Gentry points out that the primary proof for the late-date theory came from Irenaeus' book, *Against Heresies*. Irenaeus states:

This word, too, contains a certain outward appearance of vengeance, and of one inflicting merited punishment because he (Antichrist) pretends that he vindicates the oppressed. And besides this, it is an ancient name, one worthy of credit, of royal dignity, and still further, a name belonging to a tyrant. Inasmuch, then, as this name "Titan" has so much to recommend it, there is a strong degree of probability, that from among the many [names suggested], we infer, that perchance he who is to come shall be called "Titan." We will not, however, incur the risk of pronouncing positively as to the name of Antichrist; for if it were necessary that his name should be distinctly revealed in this present time, it would have been announced by him who beheld the apocalyptic vision. For that was seen no very long time since, but almost in our day, towards the end of Domitian's reign.

But he indicates the number of the name now, that when this man comes we may avoid him, being aware who he is: the name, however, is suppressed, because it is not worthy of being proclaimed by the Holy Spirit.[105]

The key phrase here, "For that was seen no very long time since" is taken to mean that from Irenaeus' time, the thing in question was recently seen. There is some controversy about this. The term translated "that" could have meant either John himself or the actual original copy of his document. I've included an unusually long quote surrounding the critical sentence to show that Irenaeus was originally trying to determine exactly what the original text said in order to discern the identity of the Antichrist. Confusion had entered over this because by the time of Irenaeus some of the texts had the number as 616 and some had 666. If Irenaeus' point was to prove precisely what the original text recorded, it makes the most sense that Irenaeus was suggesting to simply go back to John's original copy and check to see what number was recorded. But, "that," because the grammar involved is ambiguous, could have also been a reference to John himself. So Irenaeus could possibly have been suggesting that only a short time before, they could have simply asked the author. Since both are an option, dogmatism on the point is impossible.

The real problem is that the late-date authors, ancient and modern, base almost their entire case on this statement. The vast majority of the authors cite each other, and eventually this one passage, in order to make their case. This dynamic of circular reporting can become very powerful unless objectively attacked. In 2003, I was in the desert of Kuwait at the Marine Headquarters that was in charge of both the U.S. Marine and British Royal Marine invasion forces preparing to cross the border into Iraq. I was on an intelligence staff analyzing events as they unfolded. A day or so before, we'd been attacked by missiles from Basra, Iraq, and everyone was on edge that the next salvo could contain nerve gas (we fully expected to get "slimed" at any minute). Suddenly, the nerve gas alarms went off at a neighboring base. Either a missile we hadn't accounted for (we'd already had one surprise attack that missed wiping out our headquarters by about 100 meters), or some other weapon, had just released the one threat that we all feared. After a few hours in MOPP gear (full chemical warfare gear including masks, gloves, a charcoal lined suit, and rubber boots), we got the all clear. It had only been a false alarm. But then, a few hours later, the troops near the border received an alert that they themselves had been attacked. We put our gear back on. Again, a few hours later we got the all clear. And then again, after another few hours, we got word that the British Royal Marines had been hit with nerve gas. This circle of reporting repeated itself for more than a day. In the end, we were able to determine that a single, false alarm had echoed through the intel reporting system in such a way that every three to six hours (probably, at a shift change) we thought we were under attack again.

If you weren't part of the team that tracked down the error, you would think that there was a half dozen or more nerve gas attacks that the government covered up, again. Imagine what would have happened if no one had tried to get to the bottom of the problem while the raw data was still available. Now, imagine what would have happened if each unit log was public domain, and historians took them at face value a few hundred, or a few thousand years later. Finally, imagine the problem created if a few of those logs were lost to history. My bet is that you'd find a number of writers simply assuming the authority of the logs because they'd been done by military intelligence immediately after the attacks, and since some of the record was lost, it would have been nearly impossible (if anyone had ever bothered to try) to figure out that it had all come from one false alarm.

This is the danger of circular reporting. In the case of modern late-date authors, all of them either quote Irenaeus directly or quote someone who used him as a source. This body of commentary grew to appear mountainous. However, it's based on a single, shaky comment in a paragraph trying to argue for how to prove the identity of the beast and his relationship to the numbers 616 and 666. In the end, because their seeming mountain of documentation is based on the circular reporting of one ambiguous sentence, the evidence for an early date is very thin. This thin piece of evidence is hanging from a writer known to make some major mistakes. If it turns out to be wrong, then there was nothing on which to base any of their opinions. In other words, Irenaeus was known to be wrong about important details, and relying on his off-hand ambiguous comment, not intended at the time as a proof for the dating of the book of Revelation, is extremely precarious.

A powerful positive argument for an early date was made in the 2007 debate between Hank Hanegraaff and Mark Hitchcock on the dating of Revelation (Hanegraaff is an early-date advocate; Hitchcock is a late-date advocate). Hanegraaff started his argument with a verbatim quote of the first portion of the book.[106] His impassioned delivery was very powerful, making a clear point that the book was meant as a source of encouragement for that original audience who was under extreme pressure. When most people think of Revelation, they think seals, trumpets, bowls, and flying demon locust. Try to put that out of your mind. Instead, slow down and read scripture below out loud, like a head coach, as if you were giving it as a speech to team wavering in their faith:

> The revelation of Jesus Christ, which God gave him to show to his servants the things that must soon take place. He made it known by sending his angel to his servant John, who bore witness to the word of God and to the testimony of Jesus Christ, even to all that he saw. Blessed is the one who reads aloud the words of this prophecy, and blessed are those who hear, and who keep what is written in it, for the time is near. John to the seven churches that are in Asia: Grace to you and peace from him who is and who was and who is to come, and from the seven spirits who are before his throne, and from Jesus Christ the faithful witness, the firstborn of the dead, and the ruler of kings on earth. To him who loves us and has freed us from our sins by his blood and

> made us a kingdom, priests to his God and Father, to him be glory and dominion forever and ever. Amen.
>
> Behold, he is coming with the clouds, and every eye will see him, even those who pierced him, and all tribes of the earth will wail on account of him. Even so. Amen. "I am the Alpha and the Omega," says the Lord God, "who is and who was and who is to come, the Almighty."
>
> I, John, your brother and partner in the tribulation and the kingdom and the patient endurance that are in Jesus, was on the island called Patmos on account of the word of God and the testimony of Jesus. I was in the Spirit on the Lord's day, and I heard behind me a loud voice like a trumpet saying, "Write what you see in a book and send it to the seven churches, to Ephesus and to Smyrna and to Pergamum and to Thyatira and to Sardis and to Philadelphia and to Laodicea." (Rev. 1:1-2:7 ESV)

These were words of encouragement. The original audience took courage from it during the most intense persecution the church had ever seen, the attack by Nero. This persecution was so intense that Nero began to be called a beast. A great deal of the church fell away. Most of the faithful were murdered.[107] The judgment at home had begun (1 Peter 4:17), and it was followed immediately by the judgment against the persecutors.[108]

Unfortunately, futurist theologians are forced to spiritualize this advice so that it is seen as a generic admonition equally applicable to all generations. But would the original audience have seen it as such? If they could understand the warning at face value, should they have been able to take courage from the promises. And what would have happened if the promises failed, as the futurist paradigm requires?

Though it is proper to derive spiritual principles from scripture so that Christians of all eras can understand the mind of Christ on moral and spiritual issues, a slow reading of the introduction to Revelation focusing on how the original audience would have taken this advice leaves us with the obvious impression that it was meant primarily for the original audience.

Instead of relying on ambiguous or tenuous external evidence provided through a single source, we'll now turn to the unambiguous internal evidence that Revelation was written before the fall of Jerusalem. I'll start with a comparison to the other New Testament books that were written before this event. The most important in this regard is 2 Peter. Since I have a high view of scripture I have no problem believing that the Apostle Peter wrote the two letters with his name on them. What's interesting about the second epistle is how obvious it is that both Peter and his audience had read Revelation, and that his remarks seem to be a commentary on that book. This conclusion is based on an examination of the topical outline of 2 Peter and the fact that it unfolds in the same order as Revelation. I think this indicates that Peter has read the book and that he's commenting on it. As far as his commentary goes, I think it's instructive that he doesn't mention the complicated imagery of the middle, focusing instead on admonition and promise.

Peter starts with an admonition for his readers to learn how to love. This love comes as the final step of seven in a progressive program. Peter states that gaining maturity will guarantee them entry into the kingdom. Likewise, John starts with a criticism of Ephesus' lack of love, and then warns them of the consequences for not reestablishing it. John states that a failure to learn to love will result in the church's rejection. Then, Peter spends some time on false prophets such as Baalam and the sexual immorality that he brought. Likewise, John moves on in the letter to Pergamum to talk about Baalam and a disastrous sanction threatened by Jesus. Having touched on how to advance in maturity, and how to avoid "the sword of my mouth," Peter skips to the end of Revelation to talk about the climax of the story.

In the first few verses of chapter 3, Peter helps reinforce his source material:

> This is now the second letter that I am writing to you, beloved. In both of them I am stirring up your sincere mind by way of reminder, that you should remember the predictions of the holy prophets and the commandment of the Lord and Savior through your apostles . . . (2 Peter 3:1-2 ESV)

Peter is explicitly claiming that he is commenting on material revealed to them from Jesus through his Apostles. It should be no surprise, then, that 2 Peter 3 is based on the following:

> The revelation of Jesus Christ, which God gave him to show to his servants the things that must soon take place. He made it known by sending his angel to his servant John. (Rev. 1:1 ESV)

Just like 2 Peter 3 describes the burning and judging of the works of the world as well as the establishment of a new world "where righteousness dwells," Revelation 20 finishes the climax of the crisis with a description of the destruction of the old world and a judgment to match. Both passages also provide the only references to "a thousand years" in the New Testament. Finally, both passages are the only places in the New Testament to describe the end state as a new heaven and new earth. The phrase comes from Isaiah 65-66, where all sides agree the second coming is described. In my opinion, this cluster of topics cited by Peter is not coincidental. Since there is a consensus that Peter died before 68AD, it is inescapable that Revelation had to be written before that.

In addition to the direct reference to Revelation described above, there are several other books that likely have similar references. As Ed Stevens argues in his chronology of the first century, it's likely that Ephesians, Colossians, Philemon, Philippians, Hebrews, Titus, 1 and 2 Timothy, 1 and 2 Peter, and Jude were all written after Revelation.[109] Some of the more obvious allusions to Revelation among these books can be found in Hebrews.

> By faith Abraham obeyed when he was called to go out to a place that he was to receive as an inheritance. And he went out, not knowing where he was going. By faith he went to live in the land of promise, as in a foreign land, living in tents with Isaac and Jacob, heirs with him of the same promise. For he was looking forward to the city that has foundations, whose designer and builder is God . . . But as it is, they desire a better country, that is, a heavenly one. Therefore God is not ashamed to be called their God, for he has prepared for them a city. (Heb. 11:8-10, 16 ESV)

> For you have not come to what may be touched, a blazing fire and darkness and gloom and a tempest and the sound of a trumpet and a voice whose words made the hearers beg that no further messages be spoken to them. For they could not endure the order that was given, "If even a beast touches the mountain, it shall be stoned." Indeed, so terrifying was the sight that Moses said, "I tremble with fear." But you have come to Mount Zion and to the city of the living God, the heavenly Jerusalem, and to

> innumerable angels in festal gathering, and to the assembly of the firstborn who are enrolled in heaven, and to God, the judge of all, and to the spirits of the righteous made perfect, and to Jesus, the mediator of a new covenant, and to the sprinkled blood that speaks a better word than the blood of Abel. (Heb. 12:18-24 ESV)

This language is very close to the New Jerusalem described in Revelation 21-22.

> And I saw the holy city, new Jerusalem, coming down out of heaven from God, prepared as a bride adorned for her husband. And I heard a loud voice from the throne saying, "Behold, the dwelling place of God is with man. He will dwell with them, and they will be his people, and God himself will be with them as their God. He will wipe away every tear from their eyes, and death shall be no more, neither shall there be mourning nor crying nor pain anymore, for the former things have passed away. (Rev. 21:2-4 ESV)

If 2 Peter and Hebrews are referring to Revelation, then Revelation had to have been written and distributed before the deaths of Peter and Paul. Both of them were killed before 68AD in the Neronic persecution.

Next, we'll look at a few of the internal evidences from Revelation itself. The most prominent is the measuring of the temple.

> Then I was given a measuring rod like a staff, and I was told, "Rise and measure the temple of God and the altar and those who worship there, but do not measure the court outside the temple; leave that out, for it is given over to the nations, and they will trample the holy city for forty-two months. (Rev. 11:1-2 ESV)

This passage has a clear relationship to Luke's version of the Olivet Discourse.

> But when you see Jerusalem surrounded by armies, then know that its desolation has come near. Then let those who are in Judea flee to the mountains, and let those who are inside the city depart, and let not those who are out in the country enter it, for these are days of vengeance, to fulfill all that is written. Alas for women who are pregnant and for those who are nursing infants in those days! For there will be great distress upon the earth and wrath against this people. They will fall by the edge of the sword and be led captive among all nations, and Jerusalem will be trampled underfoot by the Gentiles, until the times of the Gentiles are fulfilled. (Luke 21:20-24 ESV)

Above, we have seen that the Olivet Discourse is a description of the second coming. I've argued that it is also a description of the destruction of Jerusalem in 70AD. Here, we see that Luke's version of the Olivet Discourse proposes that Jerusalem will be trampled underfoot until the times of the Gentiles is fulfilled.[110] The phrase "trampled underfoot" is specifically used to describe an ongoing military campaign, and cannot simply mean an occupation.[111] This is important because some theologians assert that Jerusalem being "trampled underfoot" simply means that Gentiles live in the city while the Jews are excluded (at least until 1948 or 1967). It does not. It means that for the period in question, there is an active military battle for the city.

In Revelation, we see that this is fulfilled after a 42-month campaign (the Roman War took exactly this long up to the point of the destruction of Jerusalem). In Revelation 11, we see that the measuring of the temple by John is done before the end of the 42 months (presumably, it's before the siege). If these elements were meant to be measured by John regarding the Roman War, then the scope and application of Revelation is established as a commentary on that war. Since it would only make sense for John to prophecy about something before it happened, and the temple is still standing in the prophecy, then it makes the simplest sense that Revelation was written before the destruction of the temple.

Futurists such as MacArthur and Hitchcock respond that there is a new temple built just for the tribulation period, and that this is what John is measuring. They recognize that there has to be a temple involved in the eschaton, but even until modern times there has been no Jewish temple. This presents a major problem for the doctrine of imminence, which states that the rapture, and thus the kicking off of the Great Tribulation, could have happened in any instant since the ascension.[112] Since "the end" must be imminent, the condition of all of human history until the moment of the rapture must always present a viable condition for that event to occur. Therefore, no event that happens before the rapture (i.e., the regathering of Israel, or the building or failure to build a Jewish temple in Jerusalem) can be a fulfillment of prophecy or can set up the conditions that will exist at the moment of the beginning of the Great Tribulation. According to premillennial dispensationalism, the church age in which we live now is only an interlude between eras of Jewish history. Since the church age was not foreseen in the Old Testament, none of the eschatology related to the Jews can unfold during the church age.[113] Immediately after the moment of the rapture there needs to be a temple in operation matching the majesty of one that took decades to build in ancient times. Because they need a future temple, and one can't be constructed before the rapture because no prophecy can be fulfilled until after the rapture, their system doesn't make sense. It points to the absurdity of the doctrine of imminence according to the pretribulation rapture paradigm.

Finally, in Revelation 17 John writes about a succession of leaders associated with the eschatological climax. He seems to be inserting his current location in time into the last portion of that list of leaders.

> And I saw the woman, drunk with the blood of the saints, the blood of the martyrs of Jesus. When I saw her, I marveled greatly. But the angel said to me, "Why do you marvel? I will tell you the mystery of the woman, and of the beast with seven heads and ten horns that carries her. The beast that you saw was, and is not, and is about to rise from the bottomless pit and go to destruction. And the dwellers on earth whose names have not been written in the book of life from the foundation of the world will marvel to see the beast, because it was and is not and is to come. This calls for a mind with wisdom: the seven heads are seven mountains on which the woman is seated; they are also seven kings, five of whom have fallen, one is, the other has not yet come, and when he does come he must remain only a little while. As for the beast that was and is not, it is an eighth but it belongs to the seven, and it goes to destruction. (Rev. 17:6-11 ESV)

If John was writing at the time that the beast was "about to rise from the bottomless pit," then we can at least say that the fulfillment of his passage has already happened. And since John places himself in the time of the sixth king, preterist commentators make the simple observation that a perfect fit for the timing of the writing of the book is in the mid-60s AD according to succession of Roman emperors in that era. I'll have more to say on this succession in the next chapter. The internal evidence clearly shows that John placed himself in the narrative of the visions in Revelation as they were unfolding in history, in the 60s AD. The internal evidence makes no sense if John was referring to events that would happen at least 2,000 years into the future.

Summary:

There is no unambiguous evidence that Revelation was written in 92-95AD. The vast majority of the external evidence of the late writing can be traced to one ambiguous sentence from a passage written by a writer known to be dramatically wrong on such basic things as the age of Christ when he died. The circular reporting anchored on this questionable single reference to a late date makes that conclusion highly suspect.

On the other hand, there are several early date traditions seen in church history. There are dozens of credible scholars who accept an early date of Revelation. The internal scriptural evidence indicates an early date of Revelation. I'm persuaded by the evidence of an early date (likely sometime in the winter of 62-63AD). Because of this, I think it's most likely that the early date of Revelation is correct.

Chapter 5 Endnotes

[101] Francis Gumerlock, *Revelation and the First Century,* p.21-37.

[102] Ibid, 24.

[103] http://livingthequestion.org/revelation/ (Last accessed 4/1/16).

[104] Kenneth Gentry, *Before Jerusalem Fell.*

[105] Philip Schaff, http://www.ccel.org/ccel/schaff/anf01.ix.vii.xxxi.html.

[106] https://www.youtube.com/watch?v=b6FOx_4wujg.

[107] Ed Stevens, *Final Decade,* p.160.

[108] If you are tempted to try to take advice like this too literally in a modern era, you'll run into all sorts of problems. You'll be challenged by having to explain who the Nicolaitans are and why they're so bad, and why a major concern for us should be persecution in synagogues. (Mark 13:9)

[109] Ed Stevens, *Final Decade,* p.18.

[110] See Don Preston's comment in his 2015 debate with Michael Brown. https://www.youtube.com/watch?v=O0Ec1GyfKxs (Last accessed 4/13/16).

[111] Ed Stevens, podcast covering "tread under foot." http://www.buzzsprout.com/11633/181738-times-of-the-gentiles-lk-21-24 (Last accessed 4/13/16).

[112] The doctrine of imminence is one of weakest in premillennial dispensationalism. It proposes that the rapture could happen at any moment. It is inextricably integrated into MacArthur's position that all of the New Testament time statements should be spiritualized to apply to every generation of the church. But if you think about what this doctrine requires, you are left scratching your head. Leaving aside for a moment that the conditions of the world need to be those at the moment of the Roman War, not the ascension, according to the doctrine of imminence it is necessary that at any moment the narrative of the Great Tribulation would be able to start up. Therefore, it makes no sense whatsoever for premillennial dispensationalists to look at current events to see how close these events might be to fulfillment. Their theology requires that absolutely no particular current event needs to happen because it is possible for the rapture to happen in any given second in the

church age. All such "newspaper eschatology" is completely disingenuous. Any idea that the migration of Jews into the modern state of Israel is equally as invalid. If the doctrine of imminence is correct, the rapture could have happened in 1947, or any time before that. Dispensationalists fail to understand that they either need to embrace their doctrine of imminence or their reliance on the central role of the modern state of Israel because the two are mutually exclusive.

[113] This presents a major problem for dispensationalists. The prophecy industry based on LaHaye's books and their progeny requires fulfillment of prophecy on a nearly daily basis. This is the basis of newspaper eschatology. But, on a systematic level, dispensationalism (the only theological program that proposes a strong separation between the Jews and Gentiles) precludes newspaper eschatology. In fact, nothing happening during our age *can* be a fulfillment of prophecy because the prophecy clock hasn't started back up. But, this causes additional problems for their position. The historical situation including an operational temple and the political subjugation of Israel has to be in place just as it was in an ancient way at the moment the pause button was pressed in the first century. Dispensationalists admit this. In fact, LaHaye has proposed that there is a quick, otherwise unknown era of history between the rapture (when the play button is pressed again) and the beginning of the Great Tribulation. Early dispensationalist authors mostly glossed over this point, but it is a serious problem. At the moment of the rapture, conditions must be very similar to those in the first century in order for the Great Tribulation to start on time. But, in their system, the rapture can happen at any time. Those conditions haven't always existed. They don't now, for that matter. In fact, since there is no temple right now in operation, it can be argued that the rapture can't happen since immediately afterwards the temple has to be functioning. Some dispensationalists have proposed prefabricating everything needed, and then falling back on a tent-based tabernacle that could be quickly set up. Their position becomes more and more desperate as critics look at it closely.

Chapter 6: Nero Wasn't the Antichrist

Calvary Chapel Statement:

The Roman emperor Nero could not have been the Antichrist.

Even though it's highly likely and even probable that Nero was a type of Antichrist, he cannot be "the Beast" that is mentioned in Revelation.

First, when we look at 2 Thessalonians 2:8, we see the demise of the coming world leader known as the Antichrist.

2 Thessalonians 2:8 says, "And then the lawless one will be revealed, whom the Lord will consume with the breath of His mouth and destroy with the brightness of His coming."

The Bible teaches that the Antichrist will be destroyed at Christ's coming. When Jesus returns at Armageddon (i.e. His Second Coming), He will capture the Antichrist along with the false prophet, and cast them alive into the lake of burning sulfur (Revelation 19:20).

Problem is, Nero committed suicide in AD 68 two years before Preterists say that Jesus returned in AD 70.

Second, when we look at Daniel 9:27, we see that the Antichrist will make a covenant with Israel for one week (i.e. seven years).

Daniel 9:27a says, "Then he shall confirm a covenant with many for one week; but in the middle of the week He shall bring an end to sacrifice and offering."

Problem is, Nero never made a covenant with Israel.

Third, when we look at 2 Thessalonians 2:3-4, we see that the Antichrist enters the temple in Jerusalem and sets himself up to be worshiped as God.

2 Thessalonians 2:3-4 says, "Let no one deceive you by any means; for that Day will not come unless the falling away comes first, and the man of sin is revealed, the son of perdition, who opposes and exalts himself above all that is called God or that is worshiped, so that he sits as God in the temple of God, showing himself that he is God."

Problem is, Nero never entered the temple in Jerusalem and in fact, he never even entered Jerusalem.

Finally, when we look at Revelation 13:16-17, we see that Antichrist's one-world government requires that everyone take a mark on their forehead or their right hand.

Revelation 13:16-17 says, "He causes all, both small and great, rich and poor, free and slave, to receive a mark on their right hand or on their foreheads, and that no one may buy or sell except one who has the mark or the name of the beast, or the number of his name."

The problem that confronts the Preterist is that this event has not happened.

Charges:

- Nero can't be the Antichrist because, according to preterism, he died two years before Jesus was prophesied to destroy him in the second coming.
- Nero never made the treaty with Israel as described in Daniel 9:27.
- Nero never entered either Jerusalem or the Temple, so he couldn't have been worshipped there.
- The mark of the Beast hasn't happened yet.

The primary problem with the Calvary Chapel position here is that they require the preterist version of eschatological events (i.e., the function of the Antichrist and the mark of the beast) to match their own. They presume that events as dispensationalists imagine them are defined within preterism in the same way. This is superficial, circular reasoning because they simply assume that they have the correct definition of the event to begin with. The reality is that not all preterists say that Nero is the Antichrist. Not all preterists agree on the identity of the beast, or the mark that he requires. It's also critical that preterists don't stipulate to the Calvary Chapel understanding of the book of Daniel. So, this chapter has a lot to untangle.

We'll start with issues related to the Antichrist. A large proportion of preterists support the theory of Nero as the fulfillment of Antichrist imagery.[114] They do so because early in the narrative he seems to fulfill a number of the criteria. An important one is that the beast was seen in the vision to die before the final events related to him. This obvious connection is behind the Nero Redivivus legend which was popular in the early church. But, because of some problems matching up all of the imagery behind Nero as the Antichrist, other traditions have been proposed.

The best solution to these problems, in my opinion, has been put forward by Duncan McKenzie in his two-volume series, *The Antichrist and the Second Coming*.[115] In it, he proposes another candidate, Titus. Titus was the Roman general who lead the army that finally overran Jerusalem in August of 70AD. He did in fact enter the Temple. According to some sources, he desecrated it by having sex with a prostitute on the altar.

However, even the option of looking to Titus doesn't fully explain what I think is going on with regards to the Antichrist. Instead, I'd argue that Paul's comment in Ephesians 6:12 should control how we look at this topic. Along with proposing Titus as the Antichrist, McKenzie does an excellent job of identifying the role of supernatural evil (Satan, demons, etc.) as important players behind the scenes in history.[116] Throughout the book he makes a powerful argument that historically the enemy is the spiritual force behind the scenes, not the human character. To explain this dynamic, he points to Daniel 10, with the angel's speech:

> And behold, a hand touched me and set me trembling on my hands and knees. And he said to me, "O Daniel, man greatly loved, understand the words that I speak to you, and stand upright, for now I have been sent to you." And when he had spoken this word to me, I stood up trembling. Then he said to me, "Fear not, Daniel, for from the first day that you set your heart to understand and humbled yourself before your God, your words have been heard, and I have come because of your words. The prince of the kingdom of Persia withstood me twenty-one days, but Michael, one of the chief princes, came to help me, for I was left there with the kings of Persia, and came to make you understand what is to happen to your people in

the latter days. For the vision is for days yet to
come. (Dan. 10:10-14 ESV)

In this passage we see that the angel that came to deliver the message was held up by the "Prince of Persia." It is commonly accepted that this prince was a demonic character capable of fighting or withstanding an angel. The fact that he is named the Prince of Persia is an indication that this demonic character is associated with the ruling of that country. Another example will help explain this perspective:

> And Micaiah said, "Therefore hear the word of
> the Lord: I saw the Lord sitting on his throne,
> and all the host of heaven standing on his right
> hand and on his left. And the Lord said, 'Who
> will entice Ahab the king of Israel, that he may
> go up and fall at Ramoth-gilead?' And one said
> one thing, and another said another. Then a
> spirit came forward and stood before the Lord,
> saying, 'I will entice him.' And the Lord said to
> him, 'By what means?' And he said, 'I will go
> out, and will be a lying spirit in the mouth of all
> his prophets.' And he said, 'You are to entice
> him, and you shall succeed; go out and do so.'
> Now therefore behold, the Lord has put a lying
> spirit in the mouth of these your prophets. The
> Lord has declared disaster concerning you. (2
> Chron. 18:18-22 ESV)

In this passage, there is a council of invisible characters that God uses to control or manage the affairs of men. This perspective has come to be known as the Divine Council theory of governance.[117] In McKenzie's works he describes in detail how the Beast that God is destroying in the eschatological climax is actually the demonic character behind the power of Rome at the time. As such, he was the power behind the powerful or dominant leaders of Rome throughout its history. As a demonic character, you might say that he possessed the governors of these countries in each generation. McKenzie points to Titus as the man this demonic character was working through in eschatological passages. Although McKenzie doesn't expand his theory this far, I propose he could have possessed (or at least influenced) any number of human leaders in the period. In other words, the Beast could have been associated with both Nero and Titus, as well as others. If this approach is correct (this is my synthesis of McKenzie's observations combined with more popular Neronic material), it would account for the destruction of the Beast outside of the destruction of its human host. It would also help to explain how elements of his identity could seem to span more than one person's reign.

To make one final point on this, let's look for a second at the destruction of the Beast in Daniel 7. There, we see four Beasts described:

> In the first year of Belshazzar king of Babylon, Daniel saw a dream and visions of his head as he lay in his bed. Then he wrote down the dream and told the sum of the matter. Daniel declared, "I saw in my vision by night, and behold, the four winds of heaven were stirring up the great sea. And four great beasts came up out of the sea, different from one another. The first was like a lion and had eagles' wings. Then as I looked its wings were plucked off, and it was lifted up from the ground and made to stand on two feet like a man, and the mind of a man was given to it. And behold, another beast, a second one, like a bear. It was raised up on one side. It had three ribs in its mouth between its teeth; and it was told, 'Arise, devour much flesh.' After this I looked, and behold, another, like a leopard, with four wings of a bird on its back. And the beast had four heads, and dominion was given to it. After this I saw in the night visions, and

> behold, a fourth beast, terrifying and dreadful
> and exceedingly strong. It had great iron teeth;
> it devoured and broke in pieces and stamped
> what was left with its feet. It was different from
> all the beasts that were before it, and it had ten
> horns. I considered the horns, and behold, there
> came up among them another horn, a little one,
> before which three of the first horns were
> plucked up by the roots. And behold, in this
> horn were eyes like the eyes of a man, and a
> mouth speaking great things. (Dan. 7:1-8 ESV)

In this passage, the four beasts are described using imagery from four animals. It should be unsurprising that in Revelation 13 we see a single composite leopard/bear/lion beast, while the fourth beast is a standalone character. The first point to see here is that the three previous beasts, connected throughout Daniel with the kingdoms of Babylon, Medo-Persia, and Greece, still exist in the time of Rome. Clearly no physical leader who had taken a role in the history of these civilizations was still alive at the time of Rome in the first century. This observation by itself should be enough to prove that the beasts in view are not human characters. But, moving to Daniel 7 we find an explanation of the beasts described above:

> These four great beasts are four kings who shall
> arise out of the earth. But the saints of the Most
> High shall receive the kingdom and possess the
> kingdom forever, forever and ever. (Dan. 7:18
> ESV)

And then a bit later:

> Thus he said: 'As for the fourth beast, there shall
> be a fourth kingdom on earth, which shall be
> different from all the kingdoms, and it shall
> devour the whole earth, and trample it down,
> and break it to pieces.' (Dan. 7:23 ESV)

In other words, the beasts seem to describe not only the kings, but the kingdoms, and since they describe kingdoms that last longer than the ones history records, they describe the demonic principalities and powers behind those kingdoms as well. This can also be seen in Daniel 7:11-12, where the beasts of Babylon, Medo-Persia, and Greece actually outlive the beast of Rome.

Having this in mind, the first charge above doesn't stand because it reflects a failure to understand a preterist position that incorporates Divine Council narrative. It is projecting the premillennial dispensational paradigm and crisis onto a different system, which results in a failure to understand the terminology under that system. To be fair to them, there have been preterist authors in the past who have focused on the human characters of Nero, Titus, and the functionaries of the Jewish Temple system in the first century. However, I don't think these approaches have kept up with developments within preterism, and so the critique of them does not threaten the paradigm I'm proposing.

The next point of contention is the covenant made between the Antichrist and the Jews during the tribulation:

> Seventy weeks are decreed about your people and your holy city, to finish the transgression, to put an end to sin, and to atone for iniquity, to bring in everlasting righteousness, to seal both vision and prophet, and to anoint a most holy place. Know therefore and understand that from the going out of the word to restore and build Jerusalem to the coming of an anointed one, a prince, there shall be seven weeks. Then for sixty-two weeks it shall be built again with squares and moat, but in a troubled time. And after the sixty-two weeks, an anointed one shall be cut off and shall have nothing. And the

people of the prince who is to come shall destroy the city and the sanctuary. Its end shall come with a flood, and to the end there shall be war. Desolations are decreed. And he shall make a strong covenant with many for one week, and for half of the week he shall put an end to sacrifice and offering. And on the wing of abominations shall come one who makes desolate, until the decreed end is poured out on the desolator. (Dan. 9:24-27 ESV)

The first thing that stands out is that the Great Tribulation is supposed to be seven years long. Some dispensational writers have gone as far as to map this out to the day. But, keep in mind that a foundational principal in dispensationalism is that no prophecy can be fulfilled before the rapture. So, if no prophecy can be fulfilled before the rapture, and the rapture can happen at any moment so that the pre-conditions are present at any point in history, when is the Antichrist supposed to negotiate a covenant with the Jews before the seven-year Great Tribulation?

Next, pay close attention to verse 27. Does it say that the Antichrist will make a deal with the Jews? No. It says, "And he shall make a strong covenant with many for one week." The identity of the person making the covenant is not explicitly stated. Gentry argues that grammatical clues indicated that it is Christ who makes this covenant:

"The covenant here is not made, it is confirmed. The usual word for the initial establishment of a covenant is karat. This is actually the confirmation of a covenant already extant, i.e., the covenant of God's redemptive grace confirmed by Christ (Rom. 15:8)." In addition, "The parallelism with verse 26 indicates that the death of the Messiah is directly related to the confirming of the covenant. He is "cut off" but "not for himself" (v.26a) for He "confirms the covenant" for the "many" of Israel (v.27a). His "cutting off" brings the confirmation of the covenant, for "without shedding of blood there is no remission" (Heb. 9:22). As Christ put it: "This is My blood of the new covenant, which is shed for many for the remission of sins" (Matt. 26:28)."[118]

In fact, many Reformed commentators insist that it's actually Christ who makes the covenant. That covenant turns out to be the New Covenant described in Jeremiah 31, Hebrews 7, and Luke 22. It was confirmed by the fulfillment of the promise to return and punish the Old Covenant nation in the Roman War.

The argument that the Antichrist didn't make a covenant with Nero is based on the dispensationalist interpretation of this passage. They assume that it is the Antichrist making the covenant, and then when preterism can't accommodate their preconceived paradigm, they declare preterism to be failed. As I've shown above, not everyone agrees with that interpretation. If the dispensational interpretation of 9:27 is wrong, then it is irrelevant whether or not Nero made a covenant.

The third point made by the Calvary Chapel writer is that Nero never entered the Temple and worshipped there. As mentioned above, many preterists identify the Beast as Titus. As McKenzie describes in detail, Titus not only entered the Temple but probably had sex with a prostitute on the altar during the sacking of the city.[119] In addition to this action, which more than fulfills the requirement that the altar was desecrated, McKenzie also points out that the language associated with the desolation could just as easily be fulfilled by the invasion of the pagan army into the land of Judah. The presence of that army on sacred land would have been seen by the Jews of the day as a desecration that made the land spiritually desolate. A comparison of Matthew 24 and Luke 21 demonstrates this:

> So when you see the abomination of desolation spoken of by the prophet Daniel, standing in the holy place (let the reader understand), then let those who are in Judea flee to the mountains. Let the one who is on the housetop not go down to take what is in his house, and let the one who is in the field not turn back to take his cloak. And alas for women who are pregnant and for those who are nursing infants in those days! Pray that your flight may not be in winter or on a Sabbath. For then there will be great tribulation, such as has not been from the beginning of the world until now, no, and never will be. (Matt. 24:15-21 ESV)

> But when you see Jerusalem surrounded by armies, then know that its desolation has come near. Then let those who are in Judea flee to the mountains, and let those who are inside the city depart, and let not those who are out in the country enter it, for these are days of vengeance, to fulfill all that is written. Alas for women who are pregnant and for those who are nursing infants in those days! For there will be great distress upon the earth and wrath against this people. They will fall by the edge of the sword and be led captive among all nations, and Jerusalem will be trampled underfoot by the Gentiles, until the times of the Gentiles are fulfilled. (Luke 21:20-24 ESV)

If you compare the location Matthew's version where the abomination of desolation is mentioned with the similar events of Luke, you find out that the abomination is likely the invasion of the land itself. There is no reason for a fantastical theory about a homosexual Jewish European leader who will make a treaty with the Jews. The text simply says that this is fulfilled with the invasion of the Romans. There are a number of ways of explaining the imagery. Again, the gap between the Calvary Chapel approach and preterism is accentuated by having significantly different ways of explaining the fulfillment.

Finally, the Calvary Chapel writer claims that the mark of the Beast was never issued, so that prophecy must be for the future. The problem here is that the Calvary Chapel writer is simply projecting the fantasy of barcodes and RFID microchips onto imagery meant for the Bronze Age. Below is an example of how nearly identical imagery had been used in the context of an eschatological disaster earlier in the history of Israel:

> Now the glory of the God of Israel had gone up from the cherub on which it rested to the threshold of the house. And he called to the man clothed in linen, who had the writing case at his waist. And the Lord said to him, "Pass through the city, through Jerusalem, and put a mark on the foreheads of the men who sigh and groan over all the abominations that are committed in it." And to the others he said in my hearing, "Pass through the city after him, and strike. Your eye shall not spare, and you shall show no pity. Kill old men outright, young men and maidens, little children and women, but touch no one on whom is the mark. And begin at my sanctuary." So they began with the elders who were before the house. Then he said to them, "Defile the house, and fill the courts

with the slain. Go out." So they went out and struck in the city. And while they were striking, and I was left alone, I fell upon my face, and cried, "Ah, Lord God! Will you destroy all the remnant of Israel in the outpouring of your wrath on Jerusalem? (Ezek. 9:3-8 ESV)

This passage in Ezekiel is the scriptural basis for the idea of marking people on the head in order to separate them before divine judgment. There is no indication that it was a literal, physical mark. Instead, just as the "hand of God" is used to describe the power to implement his will (the hand being the tool that he'd use to make things happen), the passage implies that what they thought or believed would determine their destiny. Likewise, in the New Testament, the mark of the Beast is associated with what the people believed and how they acted. Those who were dedicated followers of God would not believe in or participate in the emperor cult described in detail by Hank Hanegraaff in the debate cited above. The mark is also seen as a counterfeit sealing of the enemies of God.[120] The true mark given to the faithful is associated with the new name, the new garments, etc., found throughout Revelation.

The real problem in understanding the mark of the Beast comes from a faulty hermeneutic employed by modern theologians. They assume that the mark in question matches some technology that has now become available, and since the technology now exists to fulfill the imagery in their mind, fulfillment must be right around the corner. This is the definition of circular reasoning. But worse, if they stopped to think about it, this technology-based interpretation of the mark of the Beast completely destroys one of their key eschatological doctrines – imminence.

In all premillennial dispensational churches (all Calvary Chapels, all Pentecostals, most Southern Baptists, etc.) the time statements of the New Testament are explained away by saying that the promises are meant to keep each generation on their toes so that they will be ready since the rapture can happen at any second. But, if a certain technology, say, barcodes, had to be introduced in order to have the mark of the Beast, it is flatly untrue that the rapture could have happened before about 1980. And, if the actual technology used in the mark of the Beast (maybe it's not RFID, maybe it's nanobots of some kind) hasn't been deployed yet then the rapture can't happen until after this point. If this is so, imminence is meaningless, and their approach to explaining away the time statements is cynical and manipulative.

Like all of their hermeneutical anachronisms, the concern over the mark of the Beast reveals more about their own system than it supposedly does about preterism. There are reasonable, internally defined explanations for each similar concern so that there is no reason to go outside of scripture to establish our interpretation. The original audience was meant to understand the message, so we have to use sources and terminology that would have been available to them.

Summary:

The failure of Nero to fulfill all of the descriptions of the Antichrist is irrelevant. The true enemy in eschatology is the Satanic system behind the humans involved, not the human characters. Though the number 666 or 616 refers to a man, the Beast connected to him might be associated with several men in history. Though there are some preterists who make Nero a key figure, others are persuaded that Titus is the real human character that acts out the role of the Beast. If the demonic character behind the scenes is the real enemy, it could easily be either human in a given passage without losing continuity in the interpretation. In the case of Nero's role in a treaty with the Jews, preterists reject the entire line of thought that leads to this interpretation. Instead, preterists argue that Daniel 9:27 describes Christ confirming the New Covenant by fulfilling his promise to come in vengeance. In the case of Nero failing to enter either Jerusalem or the Temple, preterists would argue that the Roman government potentially fulfilled the idea of desolating the land simply by invading it. If a human actor behaving badly in the temple is the correct interpretation, Titus does so by entering Jerusalem, entering the Temple, and then desecrating the altar with a prostitute. Finally, the imagery surrounding the mark of the Beast was seen earlier in scripture as an invisible mark used to determine who was to be killed in a judgment sent by God. To apply this mark some sort of meaning associated with modern technology results in the implosion of the Calvary Chapel system, not preterism.

Chapter 6 Endnotes

[114] http://www.preteristcentral.com/Man%20of%20Sin.html (Last accessed 4/1/16); Francis Gumerlock, *Revelation and the First Century*, p.129.; https://adammaarschalk.com/2009/08/16/pp15-the-man-of-lawlessness-ii-thess-2-part-1/ (Last accessed 7/2/16).

[115] Duncan McKenzie, *The Antichrist and the Second Coming* (Vol. 1), p.329-360; http://planetpreterist.com/content/man-lawlessness-part-one; http://planetpreterist.com/content/man-lawlessness-part-two (Last accessed 7/2/16).

[116] Duncan McKenzie, *The Antichrist and the Second Coming* (Vols. 1-2).

[117] This system is best seen in early extra-Biblical literature such as 1 Enoch, or modern fictional work such as Brian Godawa's series *Chronicles of the Nephilim.* These works, and others, describe the spiritual forces assumed to be behind the scenes of world history. It was the accepted worldview of the Jews in the first century. This perspective helps understand some complicated elements of eschatology.; also, *Fulfilled Magazine* (Summer 2016).

[118] Kenneth Gentry on Daniel 9:27. http://www.cmfnow.com/articles/pt551.htm (Last accessed 4/13/16).

[119] Duncan McKenzie, *The Antichrist and the Second Coming* (Vol 1).

[120] David Chilton, *Days of Vengeance,* p.146.

Chapter 7: The Global Nature of Revelation

Calvary Chapel Statement:

The Tribulation Period in Revelation is just too global and cataclysmic to be attributed to the Destruction of Jerusalem in AD 70.

During the admittedly devastatingly local destruction of Jerusalem in AD 70, it did not involve "famines, pestilences and earthquakes" (verse 7), Christians being "hated by all nations" (verse 9), the "gospel... [being] preached in all the world" (verse 14), the "abomination of desolation" (verse 15), the "sun darkened, the moon not giving of its light" and the "heavens shaken" (verse 29).

Clearly, the Great Tribulation (verse 29) did not happen and Jesus certainly did not appear at that time (verses 30, 31).

When we look at some of the twenty-one judgments in the tribulation period, we can see that they are experienced over a wider geographic area then [sic] *just Jerusalem.*

For example:

1/4 of the earth's population is wiped out (Revelation 6:7, 8)

Great earth quakes and astronomical events (Revelation 6:12-14)

1/3 of the earths [sic] *vegetation is destroyed (Revelation 8:7)*

1/3 of the oceans are polluted (Revelation 8:8, 9)

1/3 of the ships will be destroyed (Revelation 8:8, 9)

1/3 of the sea life is destroyed (Revelation 8:8, 9)

1/3 of the fresh water is polluted (Revelation 8:10, 11)

1/3 of the sun, moon and stars are darkened (Revelation 8:12)

Everything in the ocean dies (Revelation 16:3)

Charges:

- Revelation's description of the Great Tribulation is too grand to be fulfilled in the Roman War.
- The Great Tribulation did not happen and Christ did not appear in that time.
- The various judgments happened over a larger area than that affected by the Roman War.

The theme of this chapter is the scale of the Great Tribulation and second coming. The Calvary Chapel writer asserts that these events will be so large that there is no way the events surrounding Judea in 70AD could have fulfilled them. We'll start by clarifying some of the language involved to demonstrate that the standard global scale of the event is an assumption they make that is not based on scripture.

Ge is translated in the King James Version as "world" 188 times, "land" 33 times, "ground" 18 times, "country" 2 times, "earthly" 1 time, and "world" 1 time.[121] Below is the Strong's citation for ge:

γῆ

gē

ghay

Contracted from a primary word; soil; by extension a region, or the solid part or the whole of the terrene globe (including the occupants in each application): - country, earth (-ly), ground, land, world.

Total KJV occurrences: 252

Since the majority of references to physical terrain in scripture refer to the land or area involved in a given narrative, unless some specific element of context requires a larger scope I suggest that the best default English term should be "land." On occasion it might make sense to expand the idea to the global scale. But in each case context will dictate, and in most of scripture the context is limited.

An example of this is found in Revelation 14:20. There, as the winepress of God's wrath is tread during the final climactic battle, the blood flows to the depth of the bridles of the horses. The blood is also described as flowing outward 1,600 furlongs, which is the size of the "whole land of Palestine" according to Wesley and others. Since this passage gives the scope of the Armageddon battle as the area of Israel, we conclude that the land in question is the land of Israel, not all of the land of the physical globe.

The next term we'll look at is oikoumene, found 15 times in the New Testament. It is almost always translated "world" in the King James Bible (the only exception is Luke 21:26 where it is translated "earth"). Below is Strong's citation for oikoumene:

οἰκουμένη

oikoumenē

oy-kou-men'-ay

Feminine participle present passive of G3611 (as noun, by implication of G1093); land, that is, the (terrene part of the) globe; specifically the Roman empire: - earth, world.

Total KJV occurrences: 15

Though oikoumene includes the idea of physical land, it also includes the idea of the civilized world. This is generally contrasted with the lands of the barbarians. Thus, by implication it always implies a limited scope with boundaries on the edge of nation in question. There is no indication in the New Testament that the scope is larger than the Roman Empire. Because of the national and political implications of this word, I prefer "empire" over "world." Using this alternative translation simplifies matters significantly.

With these two words defined for us, take a look at Revelation 3:10 and how it uses both terms in one sentence. I'm going to modify the ESV translation using "empire" and "land" in italics to reflect what I think is a clearer translation of the words oikoumene and ge (the original translation uses "world" and "earth" respectively):

> Because you have kept my word about patient endurance, I will keep you from the hour of trial that is coming on the whole *empire* to try those who dwell on the *land*. (Rev. 3:10 ESV modified)

This verse is a concise description of the scope of eschatology. The whole Roman Empire, will undergo traumatic events in order to judge those who dwell on the land. It is perfect summary of what happened in the second half of the first century in Rome and Judea. While this statement clearly limits the scope of the events to the land of Israel, the structure of it seems to preclude the option of this being a global judgment.

The final term translated "world" is kosmos. It is used 188 times in the New Testament.[122] The following is Strong's listing for Kosmos:

κόσμος

kosmos

kos'-mos

Probably from the base of G2865; orderly arrangement, that is, decoration; by implication the world (in a wide or narrow sense, including its inhabitants, literally or figuratively [morally]): - adorning, world.

Total KJV occurrences: 187

The primary meaning of Kosmos has to do with orderly arrangement. In other words, "world" translated from kosmos is usually talking about more than just the physicality of the creation. It's talking about the world system that includes unseen things and their conceptual parameters as well. In modern terms we'd probably extend this to the system of natural laws or physics that rules the universe. You'll remember that we earlier talked about the Divine Council theory of the unseen world. There, a narrative derived from scripture and other extra biblical writings describes the world as being run by invisible creatures who sit as advisors for the Ancient of Days. He uses them to execute his plan for history in time, and even seems to use their suggestions in some cases. The evil members of the Divine Council are consistently behind the idolatry of the Old Testament, and the sin and immorality associated with them is rolled into the concept of judgment against the kosmos in the New Testament.

A key part of the transition from the Old Covenant paradigm to the New Covenant paradigm is the transition of God's governance from a Divine Council system to the kingdom of God, where glorified believers replace the angels (and likely demons) as the functionaries through whom God governs (cf. Rev. 20:4-6, Heb. 2:5).[123] This is one of the reasons that the various uses of the term kosmos are so important in the New Testament. Kosmos represents the world system. It's a grand term that includes the empires that control the physical realm, the laws, customs, and morality that they promote, and the similar elements of the invisible realm. So in some cases, when kosmos is used and the destruction of the world is described, the point is to describe transitioning from the then-current world governance system to the kingdom of God, which is described as continuing forever once it is established (cf. Dan. 7:21ff, Rev. 22:5). Other times, the emphasis is on the eclipsing of the world of idolatry familiar to the New Testament generation:

> This is what I mean, brothers: the appointed time has grown very short. From now on, let those who have wives live as though they had none, and those who mourn as though they were not mourning, and those who rejoice as though they were not rejoicing, and those who buy as though they had no goods, and those who deal with the world as though they had no dealings with it. For the present form of this world [kosmos] is passing away. (1 Cor. 7:29-31 ESV)

Transactions that happen in the kosmos can be visible or invisible. This makes the arguing about their global expression in regular earth history difficult to explain to those who are only looking for helicopters spraying nerve gas.[124]

Though I've argued in most cases that the scope of "world" and "earth" should be seen in a small scope in eschatology, in the case of kosmos it represents a gigantic scope much more grand than the visible universe. The problem is that since there is no "g," "o," or "k" superscript in English Bibles above each instance of the English terms "world" and "earth" translated from "ge," "oikoumene," or "kosmos" the topic can become extremely confusing. Space precludes me from making a detailed presentation of the verses in question and their implications, but I suggest getting an interlinear

Bible and being very careful as you study to make sure you understand which term is in view. None of the terms discussed above naturally, unambiguously means the entire physical globe as we tend to think of it in 2016AD. In each case, the context of the passage should control the translation of the Greek words and their interpretation.

In the case of the second coming, or "day of the Lord," some confusion is introduced on this point because of the difference between amillennialism and premillennialism. Amillennialists use passages like 2 Peter 3 to describe the second coming, and the language there seems to be universal in nature:

> But the day of the Lord will come like a thief, and then the heavens will pass away with a roar, and the heavenly bodies will be burned up and dissolved, and the earth and the works that are done on it will be exposed. (2 Peter 3:10 ESV)

This is not a problem for amillennialists because for them the second coming is the time where the whole universe is melted. The problem for premillennialists is that this verse does not describe the second coming. For premillennialists, this verse describes the conclusion of the Gog and Magog revolution after the millennium. This happens at least 1,000 years after the second coming. John MacArthur attempts to come to the rescue of premillennialists on this point. He spoke of it directly in his 1991 broadcast of "Grace to You":

> Now, some of you are saying, "Well now wait a minute, doesn't the day of the Lord come at the end of the Tribulation?" Yes. "But aren't you describing something that happens at the end of the Millennium before the new heavens and the new earth?" Yes, because it says in verse 13, we're looking for a new heavens and

a new earth. But you say, "Wait a minute, I know a little prophecy. Isn't there a thousand years between those?" Yes. You say, "Well then does the day of the Lord last for a thousand years?"

Not really. The day of the Lord has a component that occurs at the end of the Tribulation when Jesus comes at the end of the battle of Armageddon and consumes the wicked. And the day of the Lord has another component at the end of the millennial kingdom, but don't be troubled by that because verse 8 explains it. "With the Lord, one day is," what? A thousand years," and the day of the Lord is just one day with Him. Though from a human viewpoint there's a thousand year interval between phase one and phase two. With Him it's one day of the Lord, one day of the Lord.

And in that final moment, the whole solar system and the great galaxies, will be abolished. All the elements which make up the physical world will be dissolved by heat and utterly melt away. It is an astonishing picture that really is the final act of God to destroy the remaining ungodly who have accumulated during the Millennial kingdom. He destroys those on the earth at the coming of Christ at the end of the Tribulation time, then the thousand-year kingdom.[125]

Clearly, MacArthur is scrambling to smoothly integrate 2 Peter 3 into a premillennial view of the day of the Lord. He has to split that "day" into two events separated by 1,000 years, though there are no grounds to do so other than his theological desperation.[126] On the left side of the timeline, he has to apply it to the battle of Armageddon (a straightforward military event in a single valley north of Jerusalem). Then, on the right side of the timeline 1,000 years later it becomes the melting of the universe. But, then he has to find a way to describe these as being one event. As a result, the day of the Lord ends up lasting 1,007 years, with 1,000 years in the middle being yet another pause from fulfillment.

The scopes of these two events as MacArthur describes them couldn't be more different. I propose that MacArthur is close to correct when he assigns the concept of the day of the Lord to the battle of Armageddon. Every previous use of the day of the Lord in scripture defines it as a military invasion and catastrophe. Since every other case of the day of the Lord in scripture is an example of a non-supernatural military campaign that plays out in normal history, I think we should see it the same way here. But, that severely limits the scope. No longer is the day of the Lord, or the second coming, something that could be seen from Australia. And, it can't accommodate the imagery we see in 2 Peter 3.

Using the Old Testament to establish our terminology and the basic dynamic of fulfillment (we aren't looking for a literalistic fulfillment in Old Testament terms, but we do expect the basic theme to be followed) we'll turn to Isaiah 65-66 to see how that passage handles not only the second coming but the creation of the New Heaven and new Earth. The first problem for premillennialists in Isaiah 65-66 is that they try to use it to define the millennium.[127] But the word "millennium" or the phrase "thousand years" isn't found in Isaiah. Instead, this is the only discourse in the Old Testament that explicitly talks about the "new heaven and new earth" (there are other uses of "new heaven" in the chapters of Isaiah leading up to it, but this phrase is unique to these two chapters). In premillennial doctrine, the new heaven and new earth is supposed to follow the millennium, not be parallel or synonymous with it. This has resulted in some cases of premillennialists claiming that Isaiah 65-66 is speaking of a new heaven and new earth, while Revelation 21-22 is speaking of a new new heaven and new new earth. If it hadn't been put to me personally in those terms, I might not believe it. But, in many conversations with well-educated premillennialists this is where they are forced to land. The reason is that Isaiah 65-66 clearly describes the second coming and the immediate establishment of the new heaven and new earth.

But the problems don't stop there. In Isaiah 66 the prophet claims that only a limited number of people will know that the second coming even happened!

> For by fire will the LORD enter into judgment, and by his sword, with all flesh; and those slain by the LORD shall be many. Those who sanctify and purify themselves to go into the gardens, following one in the midst, eating pig's flesh and the abomination and mice, shall come to an end together, declares the LORD. For I know their works and their thoughts, and the time is coming to gather all nations and tongues. And they shall come and shall see my glory, and I will set a sign among them. And from them I will send survivors to the nations, to Tarshish, Pul, and Lud, who draw the bow, to Tubal and Javan, to the coastlands far away that have not heard my fame or seen my glory. And they shall declare my glory among the nations. And they shall bring all your brothers from all the nations as an offering to the LORD, on horses and in chariots and in litters and on mules and on dromedaries, to my holy mountain Jerusalem, says the LORD, just as the Israelites bring their grain offering in a clean vessel to the house of the LORD. And some of them also I will take

> for priests and for Levites, says the LORD.
> (Isaiah 66:16-21 ESV)

This is one of the least appreciated, though clearly written, passages in scripture regarding the second coming. God will judge the world by fire and the sword (v.16). To judge all of the sinners, he will gather all nations and tongues to see his glory (v.18). After the sign he does (understood generally to be the second coming and judgment against those nations), God will send survivors to the coastlands far away to people who have not heard of God and who didn't know about the second coming (v.19). Once there, these survivors will evangelize those ignorant unbelievers. God will then make some of these new converts into priests.

This passage is flatly impossible, no matter how metaphorically or symbolically you take the passage, to integrate into either premillennialism or amillennialism. This is one of the reasons I think most commentators won't write about or teach it in detail. Even if you take the terms of it to be somewhat metaphorical or to contain ancient imagery that would only be figuratively applied in the future (the new converts in a future world wouldn't necessarily need to come on horses and chariots, etc.) you still have to deal with the basic dynamic that even though all nations and tongues were gathered to the judgment, the majority of the world didn't even know it happened. This is an important clue for the context of that judgment. Not only isn't it worldwide, but knowledge of it is limited.

You might say, "How can something with such far reaching implications only be known to a limited group of people?" As Don Preston is fond of pointing out, the same observation might be made of the cross, or the resurrection. In both cases only a handful of people saw the events. But, those events truly had global and eternal consequences. Just because something is not universally seen or understood at the time doesn't mean that isn't important.

Moving on to the specific catastrophes cited by the Calvary Chapel writer, it is surprising that he asserts that famines, pestilences, and earthquakes didn't happen in the first century. As a counter, I'd suggest reading the work of Ed Stevens in *Final Decade Before the End,* Marcellus Kik in *An Eschatology of Victory,* and John Bray in *Matthew 24 Fulfilled.* These authors offer extensive research on the real, historical fulfillments of the elements of the Olivet Discourse. They clearly demonstrate that wars, famines, pestilences, and earthquakes did in fact happen in the known world (potentially both ge and oikoumene) in that period. Below, I'll only mention a few of the dozens of examples found in the historical records. These start in the Biblical narrative almost immediately after the ascension of Christ.

My first example is the famous famine to strike the church as mentioned in Acts 11 (likely 44AD). Similar famine and financial hardship is described throughout the book of Acts. This hardship was so severe that Paul supervised offerings from all over the Mediterranean basin for relief to those in Judea. Examples of wars include the three-year Roman civil war starting in 66AD, which threatened the existence of the Empire itself (in the view of the times, threatening the end of the world as they knew it). Finally, the great earthquake in Laodicea in 60AD affected all seven of the cities described in Revelation. It took years to rebuild the cities afterwards, and the comment in Revelation 3 regarding the wealth and arrogance of Laodicea may have been based on the experience of this disaster.[128] There is no way to prove that these disasters are what Jesus had in mind. But to assert that there were no examples of such events in the first century is incorrect.

I could leave the topic here, and rely on the rest of my Olivet Discourse argument to define the Great Tribulation, but I want to spend a little more time on what modern Christians think about the purpose of the Great Tribulation. In dispensational teaching the Great Tribulation is a period that begins immediately after all of the Christians leave the earth via the rapture. This chapter of history restarts the Jewish calendar that had been paused at some point in the past (probably during the ministry of Christ), but then after the rapture once again begins ticking down towards the second coming.[129] But is this really what the Bible says about the Great Tribulation?

Look, for instance, at 1 Peter 4. Peter is trying to encourage his readers because of the "fiery trial" that they are expected to go through. After several powerful time statements declaring that the end is near, he gives this important admonition:

> Beloved, do not be surprised at the fiery trial when it comes upon you to test you, as though something strange were happening to you. But rejoice insofar as you share Christ's sufferings, that you may also rejoice and be glad when his glory is revealed. If you are insulted for the name of Christ, you are blessed, because the Spirit of glory and of God rests upon you. But let none of you suffer as a murderer or a thief or an evildoer or as a meddler. Yet if anyone suffers as a Christian, let him not be ashamed, but let him glorify God in that name. For it is time for judgment to begin at the household of God; and if it begins with us, what will be the

outcome for those who do not obey the gospel
of God? (1 Peter 4:12-17 ESV)

According to the chief Apostle, Peter, who recorded his thoughts in inspired scripture, it was time for judgment to begin at the household of God – in about 66AD. In other words, Peter is saying that the saints' portion of the judgment that was to come was starting at the time that he was alive. He gives no indication that this judgment would stop and start again, that there would be a separate judgment of the people of God before the judgment of the disobedient, or that the judgment of believers would last 2,000 or more years. This is extremely important. There are no passages anywhere in the New Testament that assert that either the tribulation the church should expect or the second coming should be expected outside of their lifetimes. Again, John MacArthur anchors his position of spiritualizing the text on this point, saying that all of the admonitions were simply meant to be spiritualized advice for all ages. But there isn't a hint of that in the actual text. As C.S. Lewis has already pointed out for us, the text clearly shows the Apostles thought that the second coming was going to be in their lifetimes. They thought this because Jesus taught them so. All of the leadership was unanimous that the advice they were giving their first readers was useful to prepare them for this event that they expected would happen at any minute. If it didn't happen the way that the leadership clearly asserted that it would my contention is that Christian doctrine is in far bigger trouble than it would be by accepting that it happened already, right on schedule.

I propose that the judgment mentioned by Peter fits cleanly with the pressure and falling away described in the Olivet Discourse (Matt. 24:12-13), and with another key passage in Daniel. Daniel 7 is a synopsis of the climactic time surrounding the second coming. In it, you'll notice saints being pressured by the beast.[130]

> As I looked, this horn made war with the saints and prevailed over them, until the Ancient of Days came, and judgment was given for the saints of the Most High, and the time came when the saints possessed the kingdom . . . He shall speak words against the Most High, and shall wear out the saints of the Most High, and shall think to change the times and the law; and they shall be given into his hand for a time, times, and half a time. But the court shall sit in judgment, and his dominion shall be taken away, to be consumed and destroyed to the end. And the kingdom and the dominion and the greatness of the kingdoms under the whole heaven shall be given to the people of the saints of the Most High; his kingdom shall be an everlasting kingdom, and all dominions shall serve and obey him. (Dan. 7:21-22, 25-27 ESV)

In this passage, we see the final pressure placed on the people of God before they begin to rule in the kingdom of God. This vindication is also seen in Revelation 6:

> When he opened the fifth seal, I saw under the altar the souls of those who had been slain for the word of God and for the witness they had borne. They cried out with a loud voice, "O Sovereign Lord, holy and true, how long before you will judge and avenge our blood on those who dwell on the earth?" Then they were each given a white robe and told to rest a little longer, until the number of their fellow servants and their brothers should be complete, who were to be killed as they themselves had been. (Rev. 6:9-11)

In a passage that most theologians consider parallel (though with varying explanations), Daniel 12 shows maximum pressure being brought on the people of God:

> At that time shall arise Michael, the great prince who has charge of your people. And there shall be a time of trouble, such as never has been since there was a nation till that time. But at that time your people shall be delivered, everyone whose name shall be found written in the book. And many of those who sleep in the dust of the earth shall awake, some to everlasting life, and some to shame and everlasting contempt. And those who are wise shall shine like the brightness of the sky above; and those who turn many to righteousness, like the stars forever and ever . . . And I heard the man clothed in linen, who was above the waters of the stream; he raised his right hand and his left hand toward heaven and swore by him who lives forever that it would be for a time, times, and half a time, and that when the shattering of the power of the holy people comes to an end all these things would be finished. (Dan. 12:1-3, 7 ESV)

This pressure is predicted in Revelation and given the name Great Tribulation, and is described elsewhere as the time where the beast will "overcome" the saints. It's important, then, that so many ancient sources already cited don't hesitate to declare that these portions of Daniel and the Olivet Discourse had already been fulfilled by the Roman destruction of Jerusalem. They did not seem to realize the connected nature of these events and what they conceived of as the second coming. However, we are able to do that comparative analysis quite easily. If those sources were correct, then the Great Tribulation was a combination of the Neronic persecution and the Roman War, which means that it's a thing of the past.

Why do modern Christians obsess about, even seem to hope for, such a Great Tribulation in our time? I've heard some say that it's because they can't wait for Christ to return so that they can be with him. But, each adult will experience such a presence with God sometime in the next 80 or so years, after a natural death. When I dig more into the thoughts of my adamant dispensational friends I tend to see a more biting reality: They want their enemies, and indeed the world, destroyed for what it has done to them. They feel aggrieved, and they want justification. We can't dismiss the legitimacy of this out of hand because we see some of it in Revelation 6, where the martyrs call out for justice. But none of these modern dispensationalists have been martyred, or are realistically about to be martyred, in modern Aurora, Colorado. So why the viciousness?

I propose that for many of them it's because Christianity has become a weekly exercise of asking, "What does this passage mean to me?" instead of "How does this passage explain my role in the body of Christ and the kingdom of God?" Because we have lost our connection to proper eschatology we have developed a pathologically selfish view of our place in the universe. A major reason for this is that in dispensationalist doctrine the kingdom of God is postponed. It is not a present fact. If I were to ask, "How are your actions helping to build the kingdom of God?" the proper theological response would have to be, "There is no such kingdom right now!" The inherent hopelessness of the mission of the church on earth has convinced us that we are simply polishing brass on a sinking ship. Though some are motivated to personally witness to their friends or peers, they have nothing to sell other than forgiveness of sins. Where's the kingdom of God in all of this? I'll return to this topic in my conclusion, but for now I'll end with an admonition to read what I think is a very important book on the topic, *The King Jesus Gospel* by Scott McKnight.[131]

The Calvary Chapel writer's final point is that the grand scale of seal and trumpet judgments can't be regional (he doesn't make an argument about the content of the individual judgments, only the scale). He asserts it must be literally global, though he doesn't explain why. There doesn't seem to be any engagement by this writer (or many other premillennialists that I've read) with the actual meaning of ge, oikoumene, or kosmos, so I won't be able to examine his assertions other than to give my own proposed understanding.

My first point might sound familiar. In the fourth seal, the horseman has permission to kill 1/4 of the people of the land. Likewise, in the trumpet judgments 1/3 of the vegetation of the land is destroyed, 1/3 of the ships in the sea are destroyed, 1/3 of the sea life is destroyed, 1/3 of the fresh water is polluted, and 1/3 of the sun, moon, and stars are darkened. The fact that we're dealing with round fractions such as 1/3 should set off symbolic alarm bells, but we'll come back to that in a moment. Since the terms "earth," "world," and "ocean" could just as easily have been translated "land," "sea," or "lake" there is no particular reason other than theological or translational bias for them to mean otherwise. If they do in fact mean these more limited terms, there is no reason that this judgment could not have been a regional event. All that is required of the passage is that 1/3 of the things associated with the land is destroyed.

It is also interesting that the list of destruction is very similar to the one used to describe the plagues against Egypt.[132] Dennis Johnson makes the following observation:

> The judgment in Egypt was limited in two ways: although flax and barley crops were destroyed, the later-ripening wheat and spelt survived (9:31-32); and the region of Goshen where the Israelites resided, was exempt from the hailstorm (9:26). So also the destructive fire that John sees fall to earth stays within strict boundaries set by its Sovereign.

The repetition of the pattern is remarkable. In Revelation 3:10 we see a mission statement for the judgment: The empire will be under pressure as part of judgment against the land. We see that limited destruction is determined before the land itself is dealt with in the final judgmental destruction.

F.W. Farrar (as cited by David Chilton) says something very similar when talking about this judgment:

> ... ruler after ruler, chieftain after chieftain of the Roman Empire and the Jewish nation was assassinated and ruined. Gaius, Claudius, Nero, Galba, Otho, Vitellius, all died by murder or suicide; Herod the Great, Herod Antipas, Herod Agrippa, and most of the Herodian Princes, together with not a few of the leading High Priests of Jerusalem, perished in disgrace, or in exile, or by violent hands. All these were quenched suns and darkened stars.[133]

The preceding is a good example of the types of interpretations that were common place only a generation ago. Dispensationalism brought with it a hyper literalism to interpreting scripture that did not represent the average position throughout church history. In addition to the various national leaders being represented by stars, this can be seen in the other imagery as well. The trees, vegetation, ships, and sea life, all of these are at one point or another used in prophetic literature to refer to people (Rev. 7:3, 9:4). A simple-to-understand example of this is Ezekiel 17, quoted below:

> But he rebelled against him by sending his ambassadors to Egypt, that they might give him horses and a large army. Will he thrive? Can one escape who does such things? Can he break the covenant and yet escape? "As I live, declares the Lord GOD, surely in the place where the king dwells who made him king, whose oath he despised, and whose covenant with him he broke, in Babylon he shall die. Pharaoh with his mighty army and great company will not help him in war, when mounds are cast up and siege walls built to cut off many lives. He despised the oath in breaking the covenant, and behold, he gave his hand and did all these things; he shall not escape. Therefore thus says the Lord GOD: As I live, surely it is my oath that he despised, and my covenant that he broke. I will return it upon his head. I will spread my net over him, and he shall be taken in my snare, and I will bring him to Babylon and enter into judgment with him there for the treachery he has committed against me. And all the pick of his troops shall fall by the sword, and the survivors shall be scattered to every wind, and you shall know that I am the LORD; I have spoken." Thus says the Lord GOD: "I myself will take a sprig from the lofty top of the cedar and will set it out. I will break off from the topmost of its young twigs a tender one, and I myself will plant it on a high and lofty mountain. On the mountain height of Israel will I plant it, that it may bear branches and produce fruit and become a noble cedar. And under it will dwell every kind of bird; in the shade of its branches birds of every sort will nest. And all

> the trees of the field shall know that I am the
> LORD; I bring low the high tree, and make high
> the low tree, dry up the green tree, and make the
> dry tree flourish. I am the LORD; I have spoken,
> and I will do it." (Ezek. 17 ESV)

In this passage Ezekiel is using the image of trees to represent people. At one point he even uses imagery related to catching birds for capturing the king. In the end, the tree that replaces the old one grows so that all of the birds have shade. Jesus uses similar imagery in Matthew 13:31-32, where the kingdom of God is like a plant that grows so that all of the birds can make nests in its branches. Clearly, the point of the parable is not to teach about the role of birds in the kingdom, or how high trees will grow, but about the kingdom as a resting place for people (cf. Dan. 4:26). Likewise, we've already seen that the use of sun, moon, and stars in prophetic literature is usually talking about governmental power systems (visible and invisible) as opposed to literal celestial bodies. With all of this symbolic imagery anchored elsewhere in scripture to historical events that didn't play out in a literalistic fashion, there is no need for the rest of the imagery to demand a literalistic global fulfillment at the second coming.

Finally, the Calvary Chapel writer refers to the darkening of the sun, moon, and stars and the rolling up of the sky like a scroll as a global, unprecedented disaster. But, if we turn to Isaiah 34, we can find the source of this imagery as well as a practical solution to it.

> For the Lord is enraged against all the nations,
> and furious against all their host; he has devoted
> them to destruction, has given them over for
> slaughter. Their slain shall be cast out, and the
> stench of their corpses shall rise; the mountains
> shall flow with their blood. All the host of

> heaven shall rot away, and the skies roll up like
> a scroll. All their host shall fall, as leaves fall
> from the vine, like leaves falling from the fig
> tree. For my sword has drunk its fill in the
> heavens; behold, it descends for judgment upon
> Edom, upon the people I have devoted to
> destruction. (Isaiah 34:2-5 ESV)

The kingdom of Edom was in fact destroyed as part of the Babylonian invasion. This prophecy describes that event. It was accomplished, as far as we know, by infantrymen and cavalry with spears, and chariots. There is no record of the universe melting (2 Peter 3) when the government, or power system, behind Edom was destroyed. This imagery is used to describe a military disaster. Why? Because from their point of view it was the end of their world. Likewise, Jesus and his Apostles used similar imagery to describe the impending end of the world for the nation of the Jews at the hands of the Romans. This end came exactly on time, exactly as predicted. The only problem presented to us is that we, and likely the Greek Gentile dominant early church, fail to interpret the imagery of the New Testament according to the precedent of the Old Testament. If we were more aware of the style of Old Testament prophets, and more careful about how we apply their experience and imagery to the New Testament, we would be less likely to make such mistakes.

Summary:

The language of prophecy oftentimes includes words that can be translated many different ways. While sometimes this means that "world" means the whole globe, it can mean an area as small as a country. Likewise, the Greek word used for ocean in English can also be translated lake. Wars, famines, pestilences, earthquakes and persecution are all described in both the Olivet Discourse as well as the seal judgments of Revelation. In fact, they are described in the same order in both passages. Because of this, there is no reason to give them separate fulfillments. Since the fulfillments of these events in the Olivet Discourse have been proven to have happened in the Roman War in 70AD, the burden of proof is on the premillennialist to demonstrate why it should be otherwise. Likewise, the Great Tribulation is associated with the persecution and dramatic upheaval of the first century, which is well documented in both Christian and secular sources. Finally, the language used to describe the destruction of the Roman War is repeated in the Old Testament in the judgment of Babylon against Judah and Edom. There is no textual reason for this to be a literally global judgment.

Chapter 7 Endnotes

[121] e-Sword, King James Concordance and Strong's Concordance.

[122] In two instances it is translated "adorning" in the King James Version. This has to do with women choosing different types of jewelry, etc. There seems to me to be a theme of choosing or declaring your choice of world systems based on how you present yourself. However, if this interpretation is not correct, then these two unusual uses are completely outside of eschatology.

[123] Throughout church history the dominant position on eschatology has essentially been what we call today amillennialism. Amillennialism says that there is an invisible spiritual kingdom at work in history and that this kingdom is at least partially managed by resurrected saints on thrones in heaven. The Orthodox and Roman churches fought off and on about whether a direct appeal should be made to these saints through prayer, but the basic dynamic has been assumed since the earliest times. This system is based on the assumption that Rev. 20:4-6 has been activated and is being fulfilled as a function of the church in history.

[124] Hal Lindsay, *The Late Great Planet Earth.*

[125] http://www.gty.org/resources/sermons/61-25/the-certainty-of-the-second-coming-part-3 (Last accessed 6/29/16).

[126] Preterists do not assert that the "day of the Lord" requires that the entire judgment be completed in one 24-hour period. Throughout scripture it refers to a military campaign against a nation that might last a number of months. However, there is no reason, other than theological necessity, for the "day of the Lord" to be split into two separate campaigns separated from each other by over 1,000 years.

[127] I differ subtly from traditional full preterists on this point. I see the New Heaven and New Earth as a parallel concept to the saints' portion of their thousand-year reign in Rev. 20:4-6. See, *Making Sense of the Millennium.*

[128] See, Hanegraaff debate with Hitchcock.

[129] Dispensationalists are particularly ignorant of their own system here. The idea of a clock stoppage was necessary in the 19th Century when critical examination of the time statements became widespread. If the clock didn't stop, then Jesus was a false prophet. But, it is very difficult to nail down when they think the clock actually stopped. Various authors

postulate times from Transfiguration, the Upper Room Discourse, the Cross, the Resurrection, Pentecost, Acts 9, Acts 15, and Acts 28. The Acts 28 dispensationalists are accurately called Hyper-dispensationalists because they take it as far as they can. If you were to ask them, they'd tell you that they took it as far as they needed to because the demarcation of the clock stop has to be the end of God's fulfillment of the Jewish prophetic calendar. It turns out that Acts 28 dispensationalists are the Achilles heel of the movement because they accurately point out that throughout the book of Acts, Peter and Paul claim that they are acting as a part of the fulfillment of Old Testament prophecy. In fact, Paul claims to Felix and others that he is teaching nothing other than what the prophets promised would happen. Since the Church age couldn't have been foreseen in the Old Testament according to dispensational doctrine, nothing Paul was saying while in custody could have been part of the church age. But, in Acts 28 there is an important event. For the last time on record Paul rejects the Jews and says he's going to the Gentiles. Acts 28 dispensationalists claim that this is the actual beginning of the church. And, since only Ephesians, Colossians, Philippians, and Philemon were written after this date, those are the only truly Christian texts. Most Christians I've met recoil at this proposal, but this is the only viable place for dispensational theology to go. Some efforts such as progressive dispensationalism have been tried, but they lack followers because in the end they have a similar problem. The problem is the time statements. Preterists take them seriously, which requires that they were fulfilled.

[130] Saints comes from the Greek hagios, which means holy ones. In some passages it refers to all members of the Mosaic Covenant, faithful or otherwise (Dan. 12:1-4). In this case, I think the context clearly shows that it refers to those faithful to God, though its assignment to Christians (as opposed to Jews) is not explicit.

[131] McKnight would disagree with me on my eschatological conclusions. I propose that this is because he hasn't thought through the eschatological implications of his system, which fits preterism perfectly.

[132] Dennis Johnson, *Triumph of the Lamb*, p.143. Dennis shows that the judgment imagery is taken directly from the Exodus judgment imagery.

[133] F.W. Farrar, *The Early Days of Christianity*, p.519; David Chilton, *Days of Vengeance*, p.240; cf. Isa. 13:9-11, 19; 24:19-23; 34:4-5; Ezek. 32:7-8, 11-12; Joel 2:10, 28-32; Acts 2:16-21.

Chapter 8: Gathering All Nations

Calvary Chapel Statement:

The campaign or battle that immediately precedes Jesus' Second Coming involves "all the nations" and the "kings of the earth".

Zechariah 12:3 says, "And it shall happen in that day that I will make Jerusalem a very heavy stone for all peoples; all who would heave it away will surely be cut in pieces, though all nations of the earth are gathered against it."

Zechariah 14:2 says, "For I will gather all the nations to battle against Jerusalem"

It's a well-established historical fact that the forces of Rome's emperor Vespasian (AD 9-79) led by the military commander Titus Flavius Vespasianus (AD 39-81), led the campaign against Jerusalem ultimately breaking through the walls, taking the city, burning the temple and carting off the spoils to Rome in AD 70.

This was hardly "all the nations" and "the kings of the earth and of the whole world" coming up against Jerusalem.

But this gathering of all the nations will happen in the Tribulation period for the Battle of Armageddon.

Revelation 16:14 says "For they are spirits of demons, performing signs, which go out to the kings of the earth and of the whole world, to gather them to the battle of that great day of God Almighty."

In other words, this didn't happen in the first century but it will happen at the Battle of Armageddon just before Jesus' Second Coming.

Charge:

- Armageddon includes "all nations," which is a larger group than appeared at the sacking of Jerusalem in 70AD.

The key concept to keep in mind when looking at passages such as Zechariah 14 and others that talk about "all nations" is to go back to more ancient prophetic passages that define the issue. In this case, Isaiah 66 is very helpful. Isaiah 66 comes at the climax of a criticism of the apostate members of the nations of Israel as well as the pagan nations that had seduced them into idolatry. The members of Israel are the main focus of the action, however. In that chapter we see a scene very similar to Zechariah. Pay close attention to some new information describing how the drama closes:

> Those who sanctify and purify themselves to go into the gardens, following one in the midst, eating pig's flesh and the abomination and mice, shall come to an end together, declares the Lord. "For I know their works and their thoughts, and the time is coming to gather all nations and tongues. And they shall come and shall see my glory, and I will set a sign among them. And from them I will send survivors to the nations, to Tarshish, Pul, and Lud, who draw the bow, to Tubal and Javan, to the coastlands afar off, that have not heard my fame or seen my glory. And they shall declare my glory among the nations. And they shall bring all your brothers from all the nations as an offering to the Lord, on horses and in chariots and in litters and on mules and on dromedaries, to my holy mountain Jerusalem, says the Lord, just as the Israelites bring their grain offering in a clean vessel to the house of the Lord. (Isaiah 66:17-20 ESV)

In this version of the same events described in Zechariah 14 we see that "all nations" are gathered (v.18) for the sign that God will perform. This is generally accepted to be the Battle of Armageddon and second coming of Christ. Those nations would come and see God's glory (v.18). The revealing or display of the glory of God is a very common theme in second-coming related passages. After the Battle of Armageddon and the second coming of Christ the survivors are sent out to the nations and to far-off places who've never heard of God (v.19).

Nations who've never heard of God after the second coming?!

This is flatly impossible according to regular futurist theology, whether it be premillennialism or amillennialism. According to premillennialism, after Armageddon and the second coming, all people are gathered for the sheep-and-goat judgment and only the believing survivors are allowed to stay on earth to populate world during the Millennium (Matthew 25). In conjunction with what is commonly understood in the next chapter, that "every eye will see him," it would be impossible for someone on earth not to have been aware of the second coming. This would certainly be true if every person were to be gathered to a judgment scene in Jerusalem where they were separated and then sent on to their eternal destinies according to their actions in this life.

An example of how standard evangelical premillennialism handles the idea of every eye seeing the second coming, so that there is no chance that someone could have missed it, John F. Walvoord, Chancellor of Dallas Theological Seminary, claimed that on the day of the Lord, Jesus and his armies would hover in heaven for a full day as the earth rotated underneath so that everyone would be able to see that event (therefore, there would be no need for CNN to broadcast it worldwide).[134] So, how is it that there are still people running around who haven't heard of God? At all?! And how is it that they haven't been sent to the sheep-and-goat judgment of Matthew 25?

Another, possibly more troublesome, issue is what comes next in Isaiah 66. The survivors of Armageddon who are sent to tell those far-off nations about God also evangelize people from their populations. That means that at least for the time it takes to travel to those far-off lands there are unbelievers running around after the second coming. Those people in those far-off lands who aren't believers have never even heard of the God of Israel. And, not all of the people in those lands are successfully converted (Ezek. 47:20). Those who are successfully converted travel to the new Jerusalem to pay homage to God, as seen in Zechariah 14, which ties these passages together nicely. But now look what happens in Zechariah 14 with some unbelievers who don't at least honor the new regime:

> Then everyone who survives of all the nations that have come against Jerusalem shall go up year after year to worship the King, the Lord of hosts, and to keep the Feast of Booths. And if any of the families of the earth do not go up to Jerusalem to worship the King, the Lord of hosts, there will be no rain on them. And if the family of Egypt does not go up and present themselves, then on them there shall be no rain; there shall be the plague with which the Lord afflicts the nations that do not go up to keep the Feast of Booths. This shall be the punishment to Egypt and the punishment to all the nations that do not go up to keep the Feast of Booths. (Zech. 14:16-19 ESV)

Unbelievers in the Millennium who won't worship God? And some of them remain belligerent so that punishment has to be meted out to them? And they still don't comply? Does this sound like the Millennium you have imagined? Is it possible that the traditional understanding of the world after the second coming is profoundly flawed?

This passage also points out a valuable dynamic of how terms like "all" and "everyone" are used. On the one hand, everyone from all of the nations that have come against Jerusalem will worship (v.16). But, on the other hand, those who don't worship will be punished (v.17). WAIT! I thought that according to verse 16 "everyone" will go up to worship! We see here an important, concise example of the way that such language is used in prophetic writings. When we say that "all" will see the sign, or go up to Jerusalem, we don't really, literally mean every single homo sapien. Clearly, the next portion of the passage provides a caveat for those who refuse to go. So, a later comment in the passage is intuitively understood to provide an exception to the "all" or "everyone" mentioned earlier. We see this clearly in Isaiah 66, where "all nations" are gathered, but then later we learn that some nations far off have never heard of God after the second coming. We see this very clearly in Zechariah 14 where all people will come up to worship, except for those who don't. This shouldn't be disorienting to us, and it wasn't for the generation of the Apostles because they grew up talking in such ways and reading what we call the Old Testament with this basic outlook. It's only when we turn such language into a modern scientific expression of precision that we get confused about what the scripture is trying to say.[135]

For any reader who is amillennial, and who is rejoicing at the premillennialists getting caught by Isaiah 66, look out.

The amillennial system fares even worse. According to amillennialism, our current age is a spiritual kingdom which is described in Revelation 20 as the reign of the saints from heaven. Its end comes at some point in the vague, distant future once God has decided that he's had enough with human history. Unlike postmillennialism there isn't necessarily a positive climax to history at this point. This is where amillennialism is at its weakest.

Though amillennialists are skilled at pointing out the spiritual nature of the kingdom and its presence in at least some context in church history, there doesn't seem to be a clear, coherent way to explain why and how it all eventually falls apart. They generally lean on Revelation 20:7-10 to describe the release of Satan and the Gog and Magog war, but they don't show how this dynamic fits into the scheme of the kingdom in the Old Testament, and how the kingdom of God that is described as never ending actually collapses to the point that it needs a last minute rescue of fire from heaven (Daniel 7, Revelation 20). According to Isaiah 66 (which describes this new kingdom period as the "New Heavens and the New Earth"), Zechariah 14 (where the perpetual state is one where the nations bring gifts to Jerusalem), and Daniel 7 (where the kingdom of God lasts forever), there should not be an end to this. Ezekiel 47 describes this period as one in which the river of life grows deeper and deeper as it brings new life to the earth. The connecting passages in Revelation 21-22 are clear that this period of the reign of Christ's kingdom is "forever" (Rev. 22:5; Dan. 7:21ff). So, how do you fit the collapse of the kingdom and the near extinction of believers, who are militarily pushed back into a perimeter surrounding Jerusalem, into the rest of the description of the kingdom according to scripture? The answer is that amillennialists have philosophically accepted that there will be an "end of time," and that the details are a bit fuzzy, but they have no real scriptural explanation for how it plays out in history.

An easy set of examples of this are the two passages in question, Zechariah 14 and Isaiah 66. In both cases history continues on earth. The good guys have won, and are now ruling. However, there is no such thing as an end of time. The confusion on the part of amillennialists comes from a philosophical demand to the end of the universe and time demanded by Platonic philosophy brought into Christian doctrine in the first few hundred years of the church. In more modern times, it's reinforced by bad English translations such as the King James Version Bible in passages such as Matthew 24:3, "... Tell us, when shall these things be? and what shall be the sign of thy coming, and of the end of the world?" Fortunately, more modern translations more consistently change "end of the world" to "end of the age" because of the obvious confusion that results from such a phrase. But, the assumption that the world does indeed have an end described in scripture, and the philosophical requirement that the physical universe is inherently corrupt so that it must be destroyed in order to be cleansed, has cause amillennialists to focus on "the end of time" instead of "the time of the end."[136]

Since we hear the phrase "end of time" quite a bit from pulpits and podcasts, let's consider for a minute what that would mean, or at least what it subconsciously implies. It's possible that most people who are using that phrase are simply being lazy in explaining what they mean by an end of the current world we live in. Those people might really be meaning that they expect an end of this world, but not a literal end of time. Since the Millennium continues after the second coming, or the New Heaven and New Earth continues after the Great White Throne Judgment, most of those people don't really mean that a literal end of time is really in view. I'd argue that this concept of an "end of time" is subconsciously smuggled back into their expectation of the end of the physical universe. Since in our generation we accept Einstein's observations and the physics built on them we have no problem saying that time is an element of the space time continuum, and therefore a part of the physical universe. If the physical universe were melted completely (one traditional view of 2 Peter 3), this view of physics would demand that time itself is eliminated. But since premillennialists accept a rebuilding of heaven and earth on the far side of this conflagration they should also accept a restarting of time. Even then they don't really mean that time ends. They just mean that our current clock version ends.

On the other hand, amillennialists have generally said that the end of the millennium marks the beginning of the eternal state. They very commonly use the phrase "end of time" for this. They may mean this a bit more literally since they see this eternal state as existing in heaven (as opposed to the physical universe), where the expression of time is a bit fuzzier. It's common to say that God does not experience time, and if we are to become unified with God in some way it's questionable how, exactly, we are supposed to experience time at that point. So for them, "end of time" may be a bit more literal than for a premillennialist. But again, consider that there is no description of heaven that doesn't include things occurring in succession (which requires time), and there is no passage of scripture that asserts that God himself is "outside of time," though it's popular to describe his nature and experience this way.[137]

You might accuse me of being too reductionist in my discussion on time. Maybe I'm taking the terminology "end of time" too literally. That's exactly the point. On the one hand, major interpretive mistakes can come from taking terms like "all" and "everyone" too literally. I've just shown you examples of how they can be used with exceptions. On the other hand, I've also demonstrated how the use of language can accidentally drag assumptions into the text. It's not uncommon for preterists to be challenged with, "Has time ended yet? Well, then the second coming hasn't happened!" But, of course, that's a silly position from the start. No system literally, completely expects an end to events that happen in succession.

Getting back to the nations that were gathered against Jerusalem, we need to consult some passages that address similar gatherings in the Old Testament to see the range of the language that would have been in the mind of New Testament readers. My first example is from Zephaniah:

> I said, 'Surely you will fear me; you will accept correction. Then your dwelling would not be cut off according to all that I have appointed against you.' But all the more they were eager to make all their deeds corrupt. "Therefore wait for me," declares the LORD, "for the day when I rise up to seize the prey. For my decision is to gather nations, to assemble kingdoms, to pour out upon them my indignation, all my burning anger; for in the fire of my jealousy all the earth shall be consumed. "For at that time I will change the speech of the peoples to a pure speech, that all of them may call upon the name of the LORD and serve him with one accord. (Zeph. 3:7-9)

This is an interesting example because Zephaniah is commonly understood to have been fulfilled in by the Assyrian invasion of the Northern Kingdom. In that invasion, nations were gathered and "all the earth" was consumed. If this is a correct understanding, then we are starting with a precedent that brings into question the need for the entire universe to be melted in 2 Peter 3. Clearly, from the point of view of the Jews in the New Testament era (and Peter and Paul would obviously be included in this group), for God to consume "all the earth" was a metaphorical way of saying that the whole land would be destroyed in an invasion. Likewise, "all" of the generations listed in Matthew 1:17 don't literally add up to the full genealogy recorded elsewhere; I doubt that literally all, or every single person, of Jerusalem was troubled just as Herod was in Matthew 2:3; it's unlikely that literally all of the people from Judea and the surrounding people went out to meet John the Baptist in Matthew 3:5; it's unlikely that literally all of the sick were brought to Jesus from all over Syria in Matthew 4:24; there is no indication from the Biblical record that literally all of the people hated the Disciples during the ministry, though Matthew 10:22 seems to predict it; while we know that the mustard seed is one of the very smallest ones, it's not literally the smallest seed in existence, and it doesn't grow to be literally the largest plant in the garden, though Matthew 13:22 seems to predict it; and I doubt anyone would assert that the young man had literally, perfectly kept all of the commandments he claims to have kept in Matthew 19:20. This list is just a small sample of the uses of "all" in Matthew. There are over 1,000 uses of the term throughout the New Testament. Sometimes it might plausibly have been used to literally describe an entire group, but obviously sometimes "all" is used hyperbolically, or as an exaggeration to make a point. It might come as something of a surprise to some Christians who've never looked up all of the uses of "all," but it turns out that a large percentage of the time it's being used as exaggeration. To Westerners thoroughly indoctrinated into a scientific view of the world we tend to immediately think in mathematical or scientific terms when we see such words. But, Hebrews used such words for emphasis.[138]

Though I don't think that the use of "all" was meant to be a scientifically precise description of who would take part in the battle, it might come as a surprise to most premillennialists to discover just how many nations participated in the Roman War.[139] When Rome went to war against Jerusalem in 66AD and over the next three and a half years, they brought with them troops from client nations all over the empire, including their garrison in Babylon situated on the Euphrates River. Also present were local tribes such as the Idumeans. On top of that, there were rebellious factions of Jews inside of Jerusalem who victimized the common man.[140] From their perspective it would not be exaggeration to say that armies from every nation known to them were participating. Since we've seen that "all" and "everyone" can have limited uses, and since we can show through ancient sources that the primary nations in Judah were gathered against her (so based on the definition of oikoumene the whole world did in a sense gather), there is no reason to think that the language of "all nations" being gathered wasn't fulfilled in the Roman War.

Summary:

The assertion that "all nations" weren't gathered against Jerusalem in 70AD demonstrates a number of mistakes. First, in prophetic language, "all" doesn't always literally mean "all." Second, the imagery used on prophetic scripture should not be taken as scientific descriptions. Just like our understanding and description of time does not uncritically line up with the ancient way of describing it, absolute categories such as "all," "forever," and "every" can be tricky to interpret. Finally, a large number of powerful nations, most importantly Rome, which was composed of many nations that had been absorbed into it, were in fact present for the sacking of Jerusalem.

Chapter 8 Endnotes

[134] John F. Walvoord, *Every Prophecy of the Bible*, p.524.

[135] Dale Martin, *The Corinthian Body*, chapter 6. Peter Enns, *Inspiration and Incarnation,* p.23.

[136] Kim Riddlebarger, *A Case for Amillennialism*, p.19.

[137] Gregory Ganssle, Paul Helm, Alan Padgett, William Craig, Nicholas Wolterstorff, *God and Time: Four Views.*

[138] In *The Arab Mind*, Rafael Patai makes a long argument that this is a major problem from the point of view of Westerners with all Semitic languages, including Arabic and Hebrew. Native speakers of those languages tend to use exaggeration in what he characterizes as a performance art, though the point is often lost on us. In one example of Western intelligence intercepting communication in the 1973 Arab Israeli war, the Egyptians declared victory, claiming to have killed every Jew on the battlefield. The Syrians properly took this as a face-saving admission of failure, and withdrew from the fight. The Western intelligence agencies were confused and thought it might be a trick. The goal, then, in looking at these languages, especially in ancient expressions of them, is to be careful not to confuse that performance art use of the language as deception or inaccuracy. They wouldn't have taken it as such.

[139] David Chilton, *Days of Vengeance*, p.108; Josephus, *Wars of the Jews, book 6*; John Bray, *Matthew 24 Fulfilled*, p.147.

[140] Josephus, *Wars of the Jews, Book 6*: http://sacred-texts.com/jud/josephus/war-6.htm (Last accessed 6/29/16).

Chapter 9: Every Eye Will See Him

Calvary Chapel Statement:

The Bible says that when Jesus returns at the Second Coming, "every eye shall see Him".

Revelation 1:7 says "Behold, He is coming with clouds, and every eye will see Him, even they who pierced Him. And all the tribes of the earth will mourn because of Him. Even so, Amen."

When Jesus returns at His Second Coming, every eye will see Him. This is not "a spiritual eye" or Jesus "coming in judgment and not really a physical return" but a literal, physical Second Coming of Jesus Christ.

The word every [Greek: pas] means "all, any, every, the whole".

The word eye [Greek: opthalmos] means "vision, eye, sight". In other words, there is no "spiritual eye" in the Greek language. This is where we get the word optometry or someone who is concerned with the eyes and their structure.

Vines Expository of the Old and New Testament Words says that opthalmos is "used of the physical organ".

In other words the entire world will see Jesus at His Second Coming.

Dr. John Walvoord says that "the coming of Christ...will not be an instantaneous event but will be a gigantic procession of holy angels and saints from heaven to earth."

Charge:

- Every eye did not see Christ at the sacking of Jerusalem in 70AD, therefore he could not have come yet.

As a preterist, I have been challenged with this argument more often than any other. I think the reason is that it's easy to remember, and on the face of it the charge seems impossible to refute. This point will help us get to the heart of the matter. Should we use superficial definitions of words to govern the argument as Calvary Chapel does, or should we use the words or phrases according to their scriptural precedent? Hopefully, the examination below will show you that more care should be taken in interpreting such seemingly simple English phrases.

One of the fundamental errors in dispensational theology is the failure to understand the role of Christ in his kingdom. The assumption that they make is that Christ ascended to the right hand of the father to wait until his enemies are made his footstool (Psalm 110). They propose that at this moment he is still in a flesh body in heaven, wherever that is.[141] At the moment of the second coming, they propose that he then stands up and leaves that throne in order to physically return to earth in the same flesh body he took to the cross. He then oversees the sheep-and-goat judgment and begins to reign on a physical throne in a new earthly Jerusalem.[142]

This proposition sounds reasonable enough to people raised on it. However, I think it presents a number of theological problems. The language of Christ being seated on the right hand of his Father is meant to describe him participating in a powerful rule from heaven after having become a life-giving spirit (1 Cor. 15:45; 2 Cor. 2:15; 1 John 3:2). After his resurrection, he ascends to his glory. To say that he will give up that throne at some point in order to return to earth is extremely problematic. To say that somehow heaven and earth have become unified does not solve this problem.

On the contrary, Revelation 3:21 says that those who overcome will go to be seated on Christ's throne with him after they receive a resurrection body made of spiritual material, or pneuma (1 Cor. 15:44).[143] Believers take on this new body suitable for heaven because flesh and blood cannot inherit the kingdom of God (1 Cor. 15:50).[144] Likewise, according to Matthew 19:28 when Christ is on his glorious throne in heaven at the regeneration (or, era of resurrection) he declares that the Apostles will go to be seated on thrones to rule with him (cf. Rev. 20:4, Dan. 7:9).

An example of how Paul describes the body he expected can be found in a popular chapter on the resurrection in 2 Corinthians 5. This is likely a follow up argument to 1 Corinthians 15 where Paul clarifies or expands on his point there:

> For we know that if the tent, which is our earthly home, is destroyed, we have a building from God, a house not made with hands, eternal in the heavens. For in this tent we groan, longing to put on our heavenly dwelling, if indeed by putting it on we may not be found naked. For while we are still in this tent, we groan, being burdened--not that we would be unclothed, but that we would be further clothed, so that what is mortal may be swallowed up by life. He who has prepared us for this very thing is God, who has given us the Spirit as a guarantee. So we are always of good courage. We know that while we are at home in the body we are away from the Lord, for we walk by faith, not by sight. Yes,

we are of good courage, and we would rather be away from the body and at home with the Lord. So whether we are at home or away, we make it our aim to please him. For we must all appear before the judgment seat of Christ, so that each one may receive what is due for what he has done in the body, whether good or evil. (2 Cor. 5:1-10 ESV)

Here, we see a detailed description of the resurrection body expected by Christians. If the flesh body is put off, there will be another heavenly one to put on. This heavenly body is clearly distinct from the flesh body, reinforcing Paul's point in 1 Corinthians 15 that flesh and blood cannot inherit the kingdom of God (1 John 3:2). While most people use this passage to make a point about resurrection mechanics, the climax of Paul's point speaks directly to our study.[145] He says that we would prefer to be away from this body and in the presence of the Lord so that we might be judged for what was done in the body, whether good or evil. This judgment is not done on earth, but in heaven.[146]

Clearly, the Father is never expected to leave his throne at some point to assume another one. Likewise, neither will Christ nor the saints seated with him. It is only premillennial theological assumption that drives the conclusion that Christ would leave his throne and exit heaven to come to earth to rule from another throne. The scripture never says this.[147]

On the contrary, to gain a glimpse of scripture's view of the eschatological climax in heaven we'll look at Daniel 7:9ff and Revelation 20:11-15. Here, we see a picture of the Great White Throne judgment. This judgment occurs in heaven. It also begins immediately after the second coming (when his enemies are made his footstool), and is the event in which the books are opened and the fourth beast is judged and destroyed:

> As I looked, thrones were placed, and the Ancient of Days took his seat; his clothing was white as snow, and the hair of his head like pure wool; his throne was fiery flames; its wheels were burning fire. A stream of fire issued and came out from before him; a thousand thousands served him, and ten thousand times ten thousand stood before him; the court sat in judgment, and the books were opened. I looked then because of the sound of the great words that the horn was speaking. And as I looked, the beast was killed, and its body destroyed and given over to be burned with fire. (Dan. 7:9-11 ESV) [148]

We can cross reference this to 2 Thessalonians and 1 John where we see three important references to this event:

> ...and then shall be revealed the Lawless One, whom the Lord shall consume with the spirit of his mouth, and shall destroy with the manifestation of his presence... (2 Thess. 2:8 YLT)

> ...for what is our hope, or joy, or crown of rejoicing? are not even ye before our Lord Jesus Christ in his presence? (2 Thess. 2:19 YLT)

> And now, little children, remain in him, that when he may be manifested, we may have boldness, and may not be ashamed before him, in his presence. (1 John 2:28 YLT)

These verses refer directly to the judgment scene in Daniel 7:9 and following where the books are opened for the judgment of humans, and the beast is destroyed in the presence of the Ancient of Days. This same judgment is described in Revelation 20:11-15. This judgment happens in heaven, not on earth.

This judgment also happens during the Parousia, or presence, of Christ in his kingdom. The sequence of these events can be a bit confusing when the climax of these events is stated too simplistically. In English we see only the term "coming" (literalistically used by dispensationalists to mean the touch down of Christ on the Mount of Olives); in Greek there are two distinct words used to describe the eschatological climax. The first is erchomai. This word means to arrive, and implies a distinct moment of action. The second more familiar word is parousia. This word describes an ongoing presence. Below are a few examples of parousia outside of an eschatological context, which will make it clear that it has a continuing action:

> For they say, "His letters are weighty and strong, but his bodily presence is weak, and his speech of no account." (2 Cor. 10:10 ESV)

> Therefore, my beloved, as you have always obeyed, so now, not only as in my presence but much more in my absence, work out your own salvation with fear and trembling... (Phil. 2:12 ESV)

Both of these passages (and others) describe an ongoing ministry by Paul, not just the moment of his arrival with the subjects. Likewise, Christ's Parousia describes actions that occurred during the ongoing presence of his kingdom, but not necessarily the instant that the kingdom was finally inaugurated.

Now, let's consider again an important implication of 1 Thessalonians 2:19. In this verse we have the idea that the audience's hope and joy is rewarded when finally, in the presence of the Lord Jesus Christ, who is seated on his Father's throne. We'll be considering the implications of two key words in the verse. One of them is parousia, which we've already looked at. The other is emproshen, which means to be in front of, in the presence of, or in sight of.

> For what is our hope, or joy, or crown of rejoicing? are not even ye before [emproshen] our Lord Jesus Christ in his presence [parousia]? (1 Thess. 2:19 YLT)

This verse is saying that Paul's hope is to see his followers justified and rewarded while both Paul and his followers are face to face with Christ who is on his throne in heaven during the presence of his reign in his kingdom. It's important that "before" was translated from emproshen because it carries with it the idea that the believer is now, finally, "face to face" with Christ. We see a direct parallel here with verses from Paul and Jude:

> For now we see in a mirror dimly, but then face to face. Now I know in part; then I shall know fully, even as I have been fully known. (1 Cor. 13:12 ESV)

> Now to him who is able to keep you from stumbling and to present you blameless before the presence of his glory with great joy... (Jude 1:24 ESV)

It is critical to understand that the judgment in question happens in heaven, and would happen face to face.

John's source for the imagery in Revelation 1:7 is Isaiah 52:1-2, 7-8, 10. We'll analyze it one verse at a time:

> Awake, awake, put on your strength, O Zion; put on your beautiful garments, O Jerusalem, the holy city; for there shall no more come into

you the uncircumcised and the unclean. (Isaiah
52:1 ESV)

The fulfillment of Isaiah 52 is the beginning of a new era. In
that era, no longer will uncircumcised people enter
Jerusalem (cf. Rev. 21:27). Why? Because under the
promised New Covenant, once it's open for business, only
believers will be allowed in the New Jerusalem (Ezekiel 37,
Jeremiah 31). How is that possible? Because the New
Jerusalem is itself a city built without hands (Mark 14:58, 2
Cor. 5:1ff, Heb. 9:11), "not of this creation." With the New
Jerusalem, it's impossible for the unclean to enter because
believers are the building blocks of the heavenly Jerusalem,
based on a foundation of the Apostles and prophets (or
patriarchs), and "built up as a spiritual house." (Eph. 2:20, 1
Peter 2:5, Rev. 21:14)

> Shake yourself from the dust and arise; be
> seated, O Jerusalem; loose the bonds from your
> neck, O captive daughter of Zion. (Isaiah 52:2
> ESV)

Imagery associated with resurrection is used to describe the
redemption of the nation from not only sin but subjugation
by the nations, including Assyria (Ezekiel 37, Hosea 6). The
Godly nation rises again under a New Covenant (Jeremiah
31, Ezekiel 37).[149]

> How beautiful upon the mountains are the feet
> of him who brings good news, who publishes
> peace, who brings good news of happiness, who
> publishes salvation, who says to Zion, "Your
> God reigns." (Isaiah 52:7 ESV)

Here, we find the source of the popular Christian song "Our
God Reigns." The question is prompted, "Does he reign right
now?" This passage is associated with the beginning of the
function of the New Jerusalem and the resurrection promised

to the nation of Israel and the Gentiles who join her New Covenant. If those events have not happened, the song is describing a future promise, not a present reality. In other words, standard premillennial dispensational theology would say that God does not in fact reign right now. But, "Our God Reigns at Some Point in the Indefinite Future" isn't a very catchy song title, so it's not surprising that futurist churches tend to skip over the implication of the actual lyrics.

> The voice of your watchmen—they lift up their voice; together they sing for joy; for eye to eye they see the return of the Lord to Zion. (Isaiah 52:8 ESV)

Here, the key phrase "eye to eye" (ESV, KJV, and others) is found. In addition to this translation, a number of modern translations follow the advice of the Targum (an ancient Aramaic commentary) on the meaning of the idiom. They translate it "with their own eyes" (NASB, NIV), "before their very eyes" (NLT), "for every eye will see" (HSCB). The following is a citation from Barnes' Notes on the Bible that explains the point in more detail:

> For they shall see eye to eye - Lowth renders this, 'For face to face shall they see.' Noyes, 'For with their own eyes shall they behold.' Jerome renders it, Oculo ad oculum - 'Eye to eye.' The Septuagint renders it, Ὀφθαλμοὶ πρὸς ὀφθαλμοὺς, κ.τ.λ. Ophthalmoi pros ophthalmous, etc. 'Eyes shall look to eyes when the Lord shall have mercy upon Zion.' Interpreters have been divided in regard to its meaning. The sense may be, either that they shall see face to face, that is, distinctly, clearly, as when one is near another; or it may mean that they shall be united - they shall contemplate the same object, or look steadily at the same thing.

Rosenmuller, Gesenius, Forerius, Junius, and some others, understand it in the former sense. So the Chaldee, 'For they shall see with their own eyes the great things which the Lord will do when he shall bring back his own glory to Zion.' The phrase in Hebrew occurs in no other place, except in Num. 14:14, which our translators have rendered, 'For thou, Lord, art seen face to face.' Hebrew, 'Eye to eye;' that is, near, openly, manifestly, without any veil or interposing medium.[150]

This note makes a very powerful argument that the idiom "eye to eye" is essentially the same thing as saying "every eye will see him." When those who are the target of the passage see Christ, they will do it face to face. We've already seen that scripture describes the final face to face, or eye to eye, judgment as being in heaven. Those arguments were made from comparing scripture with scripture. No similar argument is made by dispensationalists when they declare that the "face to face" language means that Christ will literally sit on a physical throne in Jerusalem while judging.

In addition to the argument above, there are also historical examples of how such language is used in the first few centuries of the church. These include Latin commentaries on Revelation as well as Ante-Nicene writings (writings made before the Council of Nicaea).[151] In those writings we see that the phrase "eye to eye" is reserved for judgment scenes in front of a throne in both secular government as well as prophetic events.[152] There are no credible examples in these writings of the phrase "eye to eye" applying to prophetic judgment on earth, as is required by the premillennial approach to the sheep-and-goat judgment of Matthew 25. Instead, they are reserved for judgment in heaven.

We'll finish our look at Isaiah 52 with verse 10 below:

> The Lord has bared his holy arm before the eyes
> of all the nations, and all the ends of the earth
> shall see the salvation of our God. (Isaiah 52:10
> ESV)

This verse makes it clear that the scope of the eyes seeing the salvation are parallel to those who saw the holy arm (or power) of God, and those who see him are associated with "all of the nations." But, we find out later in Isaiah 66:19ff that not everyone on the physical earth sees the sign that God will do, or even knows he exists when he's done doing it. That's what missionaries are for. But, those who saw the arm, or power, of God were those who were present for the final battle. The implication there is that they have died in that battle and will now be judged (Revelation 19). We also come to the conclusion that when Christ tells the Jewish leadership that they will see him "face to face," he is saying that they will be killed in the judgment and will have to face him before being cast into the Lake of Fire at the final judgment.

The clear parallel of this passage with the theme of Revelation 1 and its connection to the second coming indicates that we can consider Isaiah 52 to be one of the primary sources behind John's comment. Where else might we plug this passage into scripture? At the time of the New Testament writing, all of the dead were in the Hadean realm (either in torments or Abraham's bosom) awaiting the resurrection. At the resurrection, there would be a final judgment (Dan. 12:1-4). That judgment is popularly known as the Great White Throne judgment in Revelation 20:11-15, and the sheep-and-goat judgment in Matthew 25 (Daniel 7):

Then I saw a great white throne and him who was seated on it. From his presence earth and sky fled away, and no place was found for them. And I saw the dead, great and small, standing before the throne, and books were opened. Then another book was opened, which is the book of life. And the dead were judged by what was written in the books, according to what they had done. And the sea gave up the dead who were in it, Death and Hades gave up the dead who were in them, and they were judged, each one of them, according to what they had done. Then Death and Hades were thrown into the lake of fire. This is the second death, the lake of fire. And if anyone's name was not found written in the book of life, he was thrown into the lake of fire. (Rev. 20:11-15 ESV)

When the Son of Man comes in his glory, and all the angels with him, then he will sit on his glorious throne. Before him will be gathered all the nations, and he will separate people one from another as a shepherd separates the sheep from the goats. And he will place the sheep on his right, but the goats on the left. Then the King will say to those on his right, 'Come, you who are blessed by my Father, inherit the kingdom prepared for you from the foundation of the world. (Matt. 25:31-34 ESV)

The Revelation version of this judgment clearly states that the people undergoing it are the dead raised from Hades for final disposition. In Matthew, we see Christ on his glorious throne in heaven, which requires that the people being judged are there, not still living on earth. These passages clearly show a critical error in the dispensational view. Instead of this passage retelling the story of the Great White Throne Judgment, in their view the sheep-and-goats judgment is only supposed to apply to those who successfully lived through the Great Tribulation to be judged while still alive on earth.[153] Their doctrine says that the surviving "tribulation saints" (a category of people never described in scripture) are judged at this point by how well they treated the 144,000 Jews during that tribulation.[154] If they ministered to the Jews, they pass. If they treated them poorly, they fail.[155] In addition, the Jews themselves and the unbelieving Gentiles are judged.

Given the dispensational paradigm, no one living on earth should miss this judgment. But, in fact, the passages I listed above show exactly the opposite. Unbelieving people still living on earth continue to operate in history (Zech. 14; Isaiah 66), while Hades is emptied for the judgment of all who had died up to that point. As an example, in Zechariah 14:16-18 we learn that there are survivors from the nations who are obligated to go up year after year to give offerings during ongoing earth history.[156] There is every indication that these are people continuing to live on earth from the time before the battle of Armageddon. They are presented as subjects in this new kingdom who occasionally rebel. The implication here is that there are regular people running around on the earth who aren't part of the sheep-and-goat judgment, who haven't been judged yet, and who are actually unbelievers. This is reinforced by Zechariah 14, Isaiah 52, and Revelation 21-22 where the unbelievers aren't allowed inside of the New Jerusalem.

I propose that the sheep-and-goat judgment is synonymous to the Great White Throne judgment in Daniel 7:9-12 and Revelation 20:11-15. Connecting this with the believer's expected experience in heaven, "face to face" with Christ at the judgment, it is clear that the judgment in question is of those who had died up to that point, not those who lived through the Great Tribulation. This makes all of the final judgment passages consistent. They apply to the dead who had been raised from the Hadean realm. It makes our understanding of Revelation 1:7 rather simple. Those who pierced him would die in the judgment of the Roman destruction of Jerusalem, and they would see him face to face at his judgment seat in heaven. Every eye of those being judged in heaven would see Christ on his glorious throne, "eye to eye" so to speak, especially those who pierced him.

The assertion that "every eye" applies to those living through the second coming can't be supported by scripture. Instead, the idiom plainly states that "every eye" (or "eye to eye"; "face to face") applies to the experience of personal judgment in the afterlife. Preterists argue that this happened at the conclusion of the sacking of Jerusalem, where the Jewish leadership responsible for killing Christ were themselves killed. If futurists wanted to claim that this portion of John's vision hasn't been fulfilled yet, it wouldn't help them disprove preterism because according to scripture the event would be a heavenly one. By definition, it wouldn't be something recorded in earthly history.

But, we have a simple way to anchor this event to a past moment of history. In Revelation 1:7 we see that all the tribes will mourn for him. This is a very important clue as to which audience is primarily in view. It's not the tribes of the Eskimos, Navajos, or Incas. It's the Tribes of Israel. How do we know?

> Immediately after the tribulation of those days the sun will be darkened, and the moon will \not give its light, and the stars will fall from heaven, and the powers of the heavens will be shaken. Then will appear in heaven the sign of the Son of Man, and then all the tribes of the earth will mourn, and they will see the Son of Man

coming on the clouds of heaven with power and great glory. And he will send out his angels with a loud trumpet call, and they will gather his elect from the four winds, from one end of heaven to the other. (Matt. 24:29-31 ESV)[157]

I've already demonstrated that the Olivet Discourse is the story of the sacking of Jerusalem by the Romans in the Roman War, and that a large number of early church leaders such as Clement of Alexandria saw it as such. This phrase, "all the tribes of the earth will mourn," ties the events of Revelation 1 directly to that event. John, who had access to the gospel of Matthew by the time he wrote the introduction of Revelation, has deliberately made a reference back to this passage to make sure we didn't miss it. The same Greek word for mourn is used later to describe the fall of Babylon the Great, a name given to Jerusalem in Jesus' day:

Then I heard another voice from heaven saying, "Come out of her, my people, lest you take part in her sins, lest you share in her plagues; for her sins are heaped high as heaven, and God has remembered her iniquities. Pay her back as she herself has paid back others, and repay her double for her deeds; mix a double portion for her in the cup she mixed. As she glorified herself and lived in luxury, so give her a like measure of torment and mourning, since in her heart she says, 'I sit as a queen, I am no widow, and mourning I shall never see.' For this reason her plagues will come in a single day, death and mourning and famine, and she will be burned up with fire; for mighty is the Lord God who has judged her." And the kings of the earth, who committed sexual immorality and lived in luxury with her, will weep and wail over her when they see the smoke of her burning. They will stand far off, in fear of her torment, and say,

> "Alas! Alas! You great city, you mighty city,
> Babylon! For in a single hour your judgment
> has come." (Rev. 18:4-10 ESV)

As Don Preston has pointed out in his book, *Who is This Babylon?*, there can be no doubt that Mystery Babylon is Jerusalem in the first century.[158] It's the city that kills the prophets (cf. Matt 23) and is the city in which the Lord was crucified. Since the fall of that city in that generation is tied to the Roman War, it is impossible for Revelation 1:7 to be applied outside of that context. Let's look at Revelation 1:7 one last time:

> Behold, he is coming with the clouds, and every
> eye will see him, even those who pierced him,
> and all tribes of the earth will wail on account
> of him. Even so. Amen. (Rev. 1:7 ESV)

Allow me to paraphrase and summarize this verse and the idiom it contains: "Behold, he is coming in clouds of judgment, which have always been used by God to describe an invading army acting as an agent of God's wrath. Because of the extensive destruction of the campaign, those who pierced him will die and meet him face to face at the judgment seat. In addition, all of the Christian dead will meet him there for a judgment of their works.[159] All the tribes of the land of Israel will mourn for their failure to recognize him in his first advent. Even so. Amen."

It's not necessary to come up with wild, imaginative ways to explain how Christ could be seen by every human on earth. John F. Walvoord, the Chancellor of the Dallas Theological Seminary (one of the most powerful schools in Christian theology, and the standard bearer for dispensationalism) resorts to a fantastic explanation for this verse in which Christ's army comes out of heaven and then hovers in the air (presumably at the equator, though there is theoretically a problem for those living in the Arctic) for at least 24 hours so that everyone on earth will have a chance to see him as the earth rotates.[160] While this novel approach might seem to be satisfactory at first glance, how would it stack up against the actual description of the event, "For as the lightning comes from the east and shines as far as the west, so will be the coming of the Son of Man" (Matt. 24:27 ESV). I have found that it is common for people to interpret this verse as describing the speed, or instantaneous nature of his return. Here, Walvoord has turned that concept on its head, making the return visible but quite slow.[161] On the other hand, maybe we're supposed to rely on technology such as satellite news channels as Chad Trowell would suggest, though I doubt he's considered what this would mean to the doctrine of imminence, since that would mean the second coming couldn't have happened before the invention of CNN, or at least satellite TV feeds.[162]

I propose that simply doing a comparative analysis of the text is enough to show that the Old Testament precedent proves none of this theorizing is necessary. Christ coming in the clouds is imagery established in the Old Testament where nations that invaded others as a function of judgment from God acted as his presence in history. After the climax of the Roman War, the believers were resurrected and rewarded at the moment of their final justification. The unbelievers, who died in the judgment of the Roman invasion, did indeed see Christ face to face at the foot of his throne in heaven just before their trip to the Lake of Fire.

Summary:

The assertion in Revelation 1:7 that every eye will see Christ return must be understood within the context of the passage and those that it draws from. The passage in Revelation comes from Isaiah 52, where the context is judgment against Israel, and the language points us to an idiom that shows us "every eye" is really meant to be understood as "eye to eye," or "face to face." This is the way that the final judgment is described in numerous places in the New Testament. While preterists can argue consistently that this did in fact happen for those killed in the judgment of the Roman invasion (or possibly living Christians raptured at about this time per Ed Stevens' position), futurists are divided and indeed contradictory in their fantastic explanations of the event. The matter comes down to whether the Great White Throne judgment is a heavenly event. If it is, then "every eye" seeing Christ at the Parousia should be interpreted as a description of that judgment. Being a heavenly event, its occurrence or not in regular earth history is impossible to prove, and so is not a valid criticism against preterism.

Chapter 9 Endnotes

[141] The crisis presented by asserting that he is in a flesh body in heaven is not obvious to most Christians I've talked to. This sort of language might have made more sense back when heaven, or at least the throne of God, was considered to be a physical place, billions of miles from earth (though it's still not clear how a flesh body would exist there without some sort of space suit, etc.). But, in modern times it's commons to see heaven as a different dimension or plane of existence (whatever that's supposed to mean scientifically). If that is true, it's not at all clear what it would mean, or how it would be possible, to be in a "self-same flesh body." When most people I've talked to confront the issue, they most commonly say that Christ is right now in exactly the same flesh body he had after the resurrection, which is exactly the same flesh body he had while on the cross, though that body has been changed. I usually have to repeat out loud to them that they are saying that "it's exactly the same, but completely different" before they catch the logical failure in what they are trying to say. Eventually, they usually admit that his body is in some sort of miraculous form that isn't flesh like you and I have, at which point major problems pop up in their theology. I suggest that the topic is not as simple as it seems. A good resource for various thoughts on this topic is Murray Harris' *Raised Immortal: Resurrection and Immorality in the New Testament.*

[142] L.S. Chafer, *Major Bible Themes*, p.332-33.

[143] http://www.nakedbiblepodcast.com/naked-bible-88-what-is-the-spiritual-body-paul-talks-about-in-1-cor-15/ (Last accessed 4/11/16).

[144] This is not a position that approximates Gnosticism. As Dale Martin and Troels Enberg-Pedersen have established, pneuma in the time of the New Testament was considered a physical element, like a very thin and perfected air. Space precludes reciting their theories and arguments here, but modern academic research on Gnosticism shows that nothing I'm proposing here can be confused with it. Dale Martin, *The Corinthian Body*; Troels Engberg-Pedersen, *Cosmology and Self and the Apostle Paul: The Material Spirit.*

[145] Full preterists who emphasize the Corporate Body View (CBV) use this passage as a basis for their argument. It's important to understand that the point Paul was getting at is that he preferred to be in heaven to be judged. He was not necessarily making a detailed argument about the nature of the body in question. This can be a problem for some CBV

supporters because they don't see a literal judgment in front of a throne in heaven. This is a serious mistake in my view.

[146] Some premillennialists would assert that this particular judgment is in heaven for believers. They would see it as parallel to the so called Bema Seat judgment found in 1 Corinthians 3. The problem is that they dichotomize the Bema Seat judgment from the Great White Throne judgment. Their system requires this separation, but there are no grounds for such a dichotomy in scripture. The most obvious problem with this approach is that in 2 Cor. 5:10 the judgment is for actions done in the body "whether good or evil." According to premillennial doctrine, the Bema Seat judgment is only meant to show believers what rewards they get in heaven. There doesn't seem to be any engagement at all with the idea that they'll be judged for the evil they did on earth. But, the judgment regarding works, good or bad, is clearly described in Rev. 20:11-15. There is no reason for this judgment to be split into two events.

[147] For a detailed explanation of preterist theories on Christ's current state see the 2013 Preterist Pilgrim Weekend, "The Body of Christ." This event featured several conference speakers describing the preterist view of this doctrine.

[148] Dispensational theology insists that the Great White Throne judgment begins after the millennium, 1,000 years after the second coming. Daniel 7 is very clear that the judgment happens immediately after the beast is captured, an event clearly described in Rev. 19, which everyone agrees is an image of the final battle at the second coming. This presents an insurmountable problem for dispensationalism as a system.

[149] The Corporate Body View (CBV) of resurrection in preterism is particularly well suited to point out examples of national resurrection throughout both the Old and New Testaments. Clearly, as Wright admits in *Resurrection and the Son of God*, national regathering or rejuvenation is an important way that the Old Testament describes resurrection. He seems less aware of how this language is used in a similar way in the New Testament. The CBV provides an important lens through which to see resurrection in some places in the New Testament. However, I consider it a sort of type and shadow argument that does not exhaust the meaning of resurrection. In other words, though it is true that the nation is resurrected under a new covenant, individual pneuma resurrection is also in view. I consider the full doctrine of resurrection to be a combination of these ideas. However, the CBV passages do provide us important information for the timing of the resurrection. Since both views of resurrection would happen at the same time, nailing down the timing of the corporate resurrection will help in defining the timing of an

invisible pneuma resurrection. Clearly, the nation that is resurrected, or born again, has to do with replacing the Old Covenant nation with the New Covenant nation. And, just as clearly, this is associated with the destruction of the Old Covenant elements when the priesthood, elements of worship, and Temple were destroyed in the Roman War. Since the people of God who moved forward under the New Testament were clearly the Christians, the resurrection is assigned to this complex of events. This is the point behind Justin Martyr's argument when he invented the terms "second coming" and "second advent."

[150] Albert Barnes' *Notes on the Bible*, e-Sword.

[151] That anthology contains the oldest available Latin-based commentaries on Revelation. In the first commentary by Victorinus of Petovium (260AD) he makes no mention of Rev. 1:7 (of course, the chapter and verse markings were not invented yet, so I'm talking about the content of the passage itself). The second commentator, Apringius of Beja (approximately 500AD), takes a position similar to the Calvary Chapel one. He says:

> Therefore he now speaks of his second coming that will be in the same form and in the same body in which he suffered, died and rose again. But he will come in divine power, and not as before in human weakness, and he who showed himself for the witness of the true man that he assumed will appear to be seen by his persecutors.

He goes on to quote Zechariah 14, so we know that he's making a connection between that passage, the second coming, and Rev. 1:7. This quote might sound like a valuable discovery for the Calvary Chapel position since it seems to back them up on their view of Christ returning in a flesh body. However, it's important to keep in mind that over 400 years had passed since the writing of Revelation (more than 3/4 of the duration of the church at that point) so we begin to wonder what philosophical, linguistic, and political influences might have affected the commentary. We could also wonder why no one up to that point had commented directly in a Latin commentary on Revelation on such a key passage, and where the tradition for such a comment came from. I also think it's interesting that the theme of the commentary is that his persecutors would see him, not necessarily every person on earth. The author doesn't speculate on how everyone on earth would be able to see Christ in his flesh body at the same time. The third author cited in this text is Caesarius of Arles who wrote a series of homilies on Revelation around 500AD. Like Victorinus, he does not directly comment on Rev. 1:7.

Our final commentator in this anthology, Bede the Venerable (approximately 700AD) comments directly on the passage in question:

> Behold, he comes with clouds, and every eye will see him. He who first came in a hidden manner to be judged will then come in an open manner in order to judge. And for this reason does he recount this, that he might strengthen the church in the endurance of her sufferings, for she is now oppressed by enemies, but then she will reign with Christ.

> And those who had fought him, and all the tribes of the earth will beat themselves. When they see him as a powerful judgment in the same form in which they had judged him as someone insignificant, they will lament for themselves with a repentance that will be too late.

The important issue here is that according to both Apringius and Bede, Christ coming so that every eye will see him has to do with his universal visibility to those being judged at the final judgment, not necessarily the method of coming itself. There is no mention by Bede of connecting this passage to Zechariah 14 and Acts 1:11, so it is hard to know what he might think of the interpretive connection with these verses, or the nature of the descent. So, do Apringius and Bede reflect the average perspective on this passage as it had evolved up to that point? Where do they get this judgment theme if it wasn't the standard interpretation in his age? Or, if it was, when did we first get the idea that "every eye" seeing the second coming meant that Christ would hover over the earth for a full day as it spun underneath him?

Though he does not directly comment on Rev. 1:7, I think it's interesting that he is sensitive to the timing of the events of Revelation so that he would argue that they were already being worked out in the history of the church. This is essentially the system of historicism, though to call it that may be anachronistic because the formal school of historicism in the Reformed church expects that the events of Revelation have been slowly transpiring for 1900 or so years. From Caesarius' point of view the revealing of the Antichrist had already transpired. From the perspective of 2016AD, we'd call that a form of preterism, not historicism. The following is a long quote from him on this point (Homily 1):

> Dearest brothers, that which is contained in the Revelation of Saint John seemed to some of the ancient fathers to signify, either in the totality of the reading or certainly in its greatest part, the day of judgment or the coming of the Anti-christ. Those, however, who have more diligently commented on the revelation understand that what is contained in this Revelation had begun immediately after the passion of tour Lord and Savior and therefore was to be fulfilled to the day of judgment. As a result, only a small period of time remained for the times of the Anti-christ. Therefore, whatever you shall hear in the recitation of the reading, whether it is of the Son of man or the stars or the angels or of the lampstands, or of the four living creatures or of the eagle flying in the midheaven, understand that these and everything else are reality in Christ and in the church. Or if you will recognize that these realities have been declared by way of their types.

This quote once again reinforces two of my main points in dealing with ancient texts: First, the authors never seem to claim that their interpretation is based on anything other than analysis of the text (as opposed to inside information through oral tradition lost to us), giving them no particular advantage over us. Second, it's very difficult to find modern premillennialism (and impossible to find dispensationalism) in ancient writings, so their use by modern premillennial dispensational writers is probably cynical at best.

Thomas Oden and Gerald Bray, *Ancient Christian Texts: Latin Commentaries on Revelation*, p.3, 25, 63.

[152] Philip Schaff, http://www.ccel.org/ccel/schaff/anf04.vi.v.v.iii.html:

> Every one who participates in anything, is unquestionably of one essence and nature with him who is partaker of the same thing. For example, as all eyes participate in the light, so accordingly all eyes which partake of the light are of one nature; but although every eye partakes of the light, yet, inasmuch as one sees more clearly, and another more obscurely, every eye does not equally share in the light."

Philip Schaff, http://www.ccel.org/ccel/schaff/npnf210.iv.iv.iv.v.html:

"Behold, He cometh," saith the Scripture, "with the clouds, and every eye shall see Him, and they which pierced Him, and all the tribes of the earth shall mourn because of Him. Yea, amen. I am Alpha and Omega, saith the Lord God, Who is, and Who was, and Who is to come, the Almighty." Whom, I ask, did they pierce? For Whose coming hope we but the Son's? Therefore, Christ is Almighty Lord, and God.; Catena Aurea Vol. 4 p.19.

[153] John MacArthur, *The Second Coming,* p.177.

[154] There is no such group of people as the "tribulation saints" defined explicitly in scripture. Their role in ecclesiology becomes very tricky because they aren't part of the church, but they also aren't Jews. They usually disappear from the discussion of dispensationalists as they move into the millennium because it's not clear whether they are supposed to stay on earth (the millennium is a period where the Jews will supposedly rule the world; L. S. Chafer, *Major Bible Themes,* p.356-7) or move on to heaven to stay with the Christians (Christians, it turns out, do not dwell on the earth during this period according the classical dispensationalism).

[155] L.S. Chafer, *Major Bible Themes,* p.348-49.

[156] In a literalistic understanding of this verse, those people would be required to literally travel to Jerusalem in order to bring their gifts. From the New Testament (Romans 12) we learn that good works are spiritual sacrifices for believers. And, we learn that the New Jerusalem is an image of the church, militant and triumphant. So, preterists are not saying that unbelievers are required to physically go to Jerusalem to give gifts to Christians. They are saying that in some sense the more Christians and their ethic are honored in society, the more God will bless the unbelievers. And, in the Perpetual Millennium Preterism paradigm (the label given to my position) there is the implication that over 10,000 or a million years the Christian position will become dominant, though not in the sense of Postmillennial Dominionists. Instead, I propose that Christian spiritual expression will eventually become the dominant position in human history, though I accept as Eze. 47 and Zech. 14 indicate there will always be some element of rebellion.

[157] Interestingly, in Mark Hitchcock's *101 Answers to the Most Asked Questions about the End Times,* on p.203, in explaining the visibility of Christ's return he cites Matthew 24:23-27, but does not go as far as v.31. On the one hand, this means that he accepts that this passage is about the

second coming. But, since he doesn't connect the mourning of the tribes to Revelation 1 it is not obvious, or he may not realize, that the mourning of the Tribes of Israel is the primary fulfillment of this part of the passage (cf. Zech. 12). From his other references to "earth" it is clear that he expects this to refer to the entire physical globe. But, this would be a novel scope for the term as it shows up in prophetic writings. Generally, ge means land or ground, or the locale related to the scope of the story, as opposed to Antarctica.

[158] Don K. Preston, *Who is this Babylon?*

[159] Ed Stevens' preterist rapture position is particularly well suited to explain the experience of Christians in this situation. Throughout the New Testament Christians are told that they will be judged at the Parousia of Christ. I've shown that this means that at the time of the beginning of the presence of Christ in his kingdom, those people would be face to face with him to be judged. It's easy to explain how those who had died up to that point would do so. It's harder for non-rapture preterists to explain how the Biblical language surrounding the Parousia judgment can be fulfilled. In conversations with preterists I have typically seen arguments for this judgment based on covenant relationship, but I'm suspicious that they do not go far enough. At present, I'm undecided on Stevens' position. But, I think this "every eye"/Parousia argument is a very powerful one for his position.

[160] John F. Walvoord, *Every Prophecy of the Bible,* p.524.

[161] This can be contrasted with John MacArthur's description of the return being an instantaneous event in *The Second Coming*, p.117-118.

[162] Chad Trowell, *End Times Bible Handbook,* p.33.

Chapter 10: The Mount of Olives Split in Two

Calvary Chapel Statement:

The Bible says that when Jesus returns, the Mount of Olives will be split in two and water will flow from Jerusalem.

Zechariah 14:4 says, "And in that day His feet will stand on the Mount of Olives, Which faces Jerusalem on the east. And the Mount of Olives shall be split in two, from east to west, making a very large valley; half of the mountain shall move toward the north and half of it toward the south."

Zechariah 14:8 says, "And in that day it shall be that living waters shall flow from Jerusalem, half of them toward the eastern sea and half of them toward the western sea; in both summer and winter it shall occur."

Anybody who goes to Jerusalem today can confirm that the Mount of Olives has not been split in two and there are no rivers flowing toward the eastern sea and toward the western sea.

If Preterists claim that Jesus returned in AD 70, where did the "very large valley" go and how did the mountain get moved back into position?

Charge:

- At the second coming, the Mount of Olives will split in half, and a river will flow both west and east from the valley. Why isn't it so today?

We end with an excellent example of the difference between hermeneutics in premillennial dispensationalism and preterism. This difference can be boiled down to what premillennialists mean when they say that they always interpret scripture literally. An important defense of this is found in *Dispensationalism* by Charles Ryrie.[163] Ryrie asserts that dispensationalism, the sub-category of premillennialism followed by Calvary Chapel, is based on two principles: the literal interpretation of scripture; and a strict separation of Israel from the Church. He asserts that in any case where the plain sense of scripture can be taken literally, it should be.[164] This is a common way of describing a "literal hermeneutic." Naturally, he and other dispensational writers take the splitting of the Mount of Olives in Zechariah 14 quite literally.

But, it's not at all clear what they mean by literally. This issue can be confusing because of what we bring to the table as assumptions, and how we're used to seeing imaginative imagery played out. I mentioned earlier in this book that David was perfectly comfortable with describing the battle in which Saul was killed as one where God put his feet on angels, flew down from heaven, and shot fire from his nose. I think it's perfectly clear, then, that in ancient times they took a great deal of liberty with the imagery they used to describe important, world-shaking events.

What might be more surprising to us, though, is how we tend to do the same thing without realizing it. In modern times the primary influences are movie special effects and CGI. In the late 1980s, Sigourney Weaver became famous in sci-fi fan circles for her role in *Aliens*. As part of the preparation for that role, she was rumored to have been taught how to fire actual firearms, and to have commented on how hard it was to actually hit a target. This is a common experience for people new to guns. It illustrates that though what we see on the big screen is designed to look literally possible, in fact it is not: there is no sound in space; there are no fireballs from hand grenades; and cars have to be launched by explosives to get them to predictably roll over. We watch stylized movies as our civilizational storytelling just like those from Biblical times used radically hyperbolic language in their storytelling. Yet, because we have CGI that is used to push boundaries of believability we are sometimes subtly convinced that what we are seeing is literally happening. By nature, stunt men are supposed to make it look like normal people can do extraordinary things. In storytelling, the concept of "literal" is not as simple as it seems.

If someone from those older generations were to watch a movie like *Aliens* (one of the last sci-fi movies to use almost all natural effects and no CGI) do you think it's possible that they might see some of the events as literally possible? In the more realistic cop movie genre, where stunt men and natural effects are everywhere, do you think they might see shootout scenes as literal? But, of course, in all modern story telling you have professional stunt doubles with padded clothing, padded landing areas, blood squibs, and prop weapons shooting giant flames. Do you think that these elements of modern storytelling would give the wrong impression of the literalness of the scene they are portraying? If you saw them, and knew what you knew about movie production and special effects, you might be able to enjoy the story without being literally concerned for the safety of the actors. But if someone from 2,000BC were to go in a time machine and be brought forward, do you think they might think that people were being literally killed or maimed?

Now, reverse this. If you went back in time 4,000 years, do you think there is a chance that you might fail to understand a method of storytelling that came quite naturally to them?[165] If they said that God swooped down riding on angels and shot fire from his nose, do you think *they* would be confused about the literalness of such an event? Do you think that *you* might be confused? In such a radical example, maybe not. But, if they said that he is coming in the clouds as a means for describing foreboding, just like the character Sarah Conner saw a foreboding storm brewing on the horizon at the end of *Terminator*, do you think you might be confused by this?

The potential for confusion is the reason that we have to use the Old Testament, and examples of the way stories are told there, to establish our imagery. It was the storytelling baseline for the audience of the New Testament and its writers. I'm not implying here that the events in question didn't actually take place in history. What I'm saying is that there are obvious examples where they use a sort of rhetorical special effect to drive a point home that is usually lost on modern readers. To say that every eye would see him would have been, for them, a comparatively easy-to-decode image for every person seeing God face to face, at the final judgment. The ease of interpretation faded quickly in church history when the average Christian was no longer a Jew raised on Hebrew storytelling, but a literalistic, scientific Greek. For moderns, it takes some detailed scholarship to unlock a proper understanding of ancient Hebrew story telling techniques. That fact alone should give us pause when pretending to confidently know what it was they were trying to say. Humility should be the order of the day.

To summarize the hermeneutic (or, interpretive paradigm) I'm proposing, there are three points I'd like readers to keep in mind. First, the primary audience of Jesus' teaching (and the majority of the church in the first decade) were Jews whose story telling style was based on Hebrew literature. They spoke in those idioms and it was natural for them to understand the hyperbolic imagery that was being used. Modern Christians do not have this same background so we should not assume that we would naturally understand the plain language of scripture. Second, each of the books or letters in the New Testament was meant to be understood, at least on a basic level, by the original recipients who did not have a fully compiled New Testament canon, and only had contemporary cultural sources to use as a baseline for vocabulary. That means that in the case of the Olivet Discourse, the point of the lesson could be learned by them without confusion from any of the three versions of it. It would not have been necessary to compare the different versions to get the basic point. Comparing the three versions would have given them the richest and clearest version of the teaching. But, each of the versions would have been understandable as a standalone discourse. Third, prophetic imagery in the New Testament is based off of precedent in the Old Testament, so Old Testament examples of historic fulfillment should be our baseline for understanding how the newer prophetic language is being used.

Before we move to Zechariah and Revelation to directly answer the challenge in this chapter, we're going to look at how this dynamic plays out in Jeremiah. Jeremiah was one of the most important prophets in the Old Testament. Paul the Apostle mimics Jeremiah's call to service in the New

Testament as a way of claiming that he had similar authority to that Old Testament prophet. The majority of the book of Jeremiah directly addresses the issue of the kingdom of Judah becoming apostate and God's punishment of that nation. Jesus borrows critical language from Jeremiah 7 when he gives his teaching on gehenna (or "hell" in most English Bibles) as part of his criticism of Jews in the New Testament, who've likewise become apostate from God. Just like in Jeremiah, where the Babylonians were going to be used to execute judgment on the Jews, Jesus criticizes the Jews of his day before the Roman war. Below is some very important language used to pass on the warning of the invasion of the Babylonians (particularly important words or phrases are in bold):

> "Therefore thus says the LORD of hosts: Because you have not obeyed my words, behold, **I will send for all the tribes of the north**, declares the LORD, and for Nebuchadnezzar the king of Babylon, my servant, and **I will bring them against this land and its inhabitants, and against all these surrounding nations. I will devote them to destruction, and make them a horror, a hissing, and an everlasting desolation**. Moreover, I will banish from them the voice of mirth and the voice of gladness, the voice of the bridegroom and the voice of the bride, the grinding of the millstones and the light of the lamp. **This whole land shall become a ruin and a waste**, and these nations shall serve the king of Babylon seventy years. **Then after seventy years are completed, I will punish the king of Babylon and that nation, the land of the Chaldeans, for their iniquity, declares the LORD, making the land an everlasting waste.** I will bring upon that land all the words that I have uttered against it, everything written

in this book, which Jeremiah prophesied against all the nations. For many nations and great kings shall make slaves even of them, and I will recompense them according to their deeds and the work of their hands." Thus the LORD, the God of Israel, said to me: "**Take from my hand this cup of the wine of wrath, and make all the nations to whom I send you drink it. They shall drink and stagger and be crazed because of the sword that I am sending among them.**" So I took the cup from the LORD's hand, and made all the nations to whom the LORD sent me drink it: Jerusalem and the cities of Judah, its kings and officials, to make them a desolation and a waste, a hissing and a curse, as at this day . . . **all the kings of the north, far and near, one after another, and all the kingdoms of the world that are on the face of the earth. And after them the king of Babylon shall drink.** (Jer. 25:8-19, 26 ESV)

The passage above prophecies the initial sacking of Jerusalem as well as God's retaliation against Babylon. In it we have all sorts of imagery relating to "all . . . tribes," "everlasting waste," and "all of the kingdoms of the world that are on the face of the earth." The method used to execute this judgment is clearly a limited ancient military campaign with ancient swords and spears. Should this global, universal language be taken absolutely literally? If so, what do we make of the fact that Jerusalem and the surrounding area wasn't turned into a literal wasteland? And, neither was Babylon - forever. Finally, not all of the kingdoms on the face of the earth participated in the destruction of Babylon.

So what happens to the literal nature of this language? Obviously, it's hyperbole used to make a dramatic point about the gravity and scale of the situation. You should recognize all of this hyperbolic imagery repeated in the New

Testament in various places. If it was hyperbolic in the Old Testament, then why do we make the same language literally global in the New Testament?

Moving on to Zechariah 14:4-7, let's keep in mind what it would mean for such an event to literally happen. Below is the text, and then an analysis of what it might mean:

> On that day his feet shall stand on the Mount of Olives that lies before Jerusalem on the east, and the Mount of Olives shall be split in two from east to west by a very wide valley, so that one half of the Mount shall move northward, and the other half southward. And you shall flee to the valley of my mountains, for the valley of the mountains shall reach to Azal. And you shall flee as you fled from the earthquake in the days of Uzziah king of Judah. Then the Lord my God will come, and all the holy ones with him. On that day there shall be no light, cold, or frost. And there shall be a unique day, which is known to the Lord, neither day nor night, but at evening time there shall be light. (Zech. 14:4-7 ESV)

Notice first that it says that Jesus' feet will stand on the Mount of Olives. Most dispensational commentators would say that he descends from the clouds to do so per Acts 1:11, landing with both feet on the mountain. He does so because per Acts 1:11 he has to return in the same manner that he left. Our first problem is that he didn't ascend from the Mount of Olives. He ascended from Bethany, about a 1/2 mile to the east (Luke 24:50-53). Another problem comes from the fact that in Isaiah 63:1 the Messiah arrives on foot after walking from Bozrah, 58 miles away. I suppose that he could trudge his way to the top of the Mount of Olives before beginning to split it. But the second coming imagery normally embraced by premillennial dispensationalists is so ruined at this point that there probably is no point gained by sticking to it.

If we were to press on, it's presumed that the mountain splits in half between Jesus' feet. The river which brings restoration and life begins to flow left and right from that location, which is several hundred yards from the Temple mount. If we were to take that literally, we'd then have to find a way to combine that imagery with the imagery of Ezekiel 47 and Revelation 21-22. In Ezekiel, we find that the river only flows downhill to the east, and that it starts underneath the altar, not the Mount of Olives. In Revelation we see that the river flows to both the west and the east, again originating under the altar. In addition, it's not clear how easy such an event would be to see with the naked eye since in Zechariah 14 there is no light (v.6), though a verse later we see that that at evening there actually is light (v.7). In order to keep these verses from contradicting each other, maybe the point is that there is no light until the battle or flight of the good guys through the valley is over (though with no light, it's not clear how that remnant would find their way to and through the valley), and then at evening time some light appears. Such interpretations have the feel of trying to shoe horn an overly literalistic interpretation into something designed to make a different point.

I could go on to make point after point of the silliness of taking all of the imagery in Zechariah 14, Ezekiel 47, Isaiah 66, and Revelation 21-22 perfectly literally. At some point, it would become pointlessly obnoxious. Instead, I hope that the reader would grant me that at least some of the imagery is supposed to be taken figuratively. If that is true, we have to decide which imagery should be.

The typical dispensational answer given by people such as Ryrie is that we should take the language literally as long as there is no reason to do otherwise.[166] The problem with this definition is that it is circular. There is no objective standard used to establish when the "reason to do otherwise" kicks in. My method is to try to base it on other passages of similar types, and to realize that the original authors were only speaking in terms and style common to their day.[167] In other words, when Ryrie says to take it literally unless there is a reason to do otherwise, I suggest that a reason not to do so is that it is Old Testament apocalyptic poetry.

The champion for non-literal interpretation in the early church was Origen. He proposed a more figurative and analogous approach in interpreting scripture that is similar in many ways to the Hebrew Midrash tradition of that day. Though I think he took his approach too far in some cases, it's worth taking a minute to appreciate the way he approached the topic. Other Greek trained teachers tended to be more like modern dispensationalists as they took poetic prophetic imagery absolutely literally. The following is Origen's approach to such passages:

> And if the voices of the prophets say that God 'comes down,' who has said, 'Do I not fill heaven and earth? saith the Lord,' the term is used in a figurative sense. For God 'comes down' from His own height and greatness when He arranges the affairs of men, and especially those of the wicked.[168]

Origen goes on to describe something similar to what I call cosmological condescension. This dynamic exists when God uses the worldview (including physics, metaphysics, and language) of a given generation to explain himself. He does so in order to make his purposes understandable. But just like we now accept that heaven itself isn't literally "up" from the earth, these statements aren't designed to be taken scientifically. Origen continues:

> And as custom leads men to say that teachers 'condescend' to children, and wise men to those youths who have just betaken themselves to philosophy, not by 'descending in a bodily manner; so, if God is said anywhere in the holy Scriptures to 'come down, it is understood as spoken in conformity with the usage which so employs the word, and in like manner also with the expression, 'go up.'[169]

The final section from Origen connects overly literal interpretive styles to Celsus, a contemporary of Origen. They represent two camps in Christian interpretive tradition. Clearly, in the early years of Christianity both camps existed with wildly different positions on how to see prophetic imagery. I'll remind the reader of the argument made earlier for the value of ancient writings. In order for early writers to have unique authority, they had to be working from unique tradition passed directly from the Apostles. I have cautioned against making too much of early writings because their disagreements clearly prove that no such tradition was passed down. In this case, I'll finish the point with another quote from Origen to demonstrate that, though there was some disagreement in the early years, the very fact of the popularity of his widely followed writings means that a similar approach should at least be considered an orthodox option for preterists:

> But it is in mockery that Celsus says we speak of 'God coming down like a torturer bearing fire,' and thus compels us unseasonably to investigate words of deeper meaning, we shall make a few remarks, sufficient to enable our

> hearers to form an idea of the defense which
> disposes of the ridicule of Celsus against us, and
> then we shall turn to what follows. The divine
> word says that our God is 'a consuming fire,'
> and that 'He draws rivers of fire before Him;'
> nay, that he even entereth in as 'a refiner's fire,
> and as a fuller's herb,' to purify.[170]

For examples of how this dynamic makes my point in this chapter, let's slow down at this point and look at how the living water functions according to Ezekiel 47 and Revelation 21-22. In Ezekiel 47, at the time of the millennial kingdom after the second coming, we see water "trickling" out of the south wall before it starts to flow east (v.2). At 1,000 cubit intervals this water becomes deeper and deeper until it cannot be crossed (v.5). Wherever the water goes, it rejuvenates the world so that there is abundant life. Verse 12 provides an important glimpse of the effect of the impassable river:

> And on the banks, on both sides of the river,
> there will grow all kinds of trees for food. Their
> leaves will not wither, nor their fruit fail, but
> they will bear fresh fruit every month, because
> the water for them flows from the sanctuary.
> Their fruit will be for food, and their leaves for
> healing. (Ezek. 47:12 ESV)

Now, look at the description of the New Jerusalem in the New Heaven and New Earth of Revelation 21-22:

> Then the angel showed me the river of the water
> of life, bright as crystal, flowing from the throne
> of God and of the Lamb through the middle of
> the street of the city; also, on either side of the
> river, the tree of life with its twelve kinds of
> fruit, yielding its fruit each month. The leaves
> of the tree were for the healing of the nations.
> No longer will there be anything accursed, but

> the throne of God and of the Lamb will be in it,
> and his servants will worship him. They will see
> his face, and his name will be on their
> foreheads. And night will be no more. They will
> need no light of lamp or sun, for the Lord God
> will be their light, and they will reign forever
> and ever. (Rev. 22:1-5 ESV)

I think you can clearly see that the passage from Revelation is taken directly from the one in Ezekiel. If the dispensational paradigm is correct, this could never be the case. In fact, according to the dispensational approach, since the version of the river of life in Ezekiel is functioning in the millennium, it must be destroyed completely after failing somehow (2 Peter 3) and replaced by a better river in Revelation 22. It seems from the dispensational order of events that the first version of the river from Zechariah 14 and Ezekiel 47 was not able to heal much of anything since, after it had been functioning for 1,000 years, the world descends once again into chaos and sin.

Instead, I argue that Christ's teaching on them governs the topic and shows us some of the important spiritual truth behind these prophecies originally given as physical types and shadows of the spiritual truth that he would unveil. Peter explains this in 1 Peter 1:10ff where he says that the Old Testament writers didn't understand either the nature or the timing of what they were predicting in prophecy related to Jesus' arrival and subsequent glories. But, the arrival of Jesus fulfilled those prophecies. Those prophecies were fulfilled in him.

For instance, the function of living water is central to his ministry. When he talks to the woman at the well in John 4, he promises that if anyone drinks of the water he is offering that they will never thirst again. Is that a literal statement? It depends. As long as you understand that he was making a point about spiritual dynamics, then he is describing a literal truth. Obviously, that woman had to come to the well daily for the rest of her natural life in order not to dehydrate and die. But, the literal lesson was that Jesus was offering spiritual life that would never end.

Returning to the type and shadow of the river of life flowing from the altar, this was never going to be a literal flowing stream of water. In the Old Testament it is described as either one or two streams of water flowing across the land, bringing renewal. In John 4 the fulfillment of the living, or flowing, water imagery is actually the Holy Spirit. That water was imagery used to express salvation and spiritual life offered to all men by God. Later in John 7, we see Jesus give the true interpretation of the Feast of Tabernacles (a type and shadow of the spiritual truth about to come, Heb. 8:5, 10:1) when he says:

> Whoever believes in me, as the Scripture has
> said, 'Out of his heart will flow rivers of living
> water.' (John 7:38 ESV)

Rivers of water flowing out of the heart (literally, mind)? How are we supposed to take that literally? Clearly we're not. When we combine this with the idea from 1 Peter 2, that each believer is the new temple of God, and that we are living stones in that new, promised building, the imagery becomes clear. A literalistic understanding of Zechariah 14 becomes unnecessary, and actually impossible. After the second coming, when the new Temple made without hands has been built and is fully functional, the individual members of the New Covenant who are living stones in the temple will issue the Holy Spirit, or living water, from their minds to the people around them for the purpose of healing the people in the periphery of the believers.

The point of all of this imagery was to show that after the second coming believers would go to far-off places (from the point of view of Jerusalem) that had never heard of God as of the moment of the second coming. Our proper spiritual function would be to represent God to unsaved men. They had looked forward to this throughout the Old Testament, but in the days of the Apostles it was coming true. Christians would give these unbelievers access to the spiritual truth that would spiritually regenerate them through the work of the Holy Spirit. The imagery of stones (individual members of the new Temple), valleys (represented scars on the earth and sin), mountains (power systems in opposition to God's kingdom), abundant fish (an abundant harvest of new believers), and salt marshes (the reality of the rejection of God by some people) were never meant to be taken literally. As Paul says in Romans 12, the new spiritual function of the new class of priests under the New Covenant is our service to God and men. The old system of killing animals, which was used to teach spiritual lessons but was never an end in itself, had been done away with. The new spiritual understanding of these physical, literalistic lessons are plain to see. Jesus himself showed us how to make sense of it.

Summary:

The expectation of a literal canyon forming on the Mount of Olives, with a literal river flowing in each direction from it, is a mistake caused by a failure to follow the interpretation of these images by New Testament teaching. Jesus, Peter, and Paul are clear that these Old Testament types and shadows have been fulfilled by New Covenant spiritual realities. Literalistically following prophetic poetry in the

Old Testament results in conflicting or contradictory expectations and confusion. Accepting a spiritual fulfillment of these images using the interpretations of the Apostles as a guide leads to the proper understanding of the passages.

Chapter 10 Endnotes

[163] Charles Ryrie, *Dispensationalism*. Originally written in 1969, this book describes the basic approach of dispensationalism. Ryrie argues that dispensationalism is based on the twin pillars of a literal hermeneutic (though he doesn't develop the concept in detail) and a permanent separation between the Jews (or, more properly, Israel) and the Church. This book was very important in dispensational circles in the 1970s through the 1990s, resulting in an update in 2007.

[164] Vern Poythress, in *Understanding Dispensationalists*, addresses these foundations of dispensationalism directly. On the issue of literal interpretation, he makes the point that no system of interpretation interprets scripture literally all of the time. Dispensationalists may claim to take scripture literally, but since they have no scientific standard for defining when it is proper to do so, their standard quickly becomes arbitrary. For instance, when dispensationalists say that every prophecy would be literally fulfilled, they simply declare any prophecy that they haven't seen literally fulfilled to be yet future. Poythress spends some time showing how this circular reasoning fails.

[165] I'm not trying to imply here that the popular Old Testament stories didn't in fact happen. I am aware that in some liberal schools they doubt the historicity of important ancient events. In cases where miraculous intervention is described, I accept on face value that God was capable of causing these events to happen as described. My point is simply that if radical imagery is used to describe an event that is non-miraculous we should be cautious of how we expect the historicity of that to play out. In the case of prophetic poetry, we need to be extra careful.

[166] Charles Ryrie, *Dispensationalism,* p.91.

[167] Peter Enns, in *Inspiration and Incarnation* makes a powerful argument for the importance of audience relevance worldview. Basically, they used terminology they were familiar with and it is up to us to study their culture to figure it out. They did not seem to be worried about possible future developments like astronomy, genetics, etc. As a result, there are things from our worldview that don't seem to match up with theirs (a bottomless pit in the middle of the earth used to store people for judgment, etc.). If we can find a way to accept at face value that they were groping for ways to explain the world from their point of view without becoming anxious that their world view was wrong, we can move forward in discerning principles God meant for us.

[168] Contra Celsus, IV, xiii; Ante-Nicene Fathers, Vol IV, p.501-2; Kurt Simmons, *The Sword and Plow*, p.5-16.

[169] 4 Contra Celsus, IV, xii; Ante-Nicene Fathers, Vol. IV, p.502, 508; Kurt Simmons, *The Sword and Plow*, p.5-16.

[170] 5 Contra Celsus, IV, xiii; Ante-Nicene Fathers IV, p.502; Kurt Simmons, *The Sword and Plow,* p.5-16.

Conclusion

As I was growing up in premillennial dispensational churches in the 1970s and 80s, it was clear to me that the Great Tribulation was just over the horizon. Every day, prophecy was coming true. In the 1970s, the Israelis were once again fighting against their enemies who, this time, were being much more openly supported by the Soviet Union (interpreted to be Gog and Magog from Ezekiel and Revelation). On occasion I heard suggestions that Christians should join the Army to help Israel fight the Gog and Magog war that was right around the corner (though it never quite made sense to me how they were supposed to do that since the rapture was supposed to come first).[171]

I also heard people suggesting that we be on the lookout for the Antichrist, and speculation about the abomination of desolation was rampant. It was only a matter of time until the Temple would be rebuilt so that these events could take place. I wasn't theologically sophisticated enough to understand that the dispensationalism I was supposedly following made this approach to eschatology impossible. In dispensationalism, the next possible prophetic event is the pre-Tribulation rapture. It is impossible for any prophecy to be fulfilled between Pentecost and the rapture. Any deviation from the fundamental structure ruins the whole system. Eventually, after a few decades of watching newspapers for signs of fulfilled prophecy, with none of it really leading anywhere, I realized that if the rapture was going to happen first, I wasn't interested in the rest of the hype.

Another decade or so of study later it dawned on me: If the Apostles were constantly haranguing their readers to be ready and to look for signs, but according to dispensationalism the next sign was supposed to be an unexpected one that I couldn't see coming, there was something wrong with dispensationalism. If dispensational preachers were pointing out important prophetic events in the headlines, then they were not being true to their own system when they taught it. Clearly, the dispensational pretribulational rapture paradigm didn't fit with the tone of the New Testament.

The first step I took was to research premillennial, post-tribulation rapture positions as found in classical premillennialism. This is the traditional premillennial position held by the premillennial minority since the beginning of church history until dispensationalism was formulated in the 1800s. Classical premillennialism rejects the role that dispensationalism assigns to Jews, but embraces the second coming before the millennium. Roy Anderberg's book, *Post Tribulation Rapture* was very important for me here. I also looked at other positions such as pre-wrath rapture. H.L. Nigro's book *Before God's Wrath* is a very powerful explanation of the problems with pretribulation rapture. She effectively demolished any remaining interest that I had in a pretribulation rapture.

My next goal, since I was convinced that I might end up going through the Great Tribulation, was to figure out what it was. I decided that the best approach would be to define it through the Olivet Discourse. This seemed like the best course of action because the phrase "Great Tribulation" only exists in three places in scripture: Matthew 24:21, Revelation 2:22, and Revelation 7:14. It was clear to me that whatever was meant by the phrase was the same in each of these passages. After reading Bray and Chilton, I realized that the Olivet Discourse in Matthew 24 was talking about the events related to the destruction of Jerusalem in 70AD. The game was up.

The fulfillment didn't mean that principles related to moral living and spiritual life found in the New Testament are a thing of the past. Clearly, these were meant as timeless admonitions towards holiness based on the never-changing essence of God. This is one of the reasons that I still listen to and enjoy Calvary Chapel teaching on the radio. I'd been raised on it and still value their advice on day-to-day living.

But the problem comes from keeping people in constant expectation of the end of the world. It isn't scriptural. In the early New Testament church, around the time of Christ's ministry, they were told that sometime within that generation the prophecies would be fulfilled. About 20 years later, in the 50s, Paul told the Thessalonians that the second coming couldn't happen until after a series of future events. It wasn't about to happen at any moment. Late in the New Testament record we see John saying that it was "the last hour," and James said "the coming of the Lord is at hand." This progression of the expectation in the New Testament is ignored by premillennial theologians because the second coming was supposed to be imminent starting at Pentecost. They have no way of explaining the unanimous crescendo of the time statements. Instead, dispensational premillennialists flatten the times statements given to the early church, spiritualize them, and then hold an illegitimate hope out to their congregations. Young people decide not to go to college, get married, or have children. They see themselves literally living in the environment of 1 Corinthians 7.

If you take the prophetic times statements at face value, you are left with no other option than to conclude that they were fulfilled as promised. If you can accept this, as much as it is at odds with whatever programming you might have received up to this point, I think you'll be stunned at how simple the message of scripture is. Scripture was meant to be easily understood, especially after the issuance of the Holy Spirit, by the original audience. It was meaningful and helpful to them in their situation. We can derive lessons for how to love God and man from what they experienced, but not every specific experience of theirs will map over to our world, just like advice given by Isaiah to the population in Jerusalem is not directly applicable to us. We are not still waiting for the great apostasy, or the arrival of the man of sin. Just like the Old Testament prophecies predicting the invasion of the Assyrians or Babylonians were not meant for us, the New Testament warnings about the impending Roman judgment should not be assigned to imaginary enemies in modern newspapers. It takes careful, thoughtful, prayerful consideration to use scripture. Applying it in a ham-fisted, literalistic manner can only result in spiritual immaturity and frustration. Instead, we should strive to take on the mind of Christ, which means taking his promises seriously in their original context.

This has profound implications for the kingdom of God and the unbelieving world that we engage. In the eras of the church where spreading the kingdom of God was foremost in our minds, the church was most successful. We brought salvation, civilization, and proper spiritual principles to our world. The advent of dispensational thinking in the 1800s coincided with an implosion of this mindset in the west. In the previous worldview, the kingdom of God would expand indefinitely. In dispensationalism, no matter how hard the church might try, eventually we are removed in order to punish the world for rejecting God. The result has been atrophy of the church's confidence and sense of destiny. As a consequence of standing still, waiting to be beamed out of trouble, civilization has decayed and the church has become paralyzed over what to do about it.

Preterism provides a Biblically based rationale for switching back to the more historically successful mindset of spreading the kingdom of God to every person on the planet, with the expectation that we will win in the end. My hope is that 100 years from now we can all look down from heaven and realize that dispensationalism was a bump in the road that the church managed to overcome. In the long view, the kingdom of God is winning. It's a kingdom that will have no end.

Conclusion Endnotes

[171] The timing of the God and Magog war has been particularly difficult to nail down in premillennial thought. The problem comes from having both the Ezekiel and Revelation versions of it, trying determine if these are the same events, and then trying to determine when those events fit into the calendar. In *Epicenter*, Joel Rosenberg postulates that there are actually two Gog and Magog battles. He proposes the first one will happen before the rapture. This is a game changer because he does not follow the typical dispensational chronology. Because of this, he is listed as a false teacher by Calvary Chapel. But, what Joel is seeing correctly is the role that the Gog and Magog war plays in setting up the millennium. In Ezekiel, it occurs directly before the kingdom era described from chapter 40 forward. Though Calvary Chapel is trying to be consistent with their theology by having it after the millennium, Rosenberg's chronology seems more common sense when looking at the pattern in Ezekiel. Neither Rosenberg nor Calvary Chapel are ready to deal with what happens if this event is the same as the Battle of Armageddon in Revelation 19, much less chapter 20. If so, the Gog and Magog war happens before the millennium (just as Rev. 19 says), but then again after the millennium! See my book, *Making Sense of the Millennium* for a simple preterist answer to the problem.

Recommended Reading

Calvary Chapel Original Sources

Every Prophecy of the Bible by Dr. John Walvoord

The Popular Bible Prophecy Commentary by Tim LaHaye and Ed Hindson

The Popular Encyclopedia of Bible Prophecy by Tim LaHaye and Ed Hindson

The Second Coming by Dr. John MacArthur

Things to Come by J. Dwight Pentecost

What is the World Coming To by Chuck Smith

101 Answers to the Most Asked Questions about Bible Prophecy by Mark Hitchcock

Preterist and Other Readings

Christianity's Great Dilemma by Glenn Hill

Matthew 24 Fulfilled by John Bray

Who is This Babylon by Don Preston

Like Father Like Son, On Clouds of Glory by Don Preston

The Hymenaean Heresy: Reverse the Charges by Don Preston

Can God Tell Time by Don Preston

Final Decade Before the End by Ed Stevens

Expectations Demand a Rapture by Ed Stevens

Adumbrations by Kurt Simmons

Making Sense of the Millennium by Douglas Wilkinson

Preterist Time Statements by Douglas Wilkinson

End Times Fiction: A Biblical Consideration of the Left Behind Theology by Gary DeMar

Last Days Madness by Gary DeMar

The Lost History of Christianity by Philip Jenkins

The Corinthian Body by Dale Martin

The King Jesus Gospel: The Original Good News Revisited by Scot McKnight

Dispensationalism by Charles Ryrie

Understanding Dispensationalists by Vern Poythress

The Pilgrim Church by E.H. Broadbent

Bibliography

Alcasar, Luis de, Vestigio Arcani Sensus in Apocalypsi [An Investigation of the Secret Meaning of the Apocalypse] (Antwerp: Martinus Nutius, 1614, 1619).

Anderberg, Roy W. *Post Tribulation Rapture: A Biblical Study of the Return of Christ.* Tucson, AZ: Wheatmark, 2008.

"Apocalypse: Early Date Advocates." http://preteristarchive.com/BibleStudies/Apocalypse Commentaries/Dating/Early/index.html (Last accessed 4/3/16).

Audet, Jean-Paul. *La Didache: Instructions des Apotres.* Paris: Gabalda, 1958.

Barnes, Albert. *Notes on the Bible.* e-Sword. http://www.e-sword.net/.

Bray, Gerald L. and Thomas C. Oden. *Ancient Christian Texts: Latin Commentaries on Revelation.* Downers Grove, IL: Intervarsity Press, 2011.

Bray, John L. *Matthew 24 Fulfilled.* Atlanta, GA: American Vision, 2009.

Broadbent, E.H. *The Pilgrim Church.* Resurrected Books, 2014.

Calvary Chapel. "Ten Reasons to Reject Preterism." http://c309365.r65.cf1.rackcdn.com/TenReasonstoR ejectPreterism.doc (Original article, last accessed 7/24/15).

Chafer, Lewis Sperry. *Major Bible Themes*. Grand Rapids, MI: Zondervan, 1974.

Chilton, David. *The Days of Vengeance: An Exposition of the Book of Revelation*. Fort Worth, TX: Dominion Press, 1987.

Clement of Alexandria. *The Stromata, or Miscellanies*. http://www.earlychristianwritings.com/text/clement-stromata-book1.html (Last accessed 4/3/16).

Clement of Rome. "The First Epistle of Clement to the Corinthians." http://www.earlychristianwritings.com/text/1clement-lightfoot.html (Last accessed 5/13/16).

Currie, David B. *What Jesus Really Said About the End of the World*. San Diego, CA: Catholic Answers Press, 2012.

Curtis, David. "Spiritual Warfare Pt 1: Yahweh vs the gods (Eph 6:10-12)": https://www.youtube.com/watch?v=1IWhVVxavA4 (Last accessed 6/3/16).

DeMar, Gary. *End Times Fiction: A Biblical Consideration of the Left Behind Theology*. Nashville, TN: Thomas Nelson, 2001.

DeMar, Gary. *Last Days Madness*. Powder Springs, GA: American Vision, 1999.

DeMar, Gary. "Norman Geisler: 'This Generation' or 'This Race' Will Not Pass Away?" https://americanvision.org/1689/norman-l-geisler-generation/ (Last accessed 4/3/16).

DeMar, Gary, and Francis X. Gumerlock. *The Early Church and the End of the World*. Atlanta, GA: American Vision, 2006.

Engberg-Pedersen, Troels. *Cosmology and Self and the Apostle Paul: The Material Spirit*. New York: Oxford University Press, 2011.

Enns, Peter. *Inspiration and Incarnation: Evangelicals and the Problem of the Old Testament*. Grand Rapids, MI: Baker Academics, 2015.

Erickson, Millard. *A Basic Guide to Eschatology: Making Sense of the Millennium*. Grand Rapids, MI: Baker Books, 1998.

e-Sword. http://www.e-sword.net/.

e-Sword. *King James Concordance*.

e-Sword. *Strong's Concordance*.

"Eucharistic Canon: Anaphora." http://oca.org/orthodoxy/the-orthodox-faith/worship/the-divine-liturgy/eucharistic-canon-anaphora (Last accessed 4/3/16).

Eusebius. *The Church History*. Grand Rapids, MI: Kregel Publications, 2007.

Eusebius. *The Theophania*. http://www.tertullian.org/fathers/eusebius_theophania_01preface.htm (Last accessed 4/3/16).

Farrar, Frederic William. *The Early Days of Christianity*. Chicago, IL: Belford, Clarke and Co. Publishers, 1882.

Frend, *W.H.C. The Early Church: From the Beginnings to 461.* London: SCM Press, 2012.

Gaston, Lloyd. *No Stone on Another: Studies in the Significance of the Fall of Jerusalem in the Synoptic Gospels.* Boston, MA: Brill Academic Publications, 1970.

Gentry, Kenneth L. *Before Jerusalem Fell: Dating the Book of Revelation.* Powder Springs, GA: American Vision, 1998.

Gentry, Kenneth L. "Daniel's Seventy Weeks." http://www.cmfnow.com/articles/pt551.htm (Last accessed 4/13/16).

Gumerlock, Francis X. *Revelation and the First Century.* Powder Springs, GA: American Vision, 2012.

Gumerlock, Francis X. *The Day and the Hour: Christianity's Perennial Fascination with Predicting the End of the World.* Powder Springs, GA: American Vision, 2000.

Hall, Stuart G. *Doctrine and Practice of the Early Church.* Grand Rapids, MI: Wm. B. Eerdmans Publishing Co., 1992.

Hanegraaff-Hitchcock debate. Hank Hanegraaff vs. Mark Hitchcock. "Date of Revelation." https://www.youtube.com/watch?v=b6FOx_4wujg (Last accessed 4/13/16).

Hanson, J.W. *Universalism, the Prevailing Doctrine of the Christian Church During Its First Five Hundred Years.* 1899. Reprint. London: Forgotten Books, 2013.

Harding, Ian. *Taken to Heaven in 70AD*. Bradford, PA: International Preterist Association, 2005.

Harris, Murray. *Raised Immortal: Resurrection and Immorality in the New Testament*. Grand Rapids, MI: Wm. B. Eerdmans Publishing Co., 1985.

Heiser, Michael S. "The Divine Council in Late Canonical And Non-Canonical Second Temple Jewish Literature." 2004. http://digitalcommons.liberty.edu/cgi/viewcontent.cgi?article=1092&context=fac_dis (Last accessed 6/3/16).

Heiser, Michael S. "Naked Bible 88: What is the 'spiritual body' Paul talks about in 1 Cor. 15?" (Podcast). http://www.nakedbiblepodcast.com/naked-bible-88-what-is-the-spiritual-body-paul-talks-about-in-1-cor-15/ (Last accessed 4/11/16).

Helm, Paul, et al. *God and Time: Four Views*. Downers Grove, IL: Intervarsity Press, 2001.

Hitchcock, Mark. *101 Answers to the Most Asked Questions about the End Times*. Colorado Springs, CO: Multnomah Books, 2001.

Holmes, Michael W. *The Apostolic Fathers in English: Greek Texts and English Translations*. Grand Rapids, MI: Baker Books, 1999.

House, H. Wayne. "The Understanding of the Church Fathers Regarding the Olivet Discourse and the Fall of Jerusalem." http://www.pre-trib.org/articles/view/understanding-of-church-fathers-regarding-olivet-discourse-and-fall-jerusalem (Last accessed 4/3/16).

"Internal Evidence for an Early Date." http://www.biblestudytools.com/commentaries/revelation/introduction/internal-evidence-for-an-early-date.html (Last accessed 7/24/15).

Irenaeus. *Against Heresies.* http://www.earlychristianwritings.com/irenaeus.html (Last accessed 6/29/16).

Jenkins, Philip. *Jesus Wars: How Four Patriarchs, Three Queens, and Two Emperors Decided What Christians Would Believe for the Next 1,500 Years.* New York, NY: HarperOne, 2010.

Jenkins, Philip. *The Great and Holy War: How World War I became a Religious Crusade.* New York, NY: HarperOne, 2014.

Jenkins, Philip. *The Lost History of Christianity.* New York, NY: HarperOne, 2008.

Johnson, Dennis. *Triumph of the Lamb: A Commentary on Revelation.* Phillipsburg, NJ: P&R Publishing Company, 2001.

Jordan, James B. *Through New Eyes: Developing a Biblical View of the World.* Eugene, OR: Wipf and Stock Publishing, 1999.

Josephus. *Wars of the Jews.* http://sacred-texts.com/jud/josephus/. Original 75AD. Translated 1737.

Kik, J. Marcellus. *An Eschatology of Victory.* Phillipsburg, NJ: Presbyterian and Reformed Publishing Company, 1971.

Kratt, Jerel, et al. *Three Views on the Millennium in Preterism*. Not yet published as of 4/9/16.

Lapide, Cornelius Cornelii a, and William Frederick Cobb. *The Great Commentary of Cornelius Cornelii a Lapide: I Corinthians*. http://books.google.com/books?id=bIM9AAAAYA AJ&printsec=frontcover#v=onepage&q&f=false (Last accessed 4/3/16).

Lewis, C.S. *The World's Last Night and Other Essays*. http://archive.org/stream/worldslastnighta012859m bp/worldslastnighta012859mbp_djvu.txt (Last accessed 4/3/16).

Lindsay, Hal. *The Late Great Planet Earth*. Grand Rapids, MI: Zondervan, 1970.

Maarschalk, Adam. "PP15: The Man of Lawlessness." https://adammaarschalk.com/2009/08/16/pp15-the-man-of-lawlessness-ii-thess-2-part-1/ (Last accessed 7/2/16).

MacArthur, John. "The Certainty of the Second Coming, Part 1." http://www.gty.org/resources/sermons/61-23/the-certainty-of-the-second-coming-part-1 (Last accessed 4/3/16).

MacArthur, John. "The Certainty of the Second Coming, Part 3." http://www.gty.org/resources/sermons/61-25/the-certainty-of-the-second-coming-part-3 (Last accessed 4/3/16).

MacArthur, John. *The Second Coming*. Wheaton, IL: Crossway Books, 1999.

Martin, Brian. *Fulfilled Magazine* (Vol. 11, Issue 2). Summer 2016.

Martin, Dale. *The Corinthian Body*. London: Yale University Press, 1999.

Martyr, Justin. "Dialogue with Trypho." http://www.earlychristianwritings.com/text/justinma rtyr-dialoguetrypho.html (Last accessed 4/3/16).

Martyr, Justin. "The First Apology of Justin." http://www.earlychristianwritings.com/text/justinma rtyr-firstapology.html (Last accessed 4/3/16).

McDurmon, Joel. *Jesus v. Jerusalem: A Commentary on Luke 9:51–20:26, Jesus' Lawsuit Against Israel*. Powder Springs, GA: American Vision, 2011.

McKenzie, Duncan. *The Antichrist and the Second Coming: A Preterist Examination* (Vol. 1). Xulon Press, 2009.

McKenzie, Duncan. *The Antichrist and the Second Coming: A Preterist Examination* (Vol. 2). Xulon Press, 2012.

McKenzie, Duncan. "The Man of Lawlessness Part One." http://planetpreterist.com/content/man-lawlessness-part-one (Last accessed 7/2/16).

McKenzie, Duncan, "The Man of Lawlessness Part Two." http://planetpreterist.com/content/man-lawlessness-part-two (Last accessed 7/2/16).

McKnight, Scot. *The King Jesus Gospel: The Original Good News Revisited*. Grand Rapids, MI: Zondervan, 2011.

Moffatt, James. *Introduction to the Literature of the New Testament.* Whitefish, MT: Kessinger Publishing, 2005.

Morris, Marion. *Christ's Second Coming Fulfilled.* 1917. Reprint. BiblioBazaar LLC, 2008.

Moule, C.F.D. *The Birth of the New Testament.* London: A. & C. Black (Publishers) Ltd., 1981.

"The Nicene-Constantinopolitan Creed." http://web.mit.edu/ocf/www/nicene_creed.html (Last accessed 4/3/16).

Nigro, H.L. *Before God's Wrath: The Bible's Answer to the Timing of the Rapture.* Bellefonte, PA: Strong Tower Publishing, 2004.

Olson, Roger. *Arminian Theology: Myths and Realities.* Downers Grove, IL: InterVarsity Press, 2006.

Patai, Raphael. *The Arab Mind.* Tucson, AZ: Recovery Resources Press, 2007.

Pelikan, Jaroslav. *The Christian Tradition: A History of the Development of Doctrine, Vol I: The Emergence of the Catholic Tradition.* Chicago, IL: University of Chicago Press, 1971.

Perriman, Andrew. *Hell and Heaven in Narrative Perspective.* Self-published. Printed by CreateSpace, 2012.

Powell, Riley O'Brien. "Historic Preterist Quotes." http://livingthequestion.org/historic-quotes/ (Last accessed 4/7/16).

Powell, Riley O'Brien. "Revelation." http://livingthequestion.org/revelation/ (Last accessed 4/3/16).

Poythress, Vern S. *Understanding Dispensationalists.* Chestnut Hill, PA: Westminster Theological Seminary, 1986.

Pratt, Richard L., Jr. "Historical Contingencies and Biblical Predictions: An Inaugural Address Presented to the Faculty of Reformed Theological Seminary." http://thirdmill.org/newfiles/ric_pratt/th.pratt.historical_contingencies.pdf (Last accessed 4/3/16).

Preston, Don K. *70 Weeks are Determined for... The Resurrection!* Ardmore, OK: Jadon Management, Inc., 2010.

Preston, Don K. *The Hymenaean Heresy: Reverse the Charges.* Ardmore, OK: Jadon Management, Inc. 2014.

Preston, Don K. *Like Father Like Son, On Clouds of Glory.* Ardmore, OK: Jadon Management, Inc., 2012.

Preston, Don K. *Who is this Babylon?* Ardmore, OK: Jadon Management, Inc., 2011.

Preston, Don K., and William Bell. "Two Guys and a Bible: Zion." Podcast. http://fulfilledradio.com/ (Last accessed 4/10/16).

Preston, Don K., et al. "The Body of Christ." MP3 of the 2014 Preterist Pilgrim Weekend. http://www.store.bibleprophecy.com/2014-ppw-mp3s/ (Last accessed 4/3/16).

Preston-Brown debate. Don K.Preston vs Michael Brown. "Fullness of Times, Romans 11:25-27." 2015. https://www.youtube.com/watch?v=O0Ec1GyfKxs (Last accessed 4/13/16).

Reeves, Joe. *Second Thoughts about the Second Coming*. Bloomington, IN: AuthorHouse, 2011.

Richardson, Joel. *The Islamic Antichrist*. Los Angeles, CA: WND Books, 2015.

Riddlebarger, Kim. *A Case for Amillennialism: Understanding the End Times.* Grand Rapids, MI: Baker Books, 2013.

Robinson, John A.T. *Redating the New Testament*. Philadelphia, PA: Westminster Press, 1976.

Rosenberg, Joel. *Epicenter*. Carol Stream, IL: Tyndale House Publishers, Inc., 2006.

Ryrie, Charles. *Dispensationalism*. Chicago, IL: Moody Publishers, 2007.

Schaff, Philip. *History of the Christian Church, Vol II*. Peabody, MA: Hendrickson Publishers, Inc, 2006.

Schaff, Philip. *Proof of the Gospel Book III*. Harrington, DE: Delmarva Publications, 2013.

Schaff, Philip. *The Ante-Nicene Fathers* (Vols. 1-9). Wm. B. Eerdmans Publishing Company. Public domain. http://www.ccel.org/ccel/schaff/anf01.ii.ii.xxv.html (Last accessed 6/29/16).

Schwartz, Daniel and Zeev Weiss. *Was 70CE a Watershed in Jewish History? On the Jews and Judaism Before and After the Destruction of the Second Temple.*

Koninklijke Brill NV, Leiden, The Netherlands, 2012.

Scripture4All: Greek/Hebrew interlinear Bible software. www.scripture4all.org (Last accessed 4/3/16).

Shepherd of Hermas. http://www.earlychristianwritings.com/text/shepherd.html (Last accessed 4/18/16).

Simmons, Kurt. "Dating the Book of Revelation." http://www.preteristcentral.com/Dating%20the%20Book%20of%20Revelation.html (Last accessed 4/3/16).

Simmons, Kurt. "The Man of Sin." http://www.preteristcentral.com/Man%20of%20Sin.html (Last accessed 4/13/16).

Simmons, Kurt. "The Road Back to Preterism." http://www.preteristcentral.com/The%20Road%20Back%20to%20Preterism.html (Last accessed 4/3/16).

Simmons, Kurt. *The Sword and Plow*. Newsletter, May 2016, http://www.preteristcentral.com/index.html (Last accessed 5/13/16).

Smith, Chuck. *What is the World Coming to: A Commentary on the Book of Revelation*. http://www.ccyuma.com/chucksmithbooks/pdfbooks/whattheworldiscomingto.pdf (Last accessed 6/3/16).

Soro, Mar Bawaii. *The Church of the East: Apostolic and Orthodox*. Self-published. Printed by CreateSpace, 2014.

Stevens, Edward E. *Expectations Demand a First Century Rapture*. International Preterist Association, 2003.

Stevens, Edward E. *Final Decade Before the End*. International Preterist Association, 2014.

Stevens, Edward E. *First Century Events in Chronological Order*. Pre-publication, 2009.

Stevens, Edward E. "Times of the Gentiles (Lk 21:24)" Podcast (June 15, 2014). http://www.buzzsprout.com/11633/181738-times-of-the-gentiles-lk-21-24 (Last accessed 4/13/16).

Tertullian. "Chapter VIII. - Of the Times of Christ's Birth and Passion, and of Jerusalem's Destruction." http://www.sacred-texts.com/chr/ecf/003/0030189.htm (Last accessed 4/3/16).

Tertullian. "Preterism and the 'Church Fathers' - Part 5: Quintus Florens Tertullian." http://alt.messianic.narkive.com/MMtNY6Zv/preterism-and-the-church-fathers-part-5-quintus-florens-tertullian (Last accessed 4/3/16).

Thieme, Robert B. "Matthew audio series." (Series number 438), 1965. http://rbthieme.org/index.html# (Last accessed 6/10/16).

Toussaint, Stanley D. *Behold the King: A Study of Matthew*. Grand Rapids, MI: Kregel Academic & Professional, 2005.

Trowell, Chad. *End Times Bible Handbook*. Self-published. Printed by AuthorHouse, 2015.

Verduin, Leonard. *The Reformers and their Stepchildren.* Paris, AR: The Baptist Standard Bearer, 2001.

Walker, Williston, et al. *A History of the Christian Church.* New York, NY: Scribner, 1985.

Walvoord, John F. *Every Prophecy of the Bible.* Colorado Springs, CO: David C. Cook, 1999.

Wilkinson, Douglas. *Making Sense of the Millennium.* Self-published. Printed by CreateSpace, 2015.

Wilkinson, Douglas. *Preterist Time Statements.* Self-published. Printed by CreateSpace, 2014.

Wright, N.T. *Resurrection and the Son of God.* Minneapolis, MN: Fortress Press, 2003.

61083545R00148

Made in the USA
Charleston, SC
11 September 2016